ReFocus: The Films of Teuvo Tulio

T0333708

ReFocus: The International Directors Series

Series Editors: Robert Singer, Stefanie Van de Peer and Gary D. Rhodes

Editorial Board: Lizelle Bisschoff, Stephanie Hemelryck Donald, Anna Misiak and Des O'Rawe

ReFocus is a series of contemporary methodological and theoretical approaches to the interdisciplinary analyses and interpretations of international film directors, from the celebrated to the ignored, in direct relationship to their respective culture – its myths, values and historical precepts – and the broader parameters of international film history and theory. The series provides a forum for introducing a broad spectrum of directors, working in and establishing movements, trends, cycles and genres including those historical, currently popular, or emergent, and in need of critical assessment or reassessment. It ignores no director who created a historical space – either in or outside of the studio system – beginning with the origins of cinema and up to the present. *ReFocus* brings these film directors to a new audience of scholars and general readers of Film Studies.

Titles in the series include:

edinburghuniversitypress.com/series/refocint

ReFocus:
The Films of Teuvo Tulio

An Excessive Outsider

Henry Bacon, Kimmo Laine and
Jaakko Seppälä

EDINBURGH
University Press

Edinburgh University Press is one of the leading university presses in the UK. We publish academic books and journals in our selected subject areas across the humanities and social sciences, combining cutting-edge scholarship with high editorial and production values to produce academic works of lasting importance. For more information visit our website: edinburghuniversitypress.com

Edinburgh University Press Ltd
The Tun – Holyrood Road
12 (2f) Jackson's Entry
Edinburgh EH8 8PJ

First published in hardback by Edinburgh University Press 2020

Typeset in 11/13 Ehrhardt MT by
IDSUK (DataConnection) Ltd, and
printed and bound by CPI Group (UK) Ltd,
Croydon, CR0 4YY

A CIP record for this book is available from the British Library

ISBN 978 1 4744 4215 2 (hardback)
ISBN 978 1 4744 4218 3 (paperback)
ISBN 978 1 4744 4216 9 (webready PDF)
ISBN 978 1 4744 4217 6 (epub)

Contents

The Authors

Henry Bacon is professor of Film and Television Studies at the University of Helsinki (2004–). Previously he has worked as a research fellow at the Finnish Film Archive (1999–2004), where he also acted as project manager in charge of designing a national radio and television archive. His major research interests are transnational aspects of cinema, how audiovisual experience relates to our perception and understanding of the natural and the social world, audiovisual narratology as well as film's relation to other arts. He has also written extensively on the history of opera. From 2011 to 2014 he headed the A Transnational History of Finnish Cinema Academy of Finland research project, the results of which were published in *Finnish Cinema: A transnational Enterprise* (2016). Among his major publications are the monographs *Luchino Visconti: Explorations of Beauty and Decay* (1998), *Audiovisuaalisen kerronnan teoria* (Theory of Audiovisual Narration, 2000), *Elokuva ja muut taiteet* (Film in Relation to Other Arts, 2005) and *The Fascination of Fictional Violence* (2015). He has also published several articles in scholarly periodicals as well as anthologies such as *Studi Viscontiani* (1997), *Narration and Spectatorship in the Moving Images* (2007), *Romy Schneider: Film. Rolle. Leben* (2008), *Morte a Venezia: Thomas Mann/Luchino Visconti: un confronto* (2014), *The Films of Aki Kaurismäki: Ludic Engagements* (2018) and *Screening Characters: Theories of Character in Film, Television, and Interactive Media* (2019).

Kimmo Laine is an acting professor of Media Studies at the University of Turku and a university lecturer of Film Studies at the University of Oulu. He has published two monographs and co-edited four books on film history in Finnish. In English, he has published in, for example, *Film History*, *Journal of Scandinavian Cinema* and *Oxford Bibliographies in Cinema and Media*

Studies, as well as in several edited collections including *Nordic Genre Film: Small Nation Film Cultures in the Global Marketplace* (edited by Tommy Gustafsson and Pietari Kääpä, Edinburgh University Press, 2015), *Finnish Cinema: A Transnational Enterprise* (edited by Henry Bacon, Palgrave, 2016), *Companion to Nordic Cinema* (edited by Mette Hjort and Ursula Lindqvist, 2016) and *A Cultural History of the Avant-Garde in the Nordic Countries 1925–1950* (edited by Fredrik Hertzberg et al., 2019). Currently he is working on a book-length study on Finnish film studios, to be published in the Global Film Studios series by Edinburgh University Press.

Jaakko Seppälä is a docent (adjunct professor) in Film and Television Studies at the University of Helsinki, where he works as a university lecturer. He is one of the editors of *Nordic Noir, Adaptation, Appropriation* (edited together with Linda Badley and Andrew Nestingen, 2020) and he has published articles on Nordic cinema and television, often focusing on transnational and stylistic questions. He has contributed to anthologies including *Nordic Genre Film: Small Nation Film Cultures in the Global Marketplace* (edited by Tommy Gustafsson and Pietari Kääpä, Edinburgh University Press, 2015), *Finnish Cinema: A Transnational Enterprise* (edited by Henry Bacon, 2016) and *Aki Kaurismäki – Ludic Engagements* (edited by Thomas Austin, 2018), and journals including *Journal of Scandinavian Cinema* and *Projections: The Journal for Movies and Mind*. He is currently exploring style and meaning in Nordic noir in the context of welfare state criticism.

Acknowledgements

This study was made possible by the kind support of the National Audiovisual Institute, Finland. In particular we wish to thank the Managing Director Matti Lukkarila for granting us the use of the entire Teuvo Tulio collection in the Institute's possession, including all the surviving films and related materials. Among the many members of the personnel we especially want to thank are Timo Matoniemi, Tommi Partanen, Jorma Junttila and Juha Seitajärvi.

Many friends and colleagues have helped us in various ways with this book, notably Olof Hedling, Outi Hupaniittu, Silja Laine, Anders Marklund and Per Vesterlund. Thanks to all.

Richard Dyer and Andrew Nestingen kindly provided endorsements for this volume, as well as did one of Tulio's ardent admirers and followers, Aki Kaurismäki. Thanks also to Haije Tulokas at Sputnik Oy.

The idea of writing a volume on Tulio for the international market came from Edinburgh University Press Series Editor Robert Singer. His unquenchable enthusiasm and support have inspired us throughout the research period. He, together with his colleagues Stefanie Van de Peer and Gary Rhodes, also did a big job in providing comments on the manuscript and revising the language – this has improved the text significantly. The final stages of preparing this volume for publication were supervised by Richard Strachan.

All images are courtesy of the National Audiovisual Institute.

CHAPTER I

Introduction

As Paolo Cherchi Usai has perceptively stated, Teuvo Tulio makes 'Douglas Sirk look like Robert Bresson'.[1] In its sheer excessiveness, Tulio's brand of melodrama transcends not only other examples of this genre in Finnish cinema, but almost any other related tradition. In particular, his style utterly contravenes the national stereotype of Finns as withdrawn when it comes to emotional expression. His characters are consumed by barely, if at all, contained passions which again and again lead them to erratic, destructive behaviour. He further expanded the range of melodrama, that most transnational of genres, with his stories about obsessed characters. He developed a highly idiosyncratic style with the purpose of giving maximal emotional impact to the contorted plot twists of his films. All this makes Tulio worthy of attention even in terms of world cinema.

FROM TUGAI TO TULIO

It is difficult to trace a suitable critical attitude to Tulio's aesthetics. Having studied Tulio's films closely, we cannot quite agree with Markku Varjola, who writes: 'Tulio is able to elevate his cheap and ridiculous stories expressively to the level of archetypes, where their greatness becomes crystal clear.'[2] It would seem rather that Tulio was possessed by certain archetypes to the extent that they increasingly took over his storytelling, sometimes even reversing the pattern Varjola proposes. Tulio turns Alexandr Pushkin's sensitive and touching short story *Stationmaster* (1831) into the moralistic extravagance of *Cross of Love* (*Rakkauden risti*, 1946) and later on to that masterpiece of camp, *Sensuela* (1973), because he was possessed by the schemas of exploitation and lost innocence, which do not really appear in the original story. This is not an instance of modernisation, almost the contrary. From archetypes gone mad there emerges a surreally excessive, strangely anachronistic melodrama, way beyond its 'best before' date. On the surface it seems to hark back to what in a British context would be called Victorian morality, but in its extremity it goes far beyond even that. Judging simply by the films – as we lack substantial biographical support – we could assume that Tulio's art emerges to a great extent from a collapse of the distinction between a genuine sense of morality and the destructive power of moralism.

Moralism in Tulio's films is toxic. One archetypal category in his films is constituted by characters who in their blind fury insist on traditional codes of honour and morality, whatever the consequences. There is no pretension that such moralism would serve any good purpose whatsoever, it emerges as a purely destructive force, targeted primarily on the fatally innocent, in particular the naïvely inexperienced young woman, stained by exploitation and the betrayal she has been subjected to. She is loving and yearns for love but is cruelly ostracised even when it is acknowledged that her fall is by no means her own fault. From the point of view of the narrator – and hence also the spectator – there is an insidious sadomasochistic aspect to this: it is as if we were expected to simultaneously enjoy and abhor the unfairness and brutality. We are invited to find guilty pleasure in the iniquity of it all, yet to view it in the last instance from a supposedly moral high ground. The fallen woman's fate may be so outrageous that it transcends any even vaguely realistic framework. It is always precarious to speculate about an artist's intentions and very much so in connection with Tulio, that narratively and stylistically subversive hermit. Nevertheless, we cannot help but wonder if he really expected his melodramas to be taken seriously. Or did he at some point just cease caring?

Within the Finnish film industry, Tulio had a rather exceptional status as an independent producer at the time of the big studios. This allowed him to make just the kind of films he wanted, even if with ever-smaller budgets. Working with a small budget inevitably influenced his style, forcing him to find ways to achieve his artistic aims at the smallest cost possible. This led to aesthetic solutions that were, at their best, innovative. More often, seen with eyes attuned to polished classical style, his editing in particular is likely to appear plain clumsy. Arguably, at least most of the time, he knew what he was doing, and just did not bother about the niceties of continuity. At its most intriguing, his treatment of space, time and causality is almost hallucinatory. In this scheme of things, it just does not matter how characters are spatially or even temporally related to each other. All that matters are passionate, consuming emotional relationships, very much more so than in the stylistically more ordinary Finnish melodramas. Tulio's editing can be striking in its disregard of the classical unities, but he creates an extraordinary impact with his extraordinary images, particularly those filled with the fantastically expressive face of his closest companion, collaborator and muse, Regina Linnanheimo. She had an extraordinarily wide range of facial expressions at her command, and together they exploited those to the full.

Creative freedom did have its cost: eventually Tulio's films begun to receive only a very limited distribution. By the 1950s, both critics and audiences stopped taking his films seriously, if seeing them at all, and gradually he faded out of public memory.

Tulio was actually Latvian by birth. He settled down in Helsinki with his mother after her third marriage and changed his original name Theodor Tugai to a more Finnish form in his early adulthood. He did establish a Finnish identity of sorts, but always remained something of an outsider. In the 1950s he began to withdraw from filmmaking as well as from social life. Ironically, in a sense he became even more solitary than the proverbial taciturn and introvert Finn.

But how did Theodor Tugai (1912–2000), a Latvian country boy, become Teuvo Tulio, one of the key figures of Finnish cinema at a time when cinema was expected to contribute to the formation of a national art? His self-biographical articles published in the popular periodical *Jaana* in 1974 offer a colourful account of some aspects of his early life.[3] Apart from brief reminiscences by people who knew him, this is almost our only source as regards his private life. Having become increasingly reclusive fairly early on, he gradually ceased both making films and publicly expressing his opinions. His silence is a great loss, as it would have been of paramount interest to learn more about how his intentions as regards film style developed. We do know that at the time he started directing films, he set as his task invigorating Finnish cinema by bold use of filmic means. However, he tends to be rather casual about this as well as many other aspects of his aesthetic ideas and working practices. Little other material remains which would allow us to gain a wider and more critical perspective. Almost all the people that knew him and worked with him have passed away. He remains something of a mystery, and often we are left wondering what he could possibly have been aiming at. We can only hope that the narrative, stylistic and contextual analysis we offer in this volume will throw enough light on the extraordinary oeuvre of this exceedingly idiosyncratic director, one of the weirdest masters of melodrama ever.

APPROACHES TO MELODRAMA

The foundational problem of melodrama studies is that so many different kinds of works in literature, on stage and in film, as well as on television, have been called melodrama that in historical perspective the notion has reached the point of almost losing all coherence. Most people today probably think of melodrama more or less on the lines of the definition offered in Wikipedia: 'Melodramas are typically set in the private sphere of the home, and focus on morality and family issues, love, and marriage.' Many scholars, without unnecessarily problematising the issue, employ the notion more or less on these lines, focusing particularly on the extreme emotions that this setting allows. Carlos Monsiváis, for one, writes about the characters of melodrama: 'they exist primarily as emblems of series of feelings: compassion, pain, arrogance, evil, innocence, coquetry, cowardice, irresponsibility, resentment, generosity'.[4] Some film historians, however, are quick to object, pointing out that at certain times the word melodrama has been used in connection with action films and serials such as *Perils of Pauline* (Gasnier and Mackenzie, 1914).

In an attempt to define the 'essential element' of melodrama, Ben Singer suggests the 'certain "overwrought" or "exaggerated" quality summed up by the term *excess*'.[5] One common feature about what have been referred to as melodrama over the past two centuries is 'stimulating the sensation of agitation', either by 'the physical, visceral thrill created by situations of acute suspense', as in what may be called action melodrama, or from 'observing extreme moral injustice, the feeling of distress, of being profoundly disturbed or outraged when we see vicious power victimizing the weak, usually involving some kind of bodily violence'.[6] Further attempts at the definition of melodrama and taking into account so-called sensational melodrama requires resorting to the notion of 'cluster concept', or Wittgenstein's classification according to family resemblances. All in all, both dimensions entail viewing 'melodrama as a term whose meaning varies from case to case in relation to different configurations of a range of basic features or constitutive factors'.[7] Singer suggests that these basic features could be pathos, overwrought emotions, moral polarisation, non-classical narrative structure and sensationalism.[8] This approach provides solid ground for treating the rather amorphous notion of melodrama in an illuminating fashion.

However, certain problems of conceptualising melodrama still remain. Perhaps the issue that has caused the most confusion in recent discussions is the opposition between melodrama and the notion of 'classical'. In the nineteenth century the idea that melodrama aimed at eliciting a sense of agitation leading to visceral responses in the spectator by means of acute suspense, depictions of extreme moral injustice and the harming of the innocent and defenceless, led to the condemnation, first of stage melodrama, and subsequently of film melodrama, as entertainment for the mob.[9] This kind of melodrama was non-classical in that it had '. . . outrageous coincidence, implausibility, convoluted plotting, *deus ex machina* resolutions and episodic strings of action that stuff too many events together to be able to be kept in line by a cause-and-effect chain of narrative progression'.[10] But then again, this is not a necessary prerequisite of melodrama, not at least in the nineteenth century. As Singer points out in discussing the notion of 'situation' in connection with melodrama:

The definition of situation appears to have slipped from meaning something roughly equivalent to a 'thrill' – a highly focused charge of narrative excitement – to meaning something more like an entire scenario.
Both classical melodrama and Hollywood melodrama present human
crises, but the crises are 'situational' in different ways.[11]

The difference lies precisely in the way most Hollywood melodrama may, in
a meaningful and illuminating sense, be considered classical in that it caters
its thrills as elements of carefully constructed narratives. In other words, a
classical structure takes firm hold of the melodramatic even when not fully
taming it.

In the anthology *Melodrama Unbound* (2018), the editors Christine Gledhill
and Linda Williams argue that instead of thinking of melodrama as a genre we
should conceptualise it as a mode. They would surely not object to the use of
the notion of excess as a defining feature, but they do see it as a feature which is
antithetical to the notion of classicism. Williams makes a brave effort to define
what the criteria of the melodramatic mode from this point of view should be:

I venture to argue that the primary work of melodrama – in contrast to
the work of the 'classical' as in, say, classical tragedy – has fundamentally
been that of seeking a better justice. Enlightenment values of freedom,
equality, and justice, however perverted and corrupted, are most frequently evoked in melodramas of all sorts, as might be expected by a
mode of drama related, as Peter Brooks argues, to the principles of the
French Revolution.[12]

The problem with this definition is that Williams' understanding of classical
tragedy appears strangely distorted: the very gist of classical tragedy is in agonising debates about what is right and wrong. The style may have been digni-
fied, and certainly was so later on in French classical tragedy, but in terms of
plot, the way antagonisms are played out, we may well recognise a distinctly
melodramatic aspect. Behind Williams' thinking there is the very strong opposition she seeks to build between melodrama and classical realist style which
she was constructing already in her *Playing the Race Card* (2001). Her notion
of melodrama is based on the traditional idea that, in the words of Matthew
Buckley, 'melodrama is an excessive, uncontrolled, irrational, and crude form
of art, a form of chaos and fear'. Buckley himself sees melodrama as a 'finely-
honed, keenly synthetic, often coldly logical art of excess, developed slowly over
centuries by the combined efforts of all manner of affective arts'.[13] Achieving
melodramatic effects within a classical structure is achieved by certain narrative
and stylistic means, which in the nineteenth century were gathered under the
notion of the *well-made play*, and in twentieth-century filmmaking under the

norms of classical style, gradually formulated in Hollywood during the 1910s. As Rick Altman has put it:

> Hollywood perpetuates the menu-driven concerns of popular theater. Spectacle is needed, as are variety and strong emotions. How can these be obtained in a form that precludes overt episodicity? With no difficulty. Decide which spectacles are needed, then make it seem that they are there for internally motivated reasons.[14]

Altman further points out that the appeal of a film such as *Casablanca* (1942) is based on its linear causality on the one hand, and on its melodramatic underpinnings on the other. Our attention is guided so that, in order to enjoy the film, we do not ask too many questions about why things happen or why the characters make their decisions to act one way or the other.[15] This allows us to be guided towards the narrative resolution of 'the union of Bogie and Bergman, the beautiful couple', graced by the grander themes of 'human allegiance to things of eternal beauty and value':

> To the personal identification that pushes us forward along a suspenseful linear hermeneutic corresponds a process of cultural identification that keeps us ever-mindful of a broader set of oppositions compared to which the problems of three people don't amount to a hill of beans.[16]

Mainstream American silent cinema can indeed, as Williams argues, be largely classified as melodramatic (when it was not comedy) but in form it has for the most part been perfectly classical in the sense David Bordwell and film historians in general use this word. For Bordwell, narration in classical film is motivated, above all, compositionally, and to a lesser degree, generically.[17] There is nothing here that would in any way preclude melodrama or melodramatic features, rather it becomes a matter of degree: say, are coincidences so outrageous that narrative lacks all coherence to the degree that it does not matter what happens to the characters? Yet a considerable degree of excess, as defined in melodrama studies, can be accommodated within this framework. Realistic motivation may be suspended, but that is nothing strange to the classical style, not at least within genres that 'descend from episodic and composite forms in the American popular theatre'. It can even be demonstrated that elements such as 'big scenes favoured by stage melodrama became more compositionally motivated in film melodrama'.[18]

In a recent article, Williams actually seems to slightly change her position in this direction: 'I furthermore want to challenge the assumption, held by many – Ben Singer, as well as Brooks and Elsaesser – that melodrama's excesses challenge the "classical". Is melodrama, as it first emerged and as we know it today, really so excessive?"[19] Well, at times and in certain contexts it generally has been so, at others not. Williams is concerned that 'melodrama's developing virtues go unrecognised in the domain model of the "classical"'.[20] But this is only so if 'classical' is understood in terms of something like classical French tragedy with its defining notions of harmony and decorum. Obviously, this is not what Bordwell, Thompson and Staiger had in mind in their *Classical Hollywood Cinema* (1985), the prime target of criticism of the editors of the otherwise fine anthology *Melodrama Unbound*. Gledhill seeks to make her point by arguing how Bordwell's notion of the classical is opposed to what melodrama is all about:

> In Bordwell's model (1985, part one), causes constitute the logic of character motivation, itself key to narrative development and resolution. But from melodrama's perspective, dramatic emphasis shifts from cause to consequence. The consequences outrun its causes, flowing into new situations only marginally connected to the initiating cause, opening up areas of feeling unanticipated by character or audience.[21]

But surely, emotional reactions, so essential to melodrama, must have causes in the stream of events depicted in order to appear somehow significant – otherwise they appear plainly psychotic. They must relate to genuine human concerns as articulated within some form of narrative that may well consist of changes of fortune by factors unexpected by the characters. When could it be said that 'consequences outrun its causes'? Perhaps when a person suffers a fate disproportionate to her errors or faults, or overreacts to something unexpected and emotionally disturbing that he or she discovers. To make sense of such a pattern we have to be aware of what the situation is and how it has come about. If that situation does not seem to serve as a sufficient cause to explain it or the emotional reaction to which it gives rise, we are likely to look for other causes. Causes and consequences cannot be so easily set apart in the way we make sense of how people, or fictional characters for that matter, react to human situations. What may well happen is that the causes for character behaviour implied are not very plausible in real-life terms (or what Neoformalists called realistic motivation) and rely instead on genre expectations for their acceptability (transtextual motivation). In such a case the spectators may indeed get their pleasure from witnessing a shattering emotional outburst rather than from any insight a story might offer of the causes of such a reaction. Nevertheless, such reactions appear all the more effective when presented within the framework of a firm dramaturgy (compositional motivation), that is, for the most part, according to the paradigms of the classical style, which ensure that we at least gain the effect of reasonable causality, even if the narration might not bear much deeper scrutiny in this respect. Identification and sympathy can only emerge when we understand the situation, the narrative context and conditions in terms of which the emotional outburst takes place.

There is yet another line of definition. Thomas Elsaesser reminds us that dictionaries tend to explain melodrama as 'a dramatic narrative in which musical accompaniment marks the emotional effects'. He further points out that 'the advantage of this approach is that it formulates the problems of melodrama as problems of style and articulation'.[22] This notion is very useful in analysing the melodrama of Tulio, if not always in terms of using melodramatically apt music, very much so in the way he employs visual compositions and sequences to make his point. This is all the more remarkable considering that over most of his career he did not have at his disposal anything like the technical resources of his colleagues even in Finland, let alone in the USA. He had to rely on other kinds of stylistic means than what the latest cinematic technology would have allowed, mainly deriving from the silent era, but with a highly idiosyncratic, inimitable twist that put him into a class of his own. This inevitably set him apart also as regards the melodramatic mode in general.

At this point, having severely criticised the way Gledhill and Williams oppose classical narration and melodrama, we have to perform a partial volte-face in order to analyse and contextualise the melodramas of Tulio. This is because, if we compare his works with certain other Finnish rural melodramas, the contrast in this respect is very strong. Valentin Vaala's *They Met at the Swing* (*Keinumorsian*, 1944) is a melodrama by any account, yet it is perfectly classical in form, adhering to the standard norms of filmmaking as largely established in Hollywood in the teens. In Tulio's two first surviving rural melodramas (the three first of his films having perished in a fire at Adams Film offices) a fairly standard melodramatic pattern emerges, namely that of the prodigal son, who has to have his sexual escapades before settling down and assuming his responsibilities. With some individual sequences apart, at least in comparison with his later films, these largely conform to the norms of classical filmmaking. But as Tulio grew ever more excessive in portraying destructive emotions, it was as if he were not able to contain that excess within classical form by adhering to norms of good filmmaking. This is blatantly obvious both on the level of narrative structure and editing: he often did not care much about ensuring either a consistent causality effect or continuity. Thus, while Williams relates having concluded 'that these binaries, whether between classical and excess, or classical and modern, or classical and non-classical, are simply too crude to perform much analytical work',[23] they do help in charting how Tulio's style and approach differed from those of most of his contemporaries.

Another trait which structures the *Melodrama Unbound* anthology is criticism targeted at Peter Brooks, whose *The Melodramatic Imagination – Balzac, Henry James, Melodrama, and the Mode of Excess* (1976) is a milestone in the contemporary study of melodrama. The editors point out that although this really was a groundbreaking study, it focuses only on a thirty-year period after the French Revolution and on the authors mentioned in the title, and that some of its conclusions have been stretched too far by later scholars. As one major corrective, Matthew Buckley discusses the historical roots of melodrama, but even more importantly, challenges the notion of melodrama as a drama of morality. Brooks sees the melodramatic mode as a way of articulating spiritual values both indicated within and masked by the surface of reality. He discusses melodrama as a moral occult, 'the principle mode for uncovering, demonstrating, and making operative the essential moral universe in a post-sacred era'.[24] In this view, melodrama does not present a metaphysical system but rather serves as 'the repository of fragmentary and desacralized remnants of sacred myth'.[25] Buckley points out that there were a great number of precedents to this kind of drama of morality, and that while 'most of melodrama has laid at least a superficial claim to be moral', as the nineteenth century marched on it contained evermore morally polarised character structures. As such, it follows 'a basic trajectory of moral crises and redemptions and appeals to a shared popular moral imagination', tending evermore to be heavily moralistic.[26]

The notion of moral occult can, with some major reservations expounded by Buckley, be applied to Tulio. His characters inhabit a severely moralistic rather than a genuinely moral universe. Codes of honour, propriety and demands for strict chastity reign relentlessly over the lives of the characters. Principal male characters are typically haunted by passions and obsessions, which gnaw their sense of spirituality and lead them to depravity and destruction. Virtue is left unrecognised. Tulio's women are, as a rule, innocent, but doomed to misery, sometimes due to their own fallibility, but more often and to a much greater extent because of the lack of consideration and downright recklessness of the men who desire and seduce them. Both sexes are prone to blind passion. Indeed, blindness, literal or metaphorical, versus suddenly being able to see and then to see through deception, is a key trope in many of Tulio's films. The whirl of extreme emotions finds its expression in the stylistic means, which Tulio employs to depict how his characters are caught in ever-tightening cycles of compulsive behaviour – and as they are never just plain callous, this also serves as their all too appropriate punishment.

Gledhill, elaborating on Brooks' idea of melodrama's insistence pending on 'making the world morally legible', suggests that melodrama 'accesses the underside of official rationales for reigning moral orders – that which social convention, psychic repression, political dogma cannot articulate'.[27] In what sense might this be said about Tulio? The moral scheme is always there, depicted as a repressive social convention, flaunted by the guardians of morality and family honour, often forcing its victims either to suppress their desires or face social and spiritual degradation. The upholders of the prevailing order might acknowledge the actual moral failure of this state of affairs, but nevertheless rigidly adhere to it as if there simply was no socially accept-able or even metaphysical alternative. However, all this appears to stand in blatant contradiction with contemporary moral sense, even at the time of the making of these films. The question then remains: if the moral norms depicted were outmoded to the extent of being almost totally irrelevant, was Tulio's treatment of these themes as he recirculated them throughout his career an instance of parody – even self-parody? If not, how else might his moralistic anachronism be justified?

What is perhaps more to the point is another observation Gledhill makes following Brooks, namely that the 'spectacle, moral polarisation and dramatic reversals for which melodrama is so often criticised serves the purpose of clari-fication, identification and palpable demonstration of repressed "ethical and psychic" forces, which nevertheless constitute compelling imperatives'.[28] It could plausibly be said that Tulio by just such means expounds a critique of outmoded moral norms as 'compelling imperatives', even as it is difficult to avoid feeling that he merely exploits these moralistic schemes as plot devices, reinforced by the sensuous and the spectacular that he was so good at evoking.

In the last instance, Tulio's art contrasts significantly with Brooks' notion of melodrama as 'radically hyperbolic, the mode of bigger-than-life, reaching in grandiose reference to a noumenal realm'. 'Noumenal' refers here to the notion of a 'cosmic ethical drama', the idea that in the end metaphysical justice will prevail. This may not be in accord with our real-life experience, but all the more importantly fiction often has had the function of sustaining faith in such ultimate cosmic justice. This ethos may be seen to derive from Christianity, with its promise of a just state of affairs in an afterlife, if not here on earth. Tulio sometimes offers a slight gesture toward such consolation, but usually too much innocence has been lost in the whirl of passion for us to feel that anything like a just state of affairs has been restored – if justice ever did pre-vail. The characters are too entangled in the meshes of temptation, desire and jealousy to survive morally in a way even they themselves would find accept-able. Tulio's cosmic drama is thus much bleaker than in most traditions of melodrama, the essence of his poetics being more in the occult of moralism than in moral occult.

THE STRUCTURE OF THE STUDY

In this volume we will first contextualise Tulio's very own brand of melo-drama with some principal traditions of the melodramatic mode. We do not know how much opera or how many stage productions that still referred back to nineteenth-century melodrama he saw, but there are striking similarities between his films and certain operas as well as many general features of stage melodrama. Probably, many of these features were transmitted through silent cinema. Tulio started his career in film as an actor in silent films directed by his friend Vaala, another offspring of an immigrant family, who was to become one of the most notable Finnish filmmakers. Tulio himself directed only sound films, but most of them contain lengthy passages with no dialogue, relying heavily on silent-film aesthetics. In addition to silent melodrama, the most obvious corpus of comparison is naturally European, Scandinavian and Finnish sound-film melodrama. Finally, to provide an internationally more well-known reference point, American 1950s melodramas by Douglas Sirk and Vincente Minnelli will be discussed in order to examine how the passions that haunt their characters compare with the obsessions of Tulio's characters.

The third chapter consists of a biography based on Tulio's autobiographical articles, and the fourth is an examination of Tulio's position and possibilities as an independent producer-director in the context of the Finnish studio era. Vaala, together with certain other notable filmmakers, again provides an illuminating point of comparison.

The fifth chapter consists of an analysis of each of Tulio's films in terms of the most central themes that run through his entire oeuvre: temptation and reconciliation, loss of innocence, mad jealousy, destructive passions and female decadence. This chapter concludes with an analysis of two films that are anomalies in Tulio's oeuvre, and then of his most outrageous film, *Sensuela*.

In the sixth chapter Tulio's style will be examined systematically by means of the *Cinemetrics* Internet tool. Systematic study of style is introduced as a way of creating a firm basis for analysing how a filmmaker exploits cinematic means to articulate his concerns – or, in the case of Tulio, obsessions – in a highly individual fashion so as to evoke certain affects and emotions in the spectator. The analysis will reveal whether there are any significant changes in Tulio's style and whether these add up into discernible trends over his career. The results will be compared to film historical data that the *Cinemetrics* database provides in order to examine how Tulio's style relates to cinematic styles of the past and those of his contemporaries. Further analysis will entail a close textual analysis of the functions of certain cinematic devices Tulio kept on employing repeatedly. One of the key elements of this stylistic analysis will be comparison with relevant reference material, the most relevant being certain thematically related Finnish films of his time, above all, rural melodramas. For the most part these largely adhered to the norms of the classical style. The classical style is flexible and allows for quite idiosyncratic styles, but it could not contain Tulio.

The seventh chapter is dedicated to the exploration of one of the most distinguishing features of Tulio's oeuvre: excessive repetition. Almost all of his films are about compulsive passion and sexuality. It is not unusual for auteurs to return to the same themes, but in this respect Tulio goes significantly further than most of his colleagues in that he even circulates the same footage from one film to another, employs a comment from one film as the title of another, uses intently gazing eyes as a leitmotif of his entire output, plays the same music recurrently even from film to film, and depicts Regina Linnanheimo again and again as a young woman becoming in all her innocence a fallen and degraded woman. This chapter explores how both repetition and variation contribute to Tulio's film style, making it easily recognisable and, in its idiosyncrasy, rewarding in its own, totally unique way.

The eighth chapter focuses on Tulio's legacy, his role in the history of Finnish cinema in his own time, and contrasting his career with those of his childhood friend Vaala and another independent director, Nyrki Tapiovaara. This is followed by an examination of the vagaries of Tulio's critical reception, completed with an analysis of the major reassessment of his works that took place in the 1990s.

The volume concludes with an analysis of our understanding of Tulio's significance today. This includes a discussion of Tulio's impact on certain filmmakers such as Aki Kaurismäki, another independent filmmaker. For many of them, the main lesson has been the almost moral call to create a production context and a cinematic style that suits their need to express their own, deeply felt concerns.

NOTES

1. Lubitow, Adam: 'Film recap: The 2017 Nitrate Picture Show', *Rochester City Newspaper*, 14 May 2014, https://www.rochestercitynewspaper.com/rochester/film-recap-the-2017-nitrate-picture-show/Content?oid=3485677 (accessed 3 July 2019).
2. Varjola 1993: 346.
3. These were reprinted with minor edits in *Tulio – Levottoman veren antologia* (Toiviainen 2002) and have been used as the major source for the account of Tulio's life here and in the third chapter.
4. Monsiváis 2018: 152.
5. Singer 2001: 38–9.
6. Ibid.: 40.
7. Ibid.: 44.
8. Ibid.: 44–8.
9. Ibid.: 39–40.
10. Ibid.: 46.
11. Ibid.: 43.
12. Williams 2018: 215.
13. Buckley 2018: 23.
14. Altman 1992: 26.
15. Ibid.: 39–40.
16. Ibid.: 41.
17. Bordwell, Thompson & Staiger 1985: 24.

18. Ibid.: 71. It should be noted that the Neoformalists use the notion of excess in a slightly different way than it is employed in most melodrama studies. For them, excess signifies 'those aspects of the work which are not contained by its unifying force' (Thompson 1981: 287). The idea is that, 'The material provides perceptual play by inviting the spectator to linger over devices longer than their structured function would seem to warrant' (ibid.: 292).
19. Williams 2018: 206–7.
20. Ibid.
21. Gledhill 2018: xxi.
22. Elsaesser 1987: 50.
23. Williams 2001: 22.
24. Brooks 1985: 15.
25. Ibid.: 5.
26. Buckley 2018: 25.
27. Gledhill 1987: 33.
28. Ibid.: 30.

NEWSPAPERS

Rochester City Newspaper 2014.

BIBLIOGRAPHY

Alanen, Antti (2004), 'Nuoren Vallan kansainvälisiä vaikutteita', in Kimmo Laine, Matti Lukkarila and Juha Seitajärvi (eds), *Valentin Vaala*, Helsinki: Suomalaisen Kirjallisuuden Seura, 65–77.
Altman, Rick (1992), 'Dickens, Griffith, and Film Theory Today', in Jane Gaines (ed.), *Classical Hollywood Narrative – The Paradigm Wars*, Durham, NC and London: Duke University Press, 9–48.
Bordwell, David, Janet Staiger and Kristin Thompson (1985), *The Classical Hollywood Cinema – Film Style & Mode of Production to 1960*, London: Routledge.
Brooks, Peter (1985), *The Melodramatic Imagination – Balzac, Henry James, Melodrama, and the Mode of Excess*, New York: Columbia University Press.
Buckley, Matthew (2018), 'Unbinding Melodrama', in Christine Gledhill and Linda Williams (eds), *Melodrama Unbound – Across History, Media, and National Cultures*, New York: Columbia University Press, 15–29.
Elsaesser, Thomas (1987), 'Tales of Sound and Fury: Observations on the Family Melodrama', in Christine Gledhill (ed.), *Home is Where the Heart Is – Studies in Melodrama and the Woman's Film*, London: BFI Publishing, 43–69.
Gledhill, Christine (1987), 'The Melodramatic Field: An Investigation', in Christine Gledhill (ed.), *Home is Where the Heart Is – Studies in Melodrama and the Woman's Film*, London: BFI Publishing, 5–39.
Gledhill, Christine (2018), 'Prologue: The Reach of Melodrama', in Christine Gledhill and Linda Williams (eds), *Melodrama Unbound – Across History, Media, and National Cultures*, New York: Columbia University Press, ix–xxv.
Hupaniittu, Outi (2016), 'The Emergence of Finnish Film Production and its Linkages to Cinema Business During the Silent Era', in Henry Bacon (ed.), *Finnish Cinema – A Transnational Enterprise*, London: Palgrave Macmillan, 27–50.

Monsiváis, Carlos (2018), 'One suffers but one learns: Melodrama and the Rules of Lack of Limits', in Christine Gledhill and Linda Williams (eds), *Melodrama Unbound – Across History, Media, and National Cultures*, New York: Columbia University Press, 151–68.

Nikula, Jaana (2000), *Polttava katse – Regina Linnanheimon elämä ja elokuvat*, Helsinki: Like.

Nikula, Jaana (2002), 'Regina Linnanheimon ja Teuvo Tulion yhteistyö', in Sakari Toiviainen (ed.), *Tulio – Levottoman veren antologia*, Helsinki: Suomalaisen Kirjallisuuden Seura, 167–81.

Seppälä, Jaakko (2012), *Hollywood tulee Suomeen – Yhdysvaltalaisten elokuvien maahantuonti ja vastaanotto kaksikymmentäluvun Suomessa*, Helsingin yliopisto: Unigrafia.

Singer, Ben (2001), *Melodrama and Modernity – Early Sensational Cinema and its Contexts*, New York: Columbia University Press.

Suni, Annikki (2002), 'Fedja, ystävämme', in Sakari Toiviainen (ed.), *Tulio – Levottoman veren antologia*, Helsinki: Suomalaisen Kirjallisuuden Seura, 159–65.

Thompson, Kristin (1981), *Eisenstein's Ivan the Terrible: A Neoformalist Analysis*, Princeton: Princeton University Press.

Toiviainen, Sakari (ed.) (2002), *Tulio: Levottoman veren antologia*, Helsinki: Suomalaisen Kirjallisuuden Seura.

Uusitalo, Kari (2004), 'Valentin Vaala – "uneksivakatseinen ohjaaja"', in Kimmo Laine, Matti Lukkarila and Juha Seitajärvi (eds), *Valentin Vaala*, Helsinki: Suomalaisen Kirjallisuuden Seura, 33–43.

Varjola, Markku (1993), 'Intohimon roviot – Teuvo Tulion Sellaisena kuin sinä minut halusit, Rakkauden risti, Levoton veri', in Kari Uusitalo et al. (eds), *Suomen kansallisfilmografia 3, 1942–1947*, Helsinki: Painatuskeskus and Suomen elokuva-arkisto, 346–50.

Williams, Linda (2001), *Playing the Race Card – Melodramas of Black and White from Uncle Tom to O. J. Simpson*, Princeton: Princeton University Press.

Williams, Linda (2018), '"Tales of Sound and Fury . . ." or, The Elephant of Melodrama', in Christine Gledhill and Linda Williams (eds), *Melodrama Unbound – Across History, Media, and National Cultures*, New York: Columbia University Press, 205–18.

CHAPTER 2

Tulio and Traditions of Melodrama

Tulio was quite reticent about his sources of inspiration. In his autobiography he hardly mentions other works of art than those he actually adapted. Yet all artists have received their basic ideas, models and conceptions at least to some extent from earlier works of art, even if at times in indirect ways. Tulio's excessive brand of melodrama is, in its intensity and single-mindedness, something quite unique, but it, too, has its models in earlier traditions such as romantic opera, nineteenth-century stage melodrama and much of silent cinema. It can further be illuminatingly contrasted with its contemporary parallels, Scandinavian and Finnish rural melodrama, naturally, but also with American film melodrama of the 1950s. The relevance of each of these in respect of Tulio's oeuvre can be charted by using Ben Singer's list of five aspects of melodramas: pathos, overwrought emotions, moral polarisation, non-classical narrative structure and sensationalism.

ROMANTIC OPERA

The notion of 'operatic' is often used in a slightly condescending tone to describe films which display strong emotions. This is not entirely unfair, as in many operas the plot serves mainly to provide a chain of emotionally charged situations in which the feelings of the characters are expressed by means of maximally sensuous music. Sometimes the plots verge on the ridiculous, as characters are seen to react and then act with blind passion, often without making the slightest effort to understand why other characters are acting the way they do. Thus, often even the best of intentions can be grossly misjudged. Giuseppe Verdi *Il Trovatore* (1853) is an extreme case, as the complicated plot of the play by the Spanish Antonio García Gutiérrez has been further condensed to the point of absurdity. Between the splendid arias the events move on at breakneck speed in a highly elliptical fashion. A great deal of the tensions motivating the characters derive from traumatic past events that are only gradually and briefly revealed to other characters and the audience. Toward the end of the third act, Leonora and Manrico are singing about the 'joys of their chaste love', when a messenger storms in to inform Manrico that the old gypsy Azucena, who Manrico believes to be his mother, is in chains on an already lit stake. Manrico sings a rousing aria to summon his men to arms and they rush to save the old woman.

As the fourth act commences, it becomes apparent that the bold attack has failed and Manrico is now a prisoner. Apparently, the stake has been quenched as Manrico now meets Azucena in their prison cell. Meanwhile, Leonora has decided to save her beloved by offering herself to Count Luna, who madly desires her, in exchange for Manrico's life. Her intention is, of course, to kill herself immediately after Manrico's release. She gets to meet him once more to tell him that he is now free. Manrico, however, guesses how she has succeeded in organising this, and in a mad rage accuses her of having sold her heart, which really belongs to him. He vehemently curses her and tells her to go away, only to discover that she is already dying of poison. The Count rushes in, realises he has been betrayed, and orders the immediate execution of Manrico. His orders are fulfilled, after which Azucena informs him that Manrico was in reality his long-lost brother she had kidnapped when he was a baby.[1]

Il Trovatore is excessive to the point of untypicality, but as such offers all the more illuminating parallels with Tulio's works. The characters appear to be transported in time and place only so as to provide maximum dramatic and emotional impact without much concern about plausibility or clarity of narration. The men in particular are blinded by their passions, highly opinionated, jump to conclusions, and behave irrationally on the basis of how they mistakenly perceive the situation, either because of long- or short-term misperceptions. Above all, Manrico cursing Leonora because he mistakenly thinks she has betrayed him by selling her chastity is the stuff that Tulio's films are made of. In one of Tulio's films, *In the Fields of Dreams* (*Unelma karjamajalla*, 1940), there is even a kidnapping performed by a vengeful gypsy character, although this plot line is resolved more in the manner of another convention of nineteenth-century melodrama, with the family being finally reunited.

Another opera with a plot much reminiscent of Tulio's thematic concerns, particularly as they appear in *The Way You Wanted Me* (*Sellaisena kuin sinä minut halusit*, 1944), is Puccini's *Madama Butterfly*. The main similarities are:

- On an extra-fictional level: an innocent, embarrassingly naïve young girl is played by an adult woman trying to appear girlish (in both cases an old stage convention, and one that appears repeatedly in Tulio's films).

- The innocent-minded young woman is taken advantage of and then casually abandoned by a man.
- A mock marriage takes place in order to fool the girl herself in *Butterfly*, the girl's father in Tulio's *The Way You Wanted Me* (as well as *Sensuela*).
- She is rejected by her community.
- The man, who is not entirely a scoundrel, wants to make amends but is no longer in a position to do so (in Tulio, rather: within the moral universe of the fictional world she is beyond redemption).
- She contemptuously refuses the money offered to her in compensation.
- In the end, she gives away her child in order to guarantee him/her a better life.

The main difference is that whereas the women in Tulio's world eventually succumb to prostitution, Puccini's Cio-Cio-san retains her purity by killing herself at the tender age of eighteen.

A standard theme of opera plots almost throughout the art form's entire history has been that of jealousy. Rodolfo's feelings for Mimì in Puccini's *La Bohème* (1896) serve as a fairly good example. He has chased her away, partly because he is madly jealous as he mistakenly thinks she is a flirt, partly reasoning that she is better off with a viscount who fancies her rather than with a poor poet such as he is, even suggesting that she has got ill because of sharing his windy garret. By the final act she has left the viscount and is reunited with her bohemian friends, but she is already dying of consumption. The closest parallel in Tulio's oeuvre is with what the innocent girl has to go through in *Cross of Love* (*Rakkauden risti*, 1946). There the bohemian artist is a painter, like *La Bohème*'s Marcello. But as we shall see, jealousy is one of the foundational elements of Tulio's overly emotional universe.

One of Tulio's most persistent themes does not loom particularly large in the canons of opera, and that is the seduction of an innocent woman. Verdi's *Rigoletto* is the main exception, and *La Traviata*'s Violetta is a fallen woman with a pure soul. The more typical plot device in nineteenth-century opera is that the soprano mistakenly thinks her tenor has been unfaithful and goes mad. Thus, they can first indulge in an exquisite love duet together and then later on sing their hearts out separately in their despair of having lost their beloved. Donizetti's *Lucia di Lammermoor* and Bellini's *I Puritani* are the most famous examples. But in nineteenth-century stage and literary melodrama, seduction of an innocent woman was one of the principal plot devices. From there it found its way to silent cinema, and quite likely that is where Tulio discovered not only this but also many other central concerns of his output.

In terms of Singer's five categories, we may observe that many romantic operas seek to evoke pathos, although the transformation of opera's socio-cultural role may have diminished this aspect: plots that may have had at their time significant political urgency – as in the case of Verdi so often – have become a conventionalised part of our cultural heritage.[2] But audiences of our time still expect those overwrought emotions to be expressed at least through great singing and hopefully also compelling acting. Moral polarisations are generally not as extreme as in stage melodrama, as even the more doubtful characters are often sad victims of their own passions: a typical scheme being that baritones such as *Il Trovatore*'s Count Luna are in despair because the soprano is prepared to yield to their desire only in death. Over the nineteenth century, there was a development from classicism to romanticism, which entailed a shift toward evermore forceful emotional expression and a general darkening of the world view. Whereas in the first part of the century a happy ending was still the norm, by mid-century a tragic ending was expected.[3]

The degree of narrative classicism varies even among the works of a single romantic composer such as Verdi, whose *Masked Ball* and *Otello* are concise and classical in form whereas *Il Trovatore* and *Force of Destiny* are much more episodic and elliptical. Romantic opera could be highly extravagant, giving scope for staging huge and colourful scenes, and many works of that period can appear somewhat reduced without spectacular staging. What Tulio might have seen on the stage of the very small Alexander's Theatre, which served as the home of the Finnish Opera (Finnish National Opera since 1956) until 1993, may not have been all that grandiose, but at least emotional expression is reputed to have impressed contemporary audiences.

NINETEENTH-CENTURY MELODRAMA

Certain melodramatic features loomed large already in eighteenth-century sentimental novels such as Samuel Richardson's *Pamela, or Virtue Rewarded* (1740) and Jean-Jacques Rousseau's *Julie, ou, la nouvelle Héloise* (1761), as well as in bourgeois tragedy, most famously in Gotthold Ephraim Lessing's *Emilia Galotti* (1768) and Friedrich Schiller's *Kabale und Liebe* (1776). The melodramatic story was used to reflect the intense social and ideological crisis caused by the conflict between the rising bourgeoisie and the remnants of feudalism.[4] These works certainly gave rise to both pathos and the display of strong emotions, but mainly within a classical framework providing sensationalism by means of the emotional build-up of incidents within a focused narrative structure. Moral oppositions were structured to a great extent between representatives of different classes, one of the most common points of conflict being love that transgresses class boundaries. The key stock character is the bourgeois maiden, whose virtue is threatened by a callous aristocrat. A young woman's virtue is fetishised to the point that if not she herself, her father will kill her in order to protect it.[5] Emilia Galotti complains: 'In former days there was a father, who, to save his daughter from disgrace, plunged the first deadly weapon which he saw, into his daughter's heart – and thereby gave her life, a second time. But those were deeds of ancient times. Such fathers exist not now.' Her father, however, will not fail to observe the tradition and so he lovingly stabs her, with 'this kind parental hand', as Emilia puts it before she dies.[6]

In its nineteenth-century forms, melodrama was a predominantly bourgeois form of art in which other classes pose threats to the decent, good life of middle-class people. Among the standard themes were the loss and recovery of family unity, at least if the lost family member was a boy such as Oliver Twist in Charles Dickens' novel of that name. But if the lost family member was a young woman and she was either seduced or abused, there was not likely to be any redemption: she had become irrevocably morally contaminated and would probably have to die in shame, as happens to Lady Isabel in Ellen Wood's *East Lynne* (1861). There were violent changes of fortune often related to economical pursuits, connecting human affairs with industrialisation and the ever-more powerful rise of capitalism, such as Dickens' *Little Dorrit* and Honoré de Balzac's *Le Père Goriot*. Thus, in Peter Brooks' words, melodrama could actually serve as 'an inquest into the system responsible for the melodramatic contrasts of urban life'.[7] However, often the social reformism was generally tinged by bourgeois paternalism and was based on humanitarian sympathies rather than on an analytic study of social structures.[8]

The theatre of the post-Napoleonic restoration was in many ways a trivialisation of earlier bourgeois melodrama. Social relevance was replaced by exotic settings and escapist entertainment. Whereas before the French Revolution, plays in the melodramatic mode had generally had tragic endings, reflecting the weak social standing of the bourgeoisie under the oppression of the aristocracy, they would now rather end in a happy reconciliation and affirmation of the bourgeois social order as well as the known sympathies and antipathies of these audiences. Instead of horrible social conditions, the threat was associated with other social classes: evil aristocrats and lecherous clergymen, as well as the more conventional villains and tramps. Plots were often driven by narrative devices such as coincidences, hidden connections and *deus ex machina*-type plot twists used to reach a narrative closure. Such plot devices could be used as elements of emotional shock tactics and the narrative form as a whole was developed to minimise dead spots and to maximise suspense.[9]

This change is indicative of the wide scope of melodrama, in Thomas Elsaesser's words, 'to function either subversively or as escapism – categories which are always relative to the given historical and social context'.[10] We need not think that the writers of melodramas were just cynical: 'Even if the situations and sentiments defied all categories of verisimilitude and were totally unlike anything in real life, the structure had a truth and a life of its own, which an artist could make part of this material . . . by turning a body of techniques into a stylistic principle that carried the distinct overtones of spiritual crises, they could put the finger on the texture of their social and human material while still being free to shape this material.'[11]

While some of the great novelists of the nineteenth century could achieve astonishing effects by their employment of melodramatic narrative strategies, more generally, the ways all this worked out were not always all that subtle. Characters were not 'round' and driven by psychological motivation, rather they served as excuses for displaying extreme emotional situations. They and their problems were made for easy recognition. Conventionalised plots allowed first for thrills and sensations and then for reassuring resolutions which appeared to affirm the moral order. Justice prevailed after torment; moral elevation followed indulgence in morally dubious situations and sensations. It was still possible, in the actual working out of the fortunes of the hero or the heroine, to present more subversive attitudes, but as complex issues were simplified and fault was assigned to characters who were villains by nature, this amounted to no more than satisfying the hunger for compensatory images and giving credence to the established order.[12]

The fathers of daughters who faced the danger of the corruption of their virtue were as murderous as ever. The narrator of *East Lynne* encourages her readers concerning an astonishingly beautiful Earl's daughter:

> Admire and love her whilst you may, she is worthy of it now, in her innocent childhood; the time will come when such praise would be misplaced. Could the fate, that was to overtake his child, have been foreseen by the earl, he would have struck her down to death, in his love, as she stood before him, rather than suffer her to enter upon it.[13]

There also existed a whole sub-literature written for blatantly exploitative purposes. It had a guaranteed audience and was based on simplistic stories and characterisations, middle-class morality, genres and melodramatic plots. The writers of adventure stories would concentrate very much on action and movement, as silent film would do later on. The plot lines were often as well planned as the best stage productions or production-line films. The audience would be made to feel concerned for the well-being of the protagonist, there would be plenty of action and peaks of suspense and a final solution, which in some way had been hinted at in the beginning. And though this kind of writing was deplored by literary critics and other like-minded proponents of high culture, the cheaper media only provided in a somewhat simplified form what middle-class readers enjoyed in more sophisticated ways.[14]

Tulio's poetics is in many ways remarkably similar to this kind of melodrama. He does not provide direct social criticism. In the rural melodramas in particular there are codes of honour and morality which are rigorously enforced despite the destruction they may cause in people's lives. That is simply presented as the way of the world. Characters are easily recognised in terms of their plot functions. There is no suggestion of inner depths, everything about them is exceedingly obvious to everyone except the most innocent characters in the story. With the exception of *In the Fields of Dreams* Tulio does not employ *deus ex machina*-type plot devices and only occasionally striking coincidences, but some of his characters become victims of random events that lead them to destruction. His plot development can be as fast as that in stage melodramas, as his storytelling contains many ellipses that are never filled in. Suddenly the protagonist is seen in a new situation in which her fortunes appear to have radically changed, if only temporarily. In *The Way You Wanted Me* there is a sequence in which Maija, fallen into prostitution, appears to be saved by a wealthy elderly gentleman. But just as unexpectedly, he is arrested as a spy and Maija's downfall continues. She, like many other female characters in Tulio's films, is after all a fallen woman. Such plot twists serve at times as emotional shock tactics, inasmuch as they, coming completely unexpectedly, do not appear plainly absurd.

Tulio's plots do not amount to an inquest of a social system or class structure in the way of many of the great nineteenth-century novels. Moral issues emerge from deeply internalised moralism and vain attempts to shake off its chains, the basic pattern consisting of the reckless, rather than just plain callous, seducer, the innocent, romantically inclined young woman, and her stern, utterly uncompromising father. There are also fiercely authoritarian matrons who appear to be much more in command than their male counterparts. The thundering moralism and simple-mindedness of the fathers may make them appear somewhat comic, just like their counterpart in nineteenth-century stage melodrama. In the earlier films, the pattern could be more complex, also including a man, who in contrast to the seducer is truly loving of the young woman. However, he typically appears simply too weak to serve as a moral standard-bearer. In *The Way You Wanted Me* this character, Aarne, belongs to a family that is feuding with the young woman's, Maija's, family. His father has strictly prohibited his sons from getting involved with Maija. Aarne, however, is in love with her and they have spent a night together. His father discovers that one of his sons has slept with the girl and interrogates them to find out who has disobeyed him. All three sons deny having been with Maija. She refuses to tell who the 'culprit' is, identifying the man she has been with only as 'my *former* fiancé'.

There are very few family reconciliations in Tulio's films. Something of the kind appears in *The Song of the Scarlet Flower* and *In the Fields of Dreams*, in both of which the reckless son matures and returns to assume his responsibilities taking care of the family fortune. But the theme of an innocent woman seduced and tarnished became Tulio's veritable obsession. He returned to it again and again with just a little variation. It appears that his regular co-screenwriter and leading lady of many of his films, Regina Linnanheimo, catalysed and endorsed the treatment of this theme. With her prominent facial features, especially her big eyes, she had the appearance, dare one say, of an adult baby face. She was the perfect *ingénue*. A Wikipedia definition suits her standard role and appearance in many of Tulio's films perfectly:

> Typically, the ingénue is beautiful, kind, gentle, sweet, virginal, and often naïve, in mental or emotional danger, or even physical danger, usually a target of the Cad; whom she may have mistaken for the Hero. Due to lack of independence, the ingénue usually lives with her father, husband, or a father figure . . . The ingénue stereotypically has the fawn-eyed innocence of a child, but subtle sexual appeal as well.[15]

According to one of the most persistent patterns in stage melodrama, that 'subtle appeal', when combined with any form of female sexual activity not directed to procreation, was equated with prostitution and led to destruction.[16] Despite the ostensible concern for the treatment of innocent young women led astray by their lack of knowledge of the way of the world and their romantic aspirations, Tulio blatantly exploits this scenario in an almost sadistic fashion. In his last film, *Sensuela* (1973), it is as if he had finally done away with all pretension and the woman, referred to in the voice-over as 'a child of the nature', is shown not only in beautifully shot nude scenes during supposedly romantic encounters, but very explicitly also as a stripper in a seedy nightclub. The film may well be classified as soft porn.

There is one major stage melodrama and silent film stock character who in these contexts often served as a foil to the *ingénue*, but who does not appear to any significant degree in Tulio's films, and that is the vamp, or *femme fatale*. Again and again the male characters obsessively desire women assuming them to be pure souls, and these women certainly do not appear as seducers. Those tarnished souls resort to prostitution once they have been taken advantage of and have then been rejected from their protecting social context. But prostitutes in Tulio's world appear tired and repulsive rather than alluring and seductive. With Tulio's typical melodramatic exaggeration, these women inhabit seedy abodes which underline the sheer decadence and depravity to which they have sunk. Just as in nineteenth-century melodrama, they are socially stained, even though their fall might be a consequence of their innocence rather than moral weakness.

In view of all this, Tulio appears anachronistic even by the standards of nineteenth-century melodrama. Pirjo Lyytikäinen, in discussing Mario Praz, points out that whereas in Romanticism the standard pattern is a devilish man and an innocent female victim, by the turn of the century this has been to an extent replaced by that of the holy man and the devilish woman.[17] It would be an exaggeration to describe men in Tulio's films as devilish; they are simply self-centred and reckless, but nevertheless, the innocent women have to suffer. This pattern is never reversed. There are no holy men, or even men of thought, who succumb to the temptations of a vamp, nor are there women who would make men suffer, except if they experience at least a pang of a guilty conscious-ness for having wrecked the women's lives.

Yet another feature of nineteenth-century melodrama that does offer a per-tinent point of comparison with Tulio is the 'exhibiting [of] a truer, more "nat-ural" morality in the lower class, whose pure sensibility is presented as at once comic and admirable'.[18] The extreme of this type, to the point of parody which may or may not be intentional, looms large in the father characters of Aukusti in *The Way You Wanted Me* and Aslak in *Sensuela*. Their function is to represent stern, utterly uncompromising moralism, which effectively prevents the resto-ration of what could be left of the family (in both films, the mother is absent). Moralism thus appears as the chief obstacle to happiness, leaving the daughters ruined and fathers more embittered than they ever thought possible. In fact, another standard stage melodrama element that is entirely missing in Tulio's films is, in the words of Richard Maltby, 'the rescue of the passive heroine from men, or "devils dressed like men", embodying lust, greed, or tyranny'. What we do find is women who appear as 'corruptible vessels of spiritual value, over whose purity the man at war with himself might constantly battle'.[19] In a few instances the good and the bad elements are embodied in separate male charac-ters, but more often one single character causes evil mainly by his recklessness and lack of consideration. He might later repent, but it is always too late. The point is summarised in a line of dialogue that appears in three of Tulio's films, as well as the title of one of them: 'Here I am, the way you wanted me'.

Helen Day-Mayer and David Mayer have suggested that '[melodrama] emerges from societies where things go wrong, where suffering is not always acknowledged, and where the explanations for wrong, injustice, and suffering are not altogether understandable'.[20] However, nineteenth-century melodrama tended to exploit such concerns by providing sensational drama rather than positing actual social critique:

> Both stage and film melodramas were often structured to advance their plots at such an accelerating tempo that audiences were denied any adequate opportunity to question inconsistencies or anomalies or moral ambiguities . . . the audience has not been allowed time to note that a serious and major problem – the immediate social background to this drama – has been abruptly dispelled.[21]

By contrast, toward the end of the nineteenth century a new trend led toward dramatic realism and the 'attempt to portray fully developed, psychologically multidimensional "real" characters experiencing "real" situations'.[22] This amounted to a development which Deidre Pribram has explored as a 'cultural reconceptualization of emotions' leading to a situation in which 'externalized displays of emotion, along with melodrama in general, are increasingly considered overwrought or exaggerated'.[23] A somewhat similar pattern structured also the reception of Tulio's films. Soon after the war, if not earlier, audiences began to see his excesses in just those terms. To the very end, he was bound to the key features of an antiquated form of melodrama, far removed even from the melodramas of his contemporaries either at home or abroad.

In one important respect Tulio did succeed quite impressively in holding his ground. An interesting parallel may be seen between the visually expressive strategy of nineteenth-century stage melodrama and Tulio's cinematics. Martin Meisel has pointed out that the former was not only narrative but emphatically pictorial, 'with its situational grammar, its punctuating crystallisations into a pictorial configuration with narrative import and accent: often an impasse, sometimes a resolution, typically followed by a cut (a curtain) or a dissolve'. According to Meisel, 'even acting theory turned from a discourse based in rhetorical analysis to one that was fundamentally pictorial'.[24] These are the main elements from which arises Tulio's very own version of what Matthew Buckley has called the 'sensational expressionism' of nineteenth-century melodrama.[25]

Tulio was to a significant extent a pictorialist. This connects with the way, as opposed to the classical style, Tulio's cinema is at times characterised by blatant discontinuity taking place both on the level of dramatic structure (ellipses) and shot-to-shot continuity. Often, he seems to be rushing to the striking images that crystallise the emotional situation or the state of mind that someone, usually the (anti)-heroine, has reached. Linnanheimo provided him with an astonishing range of facial expression from *ingénue* (*Cross of Love*, 1946) and coolly calculating mistress of a country estate (*In the Grip of Passion*, 1947) to a raving maniac (*Restless Blood*, 1946) or vacuous amnesiac (*A Crooked Woman*,[26] 1952). In Tulio's films, Linnanheimo's art of acting is, for the most part, fundamentally bodily expressive rather than verbal. This is just what Tulio needed: he was no master of striking or insightful dialogue, nor a weaver of intricate dramatic patterns; he was always after the emotionally and sensationally striking situation which the actor and, above all, the actress could exploit to the full in order to satisfy his cinematic needs.[27]

Not all critics took Linnanheimo's facial acrobatics seriously. One question which has to be addressed both as it regards nineteenth-century stage melodrama and Tulio's films is that they both are likely to give rise to laughter among contemporary audiences. This may not be merely a question of these works having become outmoded. Jacky Bratton argues in connection with stage melodrama that 'we must be committing the cardinal melodramatic sin of distorting its message when we try to suppress that laughter, or misunderstand its meaning. In their own

time early melodramas easily accommodated the comic response, without embar-
rassment; it was, indeed, vital to the genre, as it should be to our understanding of
it.' According to her, in England 'comedy was a major element' of melodramas all
through the nineteenth century.[28] In discussing Edward Richardson Lancaster's
plays *Ruth, or the Lass that Loved a Sailor* and *The Devil's Daughters; or, Hell's
Belles*, Bratton notes that their 'most striking aspect . . . is their deliberate theatrical artificiality, their self-referencing, their disdain for any constricting obligation
to realism or rationality'.[29] Bratton strongly suspects that as 'these extremities are
handled with such gusto, such a switchback motion between apparently deliberate exaggeration and knowing, heavily signalled bathos, that one is tempted to see
them as the 1841 equivalent of high camp; the suspicion becomes stronger at every
climax of the action'.[30] This may seem strange in view of the moral pathos that
seems to dominate most stage melodramas. But as Matthew Buckley points out,
'as we know well today, melodrama's engagement with morality can – like that of
any genre – be exploited, rendered ironic, or simply pushed into the background
as a slight gesture in a more sensational fare'.[31]

Some reviewers of Tulio's films of the 1950s expressed their wonder about
whether these works should or even could be taken quite seriously. They
report bursts of laughter among the audience. For us it is even more difficult
to decide whether Tulio intended the almost surreally excessive emotional
reactions of his characters, the implausibility of some of the plot twists to
appear funny, or whether he just did not care as long as he could capture on
film the extremities of emotion that he could squeeze out of his actors, Regina
Linnanheimo in particular. Perhaps he cared less and less as he began to lose
his audience. In Sensuela he transcended even his own spheres of excess. The
film begins with a clumsily realised crash of a German bomber toward the end
of the Second World War, offers a politically blatantly incorrect image of Sami
people as drunkards, then suddenly transports the pilot and the young Sami
woman into the lascivious 1960s without any sign of ageing, indulges in merry
orgies among pop-culture furnishings, and shows her father (constantly
dressed in his Sami costume even when trying to find his daughter in the big
city) being fooled by what is embarrassingly obviously a mock marriage. All
of this culminates in the father castrating the former pilot with his bare teeth
(as he has been seen at the beginning of the film doing to reindeer).

Sensuela can hardly fail to appear to us as high camp, yet there remains the
uncanny suspicion that Tulio was serious all of the time. He does not appear to
have realised how silly the plot, the visual aesthetics or the overblown reactions
his characters display might appear even in the eyes of his contemporaries. The
film was not widely distributed and it even received its premiere in the small
provincial city of Kemi, with only 665 viewers on its first run. *Sensuela* was
resurrected only after Tulio's death, as the Finnish Film Archive came into
the possession of his entire legacy and then organised a full retrospective of

his surviving films. The first screening after almost thirty years was an unforgettable experience, although almost certainly not in a way Tulio would have appreciated: right from the beginning the audience was roaring with laughter and the merriment continued to the very end.

Singer's list of the defining aspects of melodrama serves again in summarising analogies and differences between Tulio and nineteenth-century melodrama. The latter most certainly sought to evoke pathos, but it appears that as this was taken to extremes, a comic momentum crept in, awarding a somewhat different kind of pleasure not necessarily incompatible with the emotion that the drama appeared to offer at face value, so to say. We can even be ironically amused by our own sentimental reactions. The same structure of experience might well apply to overwrought emotions and to the display of moral polarisation extended to absurd dichotomies. This indulgence in extremes tended to lead toward non-classical narrative structure and sensationalism, but this was by no means the necessary condition of stage melodrama, although certain standard features such as coincidences and sudden reversals of fortune have often been seen as antithetical to the principles of classical narration. Melodrama is at its most effective when it adheres to age-old wisdom about telling or presenting a story in a way in which even the most heart-rending emotions and sensational effects emerge from coherent story logic which provides the motivation for all those extravagances.

SILENT PASSIONS

Melodrama was the predominant mode of feature-length silent cinema.[32] As films grew longer and started to have more narrative scope, filmmakers began adapting works of literature and theatre for the screen. Filming celebrated novels was a way of boosting cinema's cultural prestige, although particularly in the early years of cinema a novel of great length would have to be heavily reduced, often relying on the audience's previous knowledge of the stories rather than attempting self-contained narration. Such curtailing could increase the melodramatic impact of the stories but this would take place at the expense of narrative plausibility, psychological depth and social relevance. Often, as Rick Altman has demonstrated, the literary works had first been adapted for the stage.[33] The debt to a stage tradition was, as a rule, not acknowledged, but clearly these plays served as models for dramatic condensation, which had to be taken much further in filming, even after multi-reel features became the standard. This also applies to the adaptation of more popular novels that followed the same progression. Ellen Wood's enormously popular and excessively melodramatic novel *East Lynne* was first adapted several times for the stage and then at least eight times for the screen in the years 1902–16. Screen adaptations of such popular stage melodramas had great popular appeal.

The melodramatic mode also found its way into cinema in the form of original stories. These were often heartbreaking stories of unrequited love and families torn apart for various reasons, but also stories brimming with graphic thrills and shocking sensations. Indeed, as Singer has pointed out, the notion of melodrama at the time referred to the latter rather than the former type. This kind of sensational melodrama often came in the form of the film serial, delivering 'abundant rapid action, stimulating violence, spectacular sights, and the thrills of physical peril, abductions, and suspenseful rescues'.[34] Like sensational nineteenth-century stage melodramas that preceded them, serial melodramas such as *The Perils of Pauline* (Gasnier and Mackenzie, 1914) and *Les Vampires* (Feuillade, 1916) 'relied on similar story lines emphasizing pure villainy and heroism catalysed by the villain's jealousy and/or greed and often relying on extraordinary coincidences, sudden revelations, and unexpected twists of circumstance'.[35] Instead of narrative continuity and artistic elegance, the serial melodrama emphasised exciting physical action. In some of the best-known silent melodramas, the sentimental and the sensational traditions were fused, a case in point being *Way Down East* (Griffith, 1920), an adaptation of the nineteenth-century play of the same name by Lottie Blair Parker. The film is a sentimental saga of love that features a sensational climax in which the hero rescues his beloved at the very last moment from an ice floe about to plunge over a tremendous waterfall.

The one standard narrative pattern of silent cinema that most influenced Tulio was that of the fallen woman. Russel Campbell's characterisation of it matches many of Tulio's storylines almost perfectly: 'On her own, abandoned by her lover . . ., perhaps with a baby to care for, and without a legitimate source of income, she sooner or later begins to charge for her sexual services'.[36] The main difference is that, with the exception of Tulio's last film *Sensuela*, he does not care to show how things develop after the seduction: the fall is an inexorable fact of life, its consequences take place immediately. In Tulio's films there are also traces of an alternative pattern Campbell mentions – 'a mature woman strays from the path of virtue from force of circumstance or as an act of self-sacrifice',[37] – in that Tulio does stage situations in which the fallen woman withdraws from the life of her daughter so that the child can grow up in a respectable family and hopefully avoid her own fate. On the other hand, Tulio never appeals to the narrative pattern of the cause of the fall being bad parenting, unless the inability to avoid the meshes of temptation is seen to derive from these women being almost categorically motherless. At the other end of their stories, Tulio's fallen women do not all die, but neither do they have access to the kind of spiritual regeneration that appeared in some romantic pieces of literature such as Leo Tolstoy's *Resurrection* (1899), which, again via stage productions, found its way to early silent cinema, including D. W. Griffith's film of the same name (1909). Another trait that makes Tulio different from his silent cinema predecessors is that in his films the seduced girls never really get to enjoy a life in sin, like many of their kind in the silent cinema.

There is one aspect in which both silent melodrama and Tulio's works differ from nineteenth-century melodrama: the opposition between good and evil is nowhere near as strong. Campbell detects a generally greater degree of moral and psychological complexity in the fallen woman films of the silent era, and in Tulio evil takes even more the form of a mere youthful lack of consideration for others, or the morally sterile adhering to the prevailing codes of propriety and family honour of the older generation. A thematic thread which does seem to go through a great part of all these melodramatic traditions is the 'ban on [female] sexual desire and its expression'. There is what Campbell calls 'a double discourse' at work here, the two momentums being: '1. the woman, having been done wrong by men and needing to survive (and sometimes care for a child) is an innocent victim, but, 2. the woman having been initiated into illicit sex is corrupted by the experience and hence is morally guilty when she drifts into prostitution'.[38] This duality may well have been a reflection of the incompatibility of male sexual desire and a still prevalent code of morality, however much that may have been an anachronistic residue of hypocritical Victorian notions of morality in respect to what actually was going on in the society. By contrast, in some individual silent films at least, there could be a degree of indictment of the wrongs of the social system, somewhat in the manner of great nineteenth-century novels such as Victor Hugo's *Les Misérables* (1862), but this could actually lead to problems with the critical reception and censorship.[39]

According to Russel Campbell, the fallen woman motif had virtually disappeared from world cinema by the Second World War. Tulio, however, at that time really got into full swing in his treatment of this topic, above all in his films *The Way You Wanted Me* and *Cross of Love*, returning to this theme as late as 1973 in *Sensuela*. And while in accordance with this he was partly adhering to an equally outmoded cinematic aesthetics, he also gave it a distinctly idiosyncratic twist, as analysed in the chapter on Tulio's style.

Unfortunately, although Tulio in many ways adopted prominent features of late silent cinema aesthetics, he left us no record of his taste for these films. Almost certainly he was thrilled by the Manichean world view of melodrama, with its themes of male seducers and fallen women as well as narrative elements such as unexpected turns of events and last-minute rescues, in the silent cinema of his youth. We may well assume that he must have enjoyed numerous melodramas such as *The Sheik* (Hull, 1919) and *Miss Thompson* (Maugham, 1921) in the form of film adaptations, as they circulated widely in Finland and were praised by film buffs, to whose number he certainly belonged. As he began to act in the first films of his friend Valentin Vaala in the late 1920s, Tulio modelled his performances after those of Rudolph Valentino, whose sudden death in 1926 had left the world wanting for a new Valentino.[40] By the time Tulio started his own career as a director, cinema had already converted to sound, but the power-ful model of silent melodrama was to serve in many ways as his principal guide to both content and style. He made passionate melodramas with a heavy empha-sis on the destructive power of misguided love and unrestrained sexuality. This connects also with the sensationalism of action melodrama, shamelessly appeal-ing to basic emotions, even stating a number of these literally in the production stills of his film *Jealousy* (Mustasukkaisuus, 1953): each still names one emotion with an accompanying image: love, hate, envy, hatred and so on (figures 2.1–5). At times, he even staged fierce action scenes in silent cinema fashion. Also, the narrative ellipses – or, lacunas, rather – that sometimes take the spectator by surprise, seem like vague recollections of the frequently extreme narrative con-densation of early film adaptations. This, however, might be more an instance of economic constraints of production rather than aesthetic influence.

On the purely aesthetic level, Tulio's debt to silent cinema lies above all in the visual quality of his films. The plot twists may be outrageous, coincidences blatantly implausible, the characters hardly two-dimensional, the acting hammed and the dialogue overblown, but the visualisation is often as staggering as in some of the most striking action melodramas. There are long stretches with no dialogue, the emotions being so elemental and explicit that no words are needed. One rea-son behind this may be the evermore difficult production conditions (discussed in the fourth chapter) which curtailed Tulio's options as regards recording sound, but as we shall see, he was capable of making a virtue of such necessity.

Of the five categories that Singer suggests as the defining features of melo-drama – pathos, overwrought emotions, moral polarisation, non-classical nar-rative structure and sensationalism – all, of course, apply to the silent serial film, Singer's principal target of investigation. All these are to be found in Tulio's cinema too, and this may well be where he found his principal source of inspiration in developing his own brand of truly sensational melodrama.

EUROPEAN SENSIBILITIES

While Tulio's key melodramatic influences in the 1920s seem to have come mainly, if not exclusively, from Hollywood, during the next decades the role of Central European cinema increased. Partly this was a larger trend in Finnish film culture especially in the 1930s and 1940s. Even if American films made up the bulk of the repertoire through the studio years – albeit decreasing dur-ing the Second World War years, when the Finnish film business was under the influence of the German-led International Film Chamber – many of the most popular, and definitely many of the most talked-about, films came from Europe. Critics and filmmakers looked up to and found aesthetic ideals from German and especially French films rather than Hollywood. It was not until

Figures 2.1–5

the 1950s that wide critical interest was focused on Hollywood, partly under the influence of revisionist articles which appeared in *Cahiers du Cinéma*. Among filmmakers, Vaala remained a sole exception in his enthusiasm for Hollywood aesthetics and storytelling.

As we shall see in the following chapters, Vaala's and Tulio's careers took almost diametrically opposite turns after their cooperation ended, in terms not only of production, but also aesthetics. The more Vaala adapted to classical

Hollywood storytelling, the further Tulio drifted away from it. This is exemplified by a Czech film that is said to have been one of Tulio's all-time favourites,
Gustav Machatý's *Ecstasy* (*Ekstase*, 1933) – curiously enough, one of Ingmar
Bergman's favourites too.[41] Indeed, in its silent–sound hybridity, and with its
extremely long opening with no dialogue, montage of details of objects and
body parts, expressive lighting, and avoidance of classical découpage, *Ecstasy*
is an obvious precursor of Tulio's aesthetics. No doubt also the sensational
nude scene with Hedy Kiesler (later Lamarr) inspired Tulio, as can be seen in
The Song of the Scarlet Flower that features a scene where the two protagonists
swim naked across a river – although the swim in Tulio's film is less explicit
and more expressive of the purifying quality of nature than in *Ecstasy*.[42]

The most admired French films during Tulio's formative years as a director were undeniably those that have been classified as poetic realism. Ginette
Vincendeau has argued that despite the fact that film history has usually taken
the movement's realistic premises at face value, there is a lot of common ground
between poetic realism and melodrama. Poetic realism often features fallen
woman themes and overlaps with what feminist film history has characterised
as women's films. Furthermore, both poetic realism and melodrama evoke an
everyday world that is 'dominated by fate, coincidence, circularity, and nostal-
gia';[43] all of these features can also be found in Tulio's works. As regards style
and expression, the noirish elements of Tulio's post-war films can also partly
be traced back to poetic realism. As Vincendeau emphasises, many of the key
visual motives of film noir, 'dark, low-key lighting, strong shadows, and unusual
compositions', have their roots in European cinema, not only in expressionism
but also in poetic realism.[44] In relation to acting, although poetic realism usually
tends to prefer subtle tone and expression to overwrought emotions, the famous
outbursts of Jean Gabin, for example, are perhaps not worlds apart from melodrama, nor, indeed, from the excessive expression of emotion in Tulio's films.

Maureen Turim, in her classic study on flashbacks, sees the frame story/
long flashback structure as a narrative device typical for poetic realism to express
an atmosphere of fatalism and pessimism. Starting with the (generally gloomy)
present state of things, and then showing the trajectory that has led to it, emphasises the inevitability of the events, as if the fate of the characters was prede-
termined.[45] Such a sense of fatalism is evident in those Tulio films that rely on
a long flashback structure: *The Fight over the Heikkilä Mansion*, *Silja – Fallen
Asleep when Young* (presumably, since these two films only survive in fragments),
In the Grip of Passion, *Cross of Love* and especially *The Way You Wanted Me*.
The last-mentioned opens and closes in a city port with the protagonist Maija as
a prostitute beyond all hope. The long flashback traces her journey from a small
island village to the desolate harbour as a series of mistreatments, coincidences,
bad luck and bitter fate, and the sense of inevitability looms large. Also, in terms
of atmosphere and imagery, among all of Tulio's films, *The Way You Wanted*

Me comes closest to poetic realism. Its studio-realistic harbour milieu filled with diagonal lines and expressively lit fog draws inspiration, no doubt, from port films in general, but particularly from *Port of Shadows* (*Le Quai des brumes*, Marcel Carné, 1938), one of the most admired films in 1930s Finland.

The most obvious evidence of German melodrama's influence on Tulio is *Cross of Love*, which according to the opening credits is freely based on a theme by Alexander Pushkin, but is actually intermediated by Gustav Ucicky's German film *Der Postmeister* (1940), as will be discussed in detail in chapter five. That Pushkin was credited rather than Ucicky's film was no wonder: Pushkin carried more cultural prestige than a German film melodrama and, besides, was free of copyright. Uncredited remakes and adaptations were, in fact, quite common in Finland during the studio years, even among the major producers. The most famous example is Hannu Leminen's melodrama *White Roses* (*Valkoiset ruusut*, 1943), which was adapted from Stefan Zweig's short story *Letter from an Unknown Woman* (1922), best known as Max Ophüls' Hollywood adaptation from 1948.

Not only was *Der Postmeister* left uncredited, but there is no mention of it in Tulio's memoirs either, nor of other German films, for that matter. This might still be partly due to unclear copyright issues, but perhaps also to Tulio's pre-sumably critical attitude to Nazi Germany.[46] Yet the fact remains that German cinema was very popular in Finland during the Second World War and that the best-loved and most influential German films were melodramas. The most notable of these were such Veit Harlan films as *The Golden City* (*Die Goldene Stadt*, 1942) and *Immensee: A German Folksong* (*Immensee – Ein deutsches Volkslied*, 1943). The best-known cinematic representative of the anti-urbanist tendencies prevailing in Nazi Germany, *The Golden City* tells a story of a young countrywoman who is seduced by the lure of the 'golden city', Prague, and by empty promises of men. She gets pregnant and returns home, only to be rejected by her stern father, and finally drowns herself. Whether the influence was conscious or not, German anti-urbanism must be seen at least as parallel to anti-urbanist tendencies in Finland during and after the war years, and cer-tainly the two Tulio films flirting with anti-urbanist sentiments, *The Way You Wanted Me* and *Cross of Love*, tell stories of innocent countrywomen seduced by the sinful city that are strikingly similar to that of *The Golden City*.

As idiosyncratic as Tulio's cinema is in terms of expression, a breeding ground for it was provided by traditions of Scandinavian melodrama, first by the rural melodrama that flourished to varying degrees in Finland, Sweden, Denmark and Norway during the studio era,[47] and second by the noirish 'problem dramas' that were produced in all of these countries during the post-war years. In rural melodrama, the anti-urbanist tendencies of contrasting country and city were relatively common in Finland (for example, Ville Salminen's *Leeni of Haavisto* [*Haaviston Leeni*, 1948]) and Sweden (Rune Carlsten's *Anna Lans*, 1943). Essential for rural films in all Nordic countries was the way they exploit land-scapes and nature both for spectacular scenes and as expressions of characters' inner emotions.[48] As we shall see in the analysis of *The Song of the Scarlet Flower*, both uses of nature were central for Tulio's rural films too. As regards 'problem dramas', Tulio's post-war films can be seen as a part of a Nordic – as well as an international – cinematic trend of finding interest in socially and historically relevant (albeit also sensational) themes such as crime, prostitution and venereal diseases. As has been proposed by recent film histories, these films constitute a body of Nordic film noir and, as Andrew Nestingen argues, have a strong connection not only to contemporary American and international crime films but also to French poetic realism, 'in their pessimism and bleak view of human fates but also in their melodrama and cultural politics'.[49]

Most of the rather few films Tulio mentions in his memoirs are, in fact, Swedish, usually as sources of inspiration or a possible remake: *The Song of the Scarlet Flower* (*Sången om den eldröda blomman*, first version directed by Mauritz Stiller, 1919, second by Per-Axel Branner, 1934), *Haelsingland Folks* (*Hälsingar*, directed first by William Larsson, 1923, and then by Ivar Johansson, 1933) and *King's Street* (*Kungsgatan*, Gösta Cederlund, 1943). The two first-mentioned films Tulio remade as *The Song of the Scarlet Flower* and *In the Fields of Dreams* respectively, whereas the fallen woman melodrama *King's Street* served as an inspiration for *The Way You Wanted Me*. During the 1940s, remakes of Swedish films were common in major studios too, which reminds of the close transnational relations of Finnish and Swedish cinemas. Furthermore, it is noteworthy that many of these were fallen woman films, including Toivo Särkkä's *Anja, Come Back Home!* (*Anja tule kotiin*, 1944, based on Hampe Faustman's *Sonja*, 1943), *Leeni of Haavisto* (based on *Anna Lans*) and Hannu Leminen's *Puck* (1942, based on Gunnar Widegren's Swedish novel, adapted later by Schamyl Bauman as *Puck heter jag*, 1951).

The frequent borrowing – sometimes stealing – of stories from abroad was usually justified by the lack of domestic scripts of high quality.[50] Considering many of the transnational remakes and adaptations were melodramas with controversial or sensational themes like prostitution, adultery or infanticide, it is tempting to think of an additional explanation: the most sensational themes were more easily introduced as 'foreign' than as 'domestic', as if such things did not happen here in the homeland. As we shall see in chapter four, this was a two-way process; Tulio learned how to master the delicate differences between Finnish and Swedish film cultures – permissiveness of the censorship system, the audience's appetite for 'daring' sensations – and approached the respective markets with slightly differing versions of his films.

THE AMERICAN WAY

One interesting point of comparison for Tulio's brand of film melodrama in the 1950s is that of American filmmakers such as Vincente Minnelli and Douglas

Sirk, perceptively analysed by Elsaesser in his seminal article 'Tales of Sound and Fury'. One of his starting points is that 'melodramas have a myth-making function insofar as their significance lies in the structure and articulation of the action, not in any psychologically motivated correspondence with individu-alised experience'.[51] While this may be somewhat exaggerated in view of the entire field of what may be considered to be melodrama, it captures an impor-tant point: the action works out within certain schemes, usually morally loaded, and their effectiveness is largely dependent on the persuasiveness of the articu-lation, the forceful if not exactly plausible plot, the extremities of acting, the power of the images and the emotionally arousing music. The major difference between most traditions of melodrama and the films of Minnelli and Sirk is that they depict anxiety emerging from an existential or social situation as the source of evil. In this scheme of things, individuals appear as victims of their social circumstances. Their inability to cope with actual problems results in substitute actions such as compulsive sex, bursts of bluntly targeted aggression and even violence or resorting to alcohol. According to Elsaesser's analysis:

> The critique – the questions of 'evil', of responsibility – is firmly placed on a social and existential level, away from the arbitrary and finally obtuse logic of private motives and individualized psychology. This is why the melodrama, at its most accomplished, seems capable of repro-ducing more directly than other genres the patterns of domination and exploitation existing in a given society, especially the relation between psychology, morality and class consciousness, by emphasizing so clearly an emotional dynamic whose social correlative is a network of exter-nal forces directed oppressingly inward, and with which the characters themselves unwittingly collude to become their agents.[52]

Elsaesser explores how claustrophobic spaces often serve as a metaphor of suppressed emotions. Similarly, narratively static sequences may be used to allow for focusing on strong emotional reactions. On the other hand, it really is an instance of combining 'melos' and drama, emotionally loaded music and sumptuous settings emerging from a need to express and generate feelings that can hardly be evoked by realistic stylistic means.

There is very little evident social criticism in Tulio's works, apart from the age-old pattern of the wealthy being in the position to force their will and exploit the poor country girl, childishly innocent of how men – at least in the melodra-matic universe which they share – are likely to reject the likes of her after having had their way. In the background there are, at least sketchily depicted, those 'patterns of domination and exploitation existing in a given society, especially the relation between psychology, morality and class consciousness'. But for all practices and purposes, character psychology gives way to excessive emotional dynamics within a shamelessly caricatured social framework. The purpose of all this is clearly to generate plots with extreme reversals of fortune harking back to the tradition of stage melodrama. In the film *In the Grip of Passion* this is generated by the extreme contrast between the hero Olavi (Kullervo Kalske) and Paavo (Eric Gustafsson), the man the heiress of the country estate Aino (Linnanheimo) is forced to marry. In the American melodramas of the 1950s, there could be similar contrasts between the rich weakling heir of an industrial mogul and the competent employee with a modest background, as in Sirk's *Written on the Wind* (1956). However, they are at least initially both presented as viable options for the female protagonist, whereas in Tulio's melodrama Paavo is a rude and ruthless coward prepared to destroy both his own and his wife's family fortune in order to indulge in his near-constant drunken stupor. Alcohol is not a substitute for him, as it is for the impotent protagonist of *Written on the Wind*. Rather, being an alcoholic is his mode of being. This is very typical in Tulio's melodramatic universe and not uncommon in Finnish cinema as a whole.

As regards style, Sirk's and Minnelli's melodramas function in terms of pure classical style. Continuity is perfect and the whole is governed by a strong sense of unity. Most of Tulio's films, by contrast, although their stories have a clear beginning and an end, lack narrative cohesion, stylistic continuity and aesthetic unity. Together with the sudden twists of plot, the characters might change suddenly, sometimes quite inexplicably as a part of Tulio's strategy of emotional shock tactics, his very own brand of *melodramatic montage*. This functions both on the level of scenes that appear to collide rather than follow one another in any obviously coherent fashion, as well as on the level of montage proper, which often does not follow any plausible spatio-temporal pattern: characters appear in a shot located in a certain place when they are needed there in order to generate an emotional impact, irrespective of how they could plausibly be expected to appear there; often it is pointless to speculate how far apart two locations in the fictional world are supposed to be or how long it is reasonable to expect to take to move from one place to another. The sense of spatio-temporal disorientation is further strengthened by Tulio being quite cavalier about point-of-view shots: often there is a blatant mismatch between the direction a character appears to be gazing and what is then shown as the view that he or she presumably possesses. All this creates a hallucinatory sense seldom encountered so consistently in the major traditions of melodrama (all these features will be thoroughly examined in chapters five and six).

American 1950s film melodrama does not seek to elicit pathos, but overwrought emotions loom all the more large. Moral polarisation, however, does not appear anywhere as strongly as in most traditions of melodrama, as the problem of evil is located in the system, which the characters have internalised so thoroughly that they are to a large extent themselves the agents of their own unhappiness. In a sense, Tulio's stance is somewhat similar. The evil lies in the toxic moralism of certain characters, and this poisons the human relationships around them. Such characters, parents usually, are not evil as they have simply internalised the moral notions so thoroughly that they fail to see how much evil their self-righteous attitudes produce. Thus, a huge difference remains between Sirk and Minnelli on the one hand and Tulio on the other: the principal characters of Sirk's *Written on the Wind* or Minnelli's *Two Weeks in Another Town* (1963) agonise and fail according to their own criteria, whereas Tulio's male characters cause agony because they enforce moral notions with blind self-assurance. Furthermore, Sirk and Minnelli rely on classical Hollywood narration which they execute with sovereign professionalism, whereas Tulio's style of narration is loose and relies on as much sensationalism as he could summon with his ever-decreasing budgets.

NOTES

1. Luchino Visconti actually uses the end of the third and the beginning of the fourth act of *Il Trovatore* in the very opening of his *Senso* (1954), as its performance is taking place in the La Fenice theatre in Venice. The film is set at the time of Risorgimento, the struggle for the unification of Italy in the 1860s. The opera serves as a parallel for the tendency of the main character Livia to react and behave in a melodramatic fashion, as well as for the reckless but ineffectual heroism of her cousin Ussoni, who, having participated in a demonstration against the Austrian occupation at the end of the third act, finds himself, like Manrico, in chains by the beginning of the fourth act. This creates a discreetly comic effect in counterpoint with the melodramatic behaviour of the main characters.

2. Contemporary directors may seek to revitalise this aspect, as when in a 2018 production of *Il Trovatore* at the Finnish National Opera a rape committed by soldiers represented in mime was added to the stage action.

3. Challenging the convention of the happy ending was not always easy. In Rome, Rossini was actually paid extra for adapting a duet of reconciliation for his *Otello*. Budden 1984: 7.

4. Elsaesser 1985: 167–8.

5. Things work out somewhat differently in Rousseau's *Julie, ou, la nouvelle Héloïse*. Julie is an aristocratic young lady who develops a passionate love affair with her tutor Saint-Preux, a commoner. Her father insists that she must marry not only within her own social class, but his old friend Wolmar. By astounding contrast to nineteenth-century melodrama, Julie not only accepts this arrangement but also finds her true virtuous self as an obedient daughter, a loving wife and a tender mother. And not only that, Wolmar invites Saint-Preux to join their household. As the lovers grow ever wiser, gradually their romantic passion transcends into something spiritually much more rewarding. Unsurprisingly, it appears that no film adaptations have been made. This certainly is not the sort of material melodrama is made of.

6. Translated by B. Dillon Boylan. Available at http://www.gutenberg.org/files/33435/33435-h/33435-h.htm.

7. Brooks 1985: 129.

8. Ibid.: 138

9. Ibid.: 169.

10. Elsaesser 1987: 47.

11. Ibid.: 49.

12. Fell 1986: 14.

13. Wood 1984: 9.

14. Burt 1978: 156.

15. 'Ingénue', *Wikipedia: The Free Encyclopedia*, https://en.wikipedia.org/wiki/Ing%C3%A9nue (accessed 10 September 2019).

16. Lyytikäinen 1997: 124–5.

17. Lyytikäinen 1997: 140.

18. Bratton 1994: 39.

19. Maltby 1994: 2017.

20. Day-Mayer and Mayer 2018: 101.

21. Ibid.: 102, 103.

22. Singer 2001: 49.

23. Pribram 2018: 244.

24. Meisel 1994: 67.

25. Buckley 2009: 181–2, 188.

26. This English title in the database of the National Audiovisual Institute in Finland is fundamentally misleading. The correct title would be *A Criminal Woman*.

27. In view of the current #metoo campaign, it should be noted that no evidence survives of Tulio treating his actors badly. Linnanheimo's prominent role in the screenwriting process suggests that she certainly did not object to the exploitative aspects of the storylines.

28. Bratton 1994: 38.

29. Ibid.: 45.

30. Ibid.: 47.

31. Buckley 2018: 26.

32. Nowell-Smith 1996: 194.

33. Altman 1992: 13.

34. Singer 2001: 192.

35. Ibid.

36. Campbell 1999.

37. Ibid.

38. Ibid.

39. Ibid.

40. Seppälä 2012: 354–60.

41. Salmi 2009: 118.

42. For a comparison between the two nude scenes, see Audebert 2015.

43. Vincendeau 1989: 52.

44. Vincendeau 1992: 49–58.

45. Turim 1989: 144–8.

46. See Rajala 2014: 518–19.

47. See Soila, Söderbergh Widding and Iversen 1998: 44–6, 108–13, 191.

48. Seppälä 2017.

49. Nestingen 2016: 162–3.

50. See Soila 2019: 288.

51. Elsaesser 1987: 44.

BIBLIOGRAPHY

Altman, Rick (1992), 'Dickens, Griffith, and Film Theory Today', in Jane Gaines (ed.), *Classical Hollywood Narrative – The Paradigm Wars*, Durham, NC and London: Duke University Press, 9–48.

Audebert, Pierre (2015), 'Teuvo Tulio – Le chant de la fleur écarlate + Le rêve dans la hutte bergère (1938, 1940)', *Culturopot.com* 11.10.2015. https://www.culturopoing.com/cinema/sorties-salles-cinema/teuvo-tulio-le-chant-de-la-fleur-ecarlate-le-reve-dans-la-hutte-bergere-1938-1940/20151011 (accessed 30 September 2019).

Bratton, Jacky (1994), 'The Contending Discourses of Melodrama', in Jacky Bratton, Jim Cook and Christine Gledhill (eds), *Melodrama: Stage, Picture, Screen*, London: British Film Institute, 38–49.

Brooks, Peter (1985), *The Melodramatic Imagination – Balzac, Henry James, Melodrama, and the Mode of Excess*, New York: Columbia University Press.

Burt, Daniel S. (1980), 'A Victorian Gothic: G. W. M. Reynolds's Mysteries of London', in Daniel Gerould (ed.), *Melodrama*, New York: New York Literary Forum.

Buckley, Matthew (2018), 'Unbinding Melodrama', in Christine Gledhill and Linda Williams (eds), *Melodrama Unbound – Across History, Media, and National Cultures*, New York: Columbia University Press, 15–29.

Budden, Julian (1984), *The Operas of Verdi*, Vol. I, Oxford: Oxford University Press.

Campbell, Russel (1999), '"Fallen Woman" Prostitute Narratives in the Cinema', *Screening the Past*, Issue 8 (November 1999–March 2000). https://www.academia.edu/4091082/_Fallen_Woman_Prostitute_Narratives_in_the_Cinema (accessed 24 July 2019).

Day-Mayer, Helen and David Mayer (2018), 'Performing/Acting Melodrama', in Christine Gledhill and Linda Williams (eds), *Melodrama Unbound – Across History, Media, and National Cultures*, New York: Columbia University Press, 99–113.

Elsaesser, Thomas (1987), 'Tales of Sound and Fury: Observations on the Family Melodrama', in Christine Gledhill (ed.), *Home is Where the Heart Is – Studies in Melodrama and the Woman's Film*, London: BFI Publishing, 43–69.

Fell, John (1986), *Film and the Narrative Tradition*, Berkeley, Los Angeles and New York: University of Oklahoma Press.

Lyytikäinen, Pirjo (1997), *Narkissos ja Sfinksi – Minä ja Toinen vuosisadanvaihteen kirjallisuudessa*, Helsinki: Suomalaisen Kirjallisuuden Seura.

Meisel, Martin (1994), 'Scattered Chiaroscuro – Melodrama as a Matter of Seeing', in Jacky Bratton, Jim Cook and Christine Gledhill (eds), *Melodrama: Stage, Picture, Screen*, London: British Film Institute, 65–81.

Maltby, Richard (1994), 'The Social Evil, the Moral Order and the Melodramatic Imagination, 1890–1915', in Jacky Bratton, Jim Cook and Christine Gledhill (eds), *Melodrama: Stage, Picture, Screen*, London: British Film Institute, 214–30.

Nestingen, Andrew (2016), 'Nordic Noir and Neo-noir: The Human Criminal', in Homer B. Pettey and R. Barton Palmer (eds), *International Noir*, Edinburgh: Edinburgh University Press.

Nowell-Smith, Geoffrey (1996), 'The Heyday of the Silents', in Geoffrey Nowell-Smith (ed.), *The Oxford History of World Cinema*, Oxford: Oxford University Press, 192–204.

Pribram, E. Deidre (2018), 'Melodrama and the Aesthetics of Emotion', in Christine Gledhill and Linda Williams (eds), *Melodrama Unbound – Across History, Media, and National Cultures*, New York: Columbia University Press, 237–51.

Rajala, Panu (2014), *Tulisoihtu Pimeään. Olavi Paavolaisen elämä*, Helsinki: WSOY.

Salmi, Hannu (2009), 'Hedy Lamarr, moderni ja tähteyden muutos 1933–1938', in Heta Mulari and Lauri Piispa (eds), *Elokuva historiassa, historia elokuvassa*, Turku: k&h, 115–50.

Seppälä, Jaakko (2012), *Hollywood tulee Suomeen: Yhdysvaltalaisten elokuvien maahantuonti ja vastaanotto kaksikymmentäluvun Suomessa*, Helsinki: Unigrafia.

Seppälä, Jaakko (2017), 'Following the Swedish Model: The Transnational Nature of the Finnish National Cinema in the Early 1920s', *Kosmorama* #269 (www.kosmorama.org).

Singer, Ben (2001), *Melodrama and Modernity – Early Sensational Cinema and its Contexts*, New York: Columbia University Press.

Soila, Tytti (2019), 'Valtavirtoja ja pikku puroja – liikehdintää suomalaisten ja ruotsalaisten elokuvatuotantojen välillä', in Kimmo Laine et al. (eds), *Unelmatehdas Liisankadulla – Suomen Filmiteollisuus Oy:n tarina*, Helsinki: Suomalaisen Kirjallisuuden Seura, 286–91.

Soila, Tytti, Astrid Söderbergh Widding and Gunnar Iversen (1998), *Nordic National Cinemas*, London and New York: Routledge.

Turim, Maureen (1989), *Flashbacks in Film: Memory and History*, New York: Routledge.

Vincendeau, Ginette (1989), 'Melodramatic Realism: On Some French Women's Films of the 1930s', *Screen* 30:3, 51–65.

Vincendeau, Ginette (1992), 'Noir is also a French Word. The French Antecedents of Film Noir', in Ian Cameron (ed.), *The Movie Book of Film Noir*, London: Studio Vista, 49–58.

Williams, Linda (2018). '"Tales of Sound and Fury . . ." or, The Elephant of Melodrama', in Christine Gledhill and Linda Williams (eds), *Melodrama Unbound – Across History, Media, and National Cultures*, New York: Columbia University Press, 205–18.

Wood, Mrs Henry (1984), *East Lynne*, New Brunswick, NJ: Rutgers University Press (orig. 1861).

CHAPTER 3

Biography of an Outsider[1]

Teuvo Tulio was born in 1912 as Theodor Tugai. His family roots were internationally entangled and extended as far as Turkey. His maternal grandmother appears to have come from Poland.[2] His mother Helena married three times, and Theodor was the son of her first husband, Aleksander Tugai. Soon Theodor's surname changed to that of Helene's second husband, Peter Derodzinsky, who, Tulio emphasises, did not have a drop of blue blood in his veins, despite such speculations in Finland at the time when Tulio began to make a career in the budding film industry.

Tulio assumed that his parents' marriage was one of convention. It did not last long, and Theodor, their only child, was born on a train heading for St Petersburg. At that point Helena was eighteen years old and dreamed of becoming a ballerina. As she tried to pursue a career in St Petersburg, Theodor returned to live with his grandparents in a farmhouse in Latvia. For a long time, Helena remained a remote figure for him, and he never saw her second husband, who died quite soon after the marriage. As Helena entered her third marriage with the Finn Alarik Rönnqvist, she moved to Helsinki. Theodor joined them, but he did not assume his stepfather's surname and resorted instead to his original surname, Tugai. For a long time, he remained at heart a country boy, as he spent his summers at his grandfather's farm as its prospective heir. His main interest there were the horses, and his experience with them was to be significant in his film career.

Moving to Helsinki at the age of ten meant adapting, not only to an urban environment, but also to a different language. Theodor could speak Latvian, German, English, Russian and a bit of Yiddish. Now he had to learn Finnish and Swedish. He entered the German secondary school, where he faced the further task of having to learn to write as well as speak German. Nevertheless, he enjoyed the international atmosphere of the school and the company of children from all over the world, 'except Africa'.[3] Getting along with the rough boys on the streets required a different kind of effort. Not only did he not have a full command of the local languages, he looked different and was called a Kirgizian, Chinaman or a Mongol. But he soon became streetwise. His big size and hard fists helped a lot. As he realised how well the power of fists compensated for the lack of linguistic skills, for a while he took boxing seriously. He won in the junior league, but as he felt that in a crucial match he succeeded to a great extent because his competitor was really quite weak, he did not bother to continue boxing except as an occasional pastime. This anecdote demonstrates a rather charming trait in Tulio's character: though proud of his achievements, he was not one to boast.

Soon popular cinema caught his attention and imagination, to the extent that together with a new friend, Valentin Ivanoff – Russian by descent and later known as Valentin Vaala – Tugai (as he was still known at the time) began his career in cinema as an actor. Taking advantage of his slightly exotic looks, he styled himself as Finland's Valentino in three films directed by Vaala, *Dark Eyes* (*Mustat silmät*, 1929), *The Gypsy Charmer* (*Mustalaishurmaaja*, 1929) (figures 3.1–2) and *The Wide Road* (*Laveata tietä*, 1931). The first two films are set in the world of the Romani people, and particularly the latter film allowed Tugai to display his horse-riding skills. In both films Tugai has the role of a son of a well-respected Romani family, but struggling against their traditions: in *Dark Eyes* he falls in love with the blonde daughter of a stately home, and in *The Gypsy Charmer* he tries to escape an arranged marriage to the daughter of another wealthy Romani family.

Dark Eyes survives only in fragments; Vaala is reputed to have thrown the original negative and the only copy of what he later called 'school kids' first effort' into the sea.[4] This seems to have been an exaggerated gesture, as the film did have its supporters. Tugai and Vaala had connections with the mainly literary avant-garde movement Tulenkantajat (The Torch Bearers).[5] Its members were critical about the still-young tradition of Finnish cinema and greeted the efforts of the young Vaala and Tugai with a degree of enthusiasm. On the basis of *Dark Eyes* the critic Yrjö Kivimies recognised Vaala as Finland's most promising young film director. It is indicative of the prevailing sentiment that in the nationalistic-minded press, Kivimies was criticised for supporting foreigners.[6] In the long run, Vaala succeed in integrating into Finnish culture more smoothly than Tugai, and he was soon recognised as one of Finland's most sophisticated filmmakers.

Vaala and Tugai made two more films together. In *The Wide Road* Tugai had the role of Antti, known internationally as Anton Lardozo, a world-famous violinist. On his visit to Finland, his home country, he romances Kirsti (Eeva Virtanen), a poor relative of his friend, but then leaves her for Tanita, a society lady whom he

Figures 3.1–2

has impressed with his art to the extent that she is prepared to leave her husband Matti and elope with Antti to Paris. But he soon grows tired of her and continues to womanise. Years later he returns to Helsinki and discovers that Kirsti has married his friend Eero. He tries to seduce her, but she scornfully rejects him. In the final scene, Kirsti and Eero are decorating a Christmas tree, while Antti walks dejectedly into the darkness. There is a lot in the plot that foreshadows Tulio's obsession with certain melodramatic plot developments, but with one crucial difference: the badly treated woman is not doomed and she still has a genuine chance to live a decent life. Tulio would not extend such grace to many of his female protagonists. The film was well received by critics, who in the spirit of the Tulenkantajat group saw the urban scenes as the cinematic equivalent of 'opening the windows towards Europe'. Two prominent members of the group, Olavi Paavolainen and Mika Waltari, both wrote enthusiastic reviews, assuring their readers that Finnish cinema had now attained an international level.[7]

The Blue Shadow (*Sininen varjo*, 1933), based on an unpublished novella by Waltari,[8] was Vaala and Tugai's first film with recorded dialogue; *The Wide Road* was released both in a silent and a sound version, the latter containing music, songs and sound effects. *The Blue Shadow*, only one reel of which survives, is an adventure film featuring Tugai in a double role, as a mysterious burglar and his lookalike, an assumed-to-be innocent man who has to prove his innocence. According to the surviving parts and stills, the action takes place in a similar, 'international' high-class milieu of fancy restaurants and luxurious art deco-style apartments to that of *The Wide Road*.

Tugai must have been remarkably able to convince people about his ideas, as he got to direct his first film at the age of twenty-three. The producer, one of the most prominent film distributors in Finland at the time, was Abel Adams, born as Aapeli Korhonen, son of a poor peasant. In 1902, when he was in his early twenties, he left for America to make his fortune, and apparently was quite successful.[9]

Adams returned to Finland in 1912, according to Tulio with his pockets 'full of dollars',[10] and could afford to buy a biograph theatre in Helsinki. This was the beginning of what in the Finnish context amounted to a film empire. It was modest by international standards but became one of the key players in the Finnish film scene. The company he established, Adams-Filmi, survived as an independent company until 1986, when the much bigger Finnkino bought the majority of its shares. Adams-Filmi concentrated mainly on the import, distribution and exhibition of films, but Adams did also try his hand at producing films. Among these were Tulio's three first films, *The Fight over the Heikkilä Mansion* (*Taistelu Heikkilän talosta*, 1936), *Silja – Fallen Asleep When Young* (*Nuorena nukkunut*, 1937) and *Temptation* (*Kiusaus*, 1938). Sadly, together with a significant part of Finnish film history, they were destroyed in 1959, when a fire burned down Adams' film warehouse. Fragments of *The Fight over the Heikkilä Mansion* and *Silja – Fallen Asleep when Young* have been rediscovered in the 2000s though, one reel of the latter from the Cinémathèque française in Paris in 2015. Echoes of *The Fight over the Heikkilä Mansion* can also be seen in Tulio's later film *In the Grip of Passion* (*Intohimon vallassa*, 1947), which is really a remake of it. Further, the themes of jealousy and obsession that permeate all these films were to haunt Tulio throughout his career.

At this time Tulio started a lifelong collaboration with his old schoolfriend Regina Linnanheimo, who had already had a few parts in Vaala's films. Giving her a leading role was considered to be something of a risk, as she had neither education in acting nor experience in big dramatic roles. Tulio's faith in her was rewarded. *The Fight over the Heikkilä Mansion* was well received and together with the next two films they made together it lifted Linnanheimo to fame: during the late 1930s and 1940s, she became the best-paid female actor in Finland, working in turn for both of the major studios of the era, Suomi-Filmi and Suomen Filmiteollisuus. Tulio also invited Linnanheimo to participate as a screenwriter and a typist. She was to write or co-write the scripts to at least six of Tulio's films, although she was often credited under a pseudonym, if at all. Her motivation appears to have been to create roles for herself that would have depth rather than just playing an ethereal beauty in costume dramas.[11]

Remarkably, Tulio succeeded in engaging one of Finland's major composers, Leevi Madetoja, to create the music for his first film. The young man explained to the old master what he wanted. Madetoja composed and the music was played. But when Tulio tried to mix it with the film, he soon became distraught: the music was just too beautiful. He plucked up the courage to explain the problem to Madetoja. He turned out to be understanding and composed some new music, but it still did not offer anything that Tulio could use for the more violent scenes. One of the players of the orchestra came to the rescue, promising that he and the other musicians could fill in for the scenes in which Madetoja's music was of no use. As the film survives only in fragments, we cannot know how effectively this worked out. In any case, the ad hoc working method does appear to be the first instance of the idiosyncratic and intuitive attitude Tulio would adopt to using music in his later films.

Filming *Silja – Fallen Asleep When Young* entailed approaching the prominent author Frans Emil Sillanpää to negotiate filming rights of his highly acclaimed novel. This would not have been strictly necessary, as the publisher had already granted the rights in order to cover the great author's debts to the company. Out of respect, however, Tulio wanted the approval of the senior artist. This turned out to be surprisingly easy. Sillanpää confessed he knew nothing about filmmaking, and stated that 'if this young man makes a bad film of *Silja*, it will be his shame, not mine'.[12] The negotiation proceeded on this mutual understanding, and eventually Sillanpää even agreed to write the new pieces of dialogue that were needed. According to Tulio, he did this very well, and had his commission doubled. After the film was released and met with a storm of debate, Sillanpää defended it, saying that it was not his work but Tulio's, and as such it was good.

With this film Tulio also claimed to have invented a type of scene that was to become a standard, or even clichéd, feature of many Finnish films with rural settings: young man and a woman having an amorous encounter, possibly – this would often be discreetly suggested – also making love, in a hay barn. This was somewhat exaggerated, as a similar scene had been seen already in, for example, Mauritz Stiller's *The Song of the Scarlet Flower* (*Sången om den eldröda blomman*, 1919), a film which enormously influenced Finnish filmmaking in the 1920s,[13] and which Tulio would have seen. Also, as Raija Talvio reminds us, although amorous haystack scenes were considered a cliché of Finnish cinema, such scenes were already familiar from literature, including Sillanpää's original novel.[14]

Silja – Fallen Asleep When Young was at first passed by the Film Classification Board, but after its release a number of letters were sent to the readers' columns of major newspapers criticising its morality. The criticism mainly targeted the love scene in the hay (figure 3.3), and a scene where an older man spies on Silja bathing in a sauna. According to a columnist of the conservative newspaper *Uusi Suomi*, films such as *Silja* were 'morally reprehensible. They aim to depict mainly sexual life – what else! – "from the inside", psychologically, as well as such mental phenomena as extreme repulsiveness, bitterness and hatred'.[15] The debate soon heated up, and as a result Adams-Filmi shortened the two controversial scenes following negotiations with the Classification Board.

With hindsight, the debate surrounding *Silja* can be seen as part of a larger controversy over art and morality that took place in Finland during the late 1930s, often referred to as the 'cultural crisis'. The controversy concerned such oppositions as tradition/modernity, nationalism/internationalism, idealism/materialism and Christian morality/vitalism. As Anu Koivunen has remarked,

Figure 3.3

at the core of the debate was often sexuality, and more specifically the female body,[16] as in the case of *Silja*. The debate was also highly politicised, as from the conservative perspective, controversial representations of sexuality were readily associated with Bolshevism. To a degree, the *Silja* debate can be traced back to the author Sillanpää: as valued as he was from the nationalist point of view as a rumoured Nobel Prize candidate, he was also fascinated by modernist literary techniques and psychoanalysis. Indeed, both controversial scenes are already there in Sillanpää's novel. Tulio's adaptation, however, foregrounded the potentially controversial elements: the haystack scene is even depicted not only in many of the production stills, but also in the best-known, hand-painted poster of the film. This may not have been a coincidence, as the stormy debate naturally boosted attendance figures. It also gave Tulio a public image that he was to retain throughout his career: he had established his reputation as a director of erotic and sensational films.[17]

Tulio's third film, *Temptation* (1938), a melodrama about a priest who falls in love with a fisherman's wife, did not fare well at the box office, and with it his collaboration with Adams came to an end. His first effort as an independent producer daringly invited comparison with two highly regarded Swedish films, the two earlier adaptations of Johannes Linnankoski's novel *The Song of the Blood-Red Flower* (*Laulu tulipunaisesta kukasta*, 1905).[18] The novel has been referred to as the first Finnish-language bestseller.

The filming rights had been sold to Sweden for an indefinite period, and although with some legal advice Tulio was able to secure rights for a Finnish-language production, he was not able to shoot a Swedish-language version. He invested in what was to be the great draw of his film, the shooting of the rapids. He found a sufficiently impressive location near the city of Lahti. However, it was more difficult to find anyone hot-headed enough to brave the wild Mankala rapids.[19] Kille Oksanen, the actor cast in the role of Olavi, was a sportsman, but the challenge was far beyond his abilities. Finally, a local young man was found who was prepared to act as a stand-in for Oksanen. He had shot most of the sections of the rapids, although not the fiercest of them, standing on a single log, as he was to do now. Even with full safety precautions the stunt was extremely dangerous, but the body double was eager to try it as many times as necessary to obtain images worth his effort. He fell into the rapids a few times, fortunately without injury, and Tulio's twelve cameramen captured some great shots – so great, in fact, that he recycled them in many of his later films. In some of the shots it is possible to see briefly safety ropes, but this does not spoil the sense of a foolishly daring exploit.

Oksanen himself appeared in a potentially dangerous sequence. He could use an axe skilfully, so he took on the scene where Olavi saves the day by cutting a log which has caused a blockage in the river. Had the logs started moving more quickly than expected, he would probably have been crushed between them. As it happened, because of a misunderstanding, even more logs had been released upstream and eventually explosives were needed to release the block.[20]

The film received mixed reviews. As was to happen in connection with many later Tulio films, the cinematography received mainly positive attention. But as with some other of his films, the adaptation was not thought to match the sensitivity of the original literary work. The most venomous critic, writing for the extreme right-wing newspaper *Ajan Suunta*, stated: 'If Mr Tulio continues to make films depicting the life of the Finnish people, as a foreigner ignorant of these things, he really should get to know this field better.'[21]

Tulio's next effort was a far cry from depicting the national character, and the least characteristic film of his entire output. It was an adaptation of George McManus' *Bringing Up Father* comic strip, known in Finland as *Vihtori and Klaara* (*Jiggs and Maggie*). The suggestion came from Eino Jurkka, who had had great success as an actor depicting Vihtori in many stage productions, as well as in Nyrki Tapiovaara's film *Two Henpecked Husbands* (*Kaksi Vihtoria*), which premiered in early 1939.

As would always be the case with Tulio's productions, the budget for *Jiggs and Maggie* was small. In this case it was more of a problem than in the later films, as creating some of the comic effects required elaborate tricks. At the time there was not much expertise in this field in Finland, so imagination was required. The most challenging scene was one in which Maggie chases Vihtori across the rooftops. Lots of tricks and a pair of body doubles were used, but eventually Tulio was satisfied that 'the illusion was perfect'.[22]

In the Fields of Dreams (*Unelma karjamajalla*, 1940) was the third adaptation of the Swedish playwright Henning Ohlson's play *Hälsingar* (1922). Tulio had probably seen the first one by William Larsson (1923) and, even more likely, the second by Ivar Johansson (1933). He succeeded in gaining the rights, and with them came the script the Swedes had been using. It was set in the Swedish province of Dalarna and contained scenes with national costumes and country dances. Tulio thought it was too much like a stage play, but that it could easily be made more modern and adapted to a Finnish setting. *In the Fields of Dreams* was reasonably well received, and again critics especially appreciated its cinematic quality.

In the Fields of Dreams was shot in 1939, but because of the outbreak of war, the premiere was delayed to the autumn of 1940. Tulio had further plans, but the war interrupted his new film project. He lost a substantial amount of money and was not able to finish another film until 1944. Much more sadly, as Tulio points out, Kille Oksanen, who was supposed to appear in the main role of the unfinished film, died in the war in 1941.

In Finland the Second World War took place in three phases: the Winter War 1939–40 and the Continuation War 1941–4 against Soviet Union; and the Lapland War 1944–5 against the former ally, Germany. Tulio's account of his own contribution to the war effort is quite self-deprecating. He depicts himself as an anti-hero and titles the appropriate chapter in his autobiography 'I served in the war as a coward'.[23] Like the autobiography as a whole, it is filled with amusing anecdotes, the veracity of which should be taken with a pinch of salt. At points a touch of self-irony suggests that though evermore determined to follow his own, highly idiosyncratic line, Tulio – at least at the time of writing the autobiography – did not take himself too seriously. Officially, he served as a cinematographer in an information unit, like many other Finnish filmmakers, and he participated in some of the decisive battles of the Continuation War. He was also decorated with the Cross of Liberty for his bravery and his work as a cinematographer. Nevertheless, he emphasises that the work of the cinematographers even at its most perilous could not be compared with the hardships faced by the infantrymen. His ambivalent attitude toward the war is further stressed by the fact that he was, along with, for example, Olavi Paavolainen, the former leading figure of the Tulenkantajat, part of an unofficial group of intellectuals in the information unit who called themselves a 'pessimistic and anti-Nazi salon'.[24]

The only actual combat incident Tulio relates was surviving an ambush in which, due to his quick reflexes, he was able to duck in time, while two of his comrades were shot dead. For the most part, instead of relating military events, Tulio lists all the interesting people he met while serving at the front, ranging from scientists through authors, comedians and future politicians, to Gustav Adolph, the Crown Prince of Sweden. He also relates how he twice happened to be present when Marshal Mannerheim came to inspect the front. The Field Marshal exposed himself to enemy sharpshooters but, it seems, not to being shot by a friendly camera. According to Tulio, Mannerheim was somewhat camera-shy. Before the war, Tulio relates, during a Red Cross charity event at which the Marshal was guest of honour, a picture of him was needed for a newsreel about the occasion. As Tulio pointed the lights toward the Marshal, he covered his face with his hand. Tulio then had the audacity gently and firmly to lower the hand. The Marshal turned angrily, but realising he was on camera, adopted a gentler expression and finally, actually smiled.

Immediately after the Continuation War, there was a shortage of film stock and other infrastructure needed for making and exhibiting films, causing problems for both the major film companies and independent producers like Tulio. But there was a market for domestic films, as foreign films had not yet started to flood in, because the war raged on in the rest of Europe. Tulio took his cue from a line in his *Song of the Scarlet Flower*. One of the girls previously seduced by the protagonist Olavi, whose life he has wrecked, appears in his life again as a prostitute. She announces: 'Here I am, just the way you wanted me'. Such was the starting point of *The Way You Wanted Me* (*Sellaisena kuin sinä minut halusit*, 1944).

However, after the war Tulio failed to maintain the stature he had achieved in the thirties. By the fifties he was already out of fashion, and by the time the new wave hit Finland's cinematic shores in the sixties, he had sunk into oblivion. Regina Linnanheimo's dedication was to no avail, even though she had left the major studios after the war and devoted herself almost exclusively to Tulio's films. Most of Tulio's late films did not receive a decent critical reception, and he was only able to continue because he had developed a way of making films very cheaply.

Toward the end of his life, Tulio became increasingly reclusive. For more than twenty years he withdrew from public life, but continued a close relationship with Linnanheimo until her death in 1995.[25] He remained a dandy to the very end, faithfully sticking to the style he had adopted decades earlier, always careful to place his Basque beret carefully on his head at the right angle. He spent the last two years of his life in a hospital in Helsinki. Another faithful friend, Annikki Suni, visited him regularly. One of her duties was to give careful accounts of the films she had seen, and she also read to him his young colleague Aki Kaurismäki's account of how Tulio had inspired him.[26] Teuvo Tulio died in a hospital on 8 June 2000, at the age of eighty-seven, having witnessed the beginning of his rehabilitation as a master of melodrama.

NOTES

1. The basic biographical facts in this chapter come mainly from Tulio's autobiography, first published in 1974 and reprinted in a slightly edited form in Toiviainen 2002. References to the autobiography are left out from this chapter, except for direct quotations. However, references to other sources are provided as elsewhere in this book.

2. Historically, the border between Latvia and Poland is one of the many contested areas in Europe, so over different phases of history the area Tulio's mother came from might have belonged to either of these nations.

3. Tulio 2002: 42.

4. Uusitalo et al. 1996: 405.

5. Tulenkantajat was a fairly loose group consisting mainly of writers associated with a periodical of the same name. Active from around the mid-1920s, the group conceived of a more urban kind of Finnishness, as opposed to the predominantly rural ideals of nationhood that had dominated the formation of the national identity during the struggle for independence. Above all, the Tulenkantajat wanted to bring contemporary European trends such as expressionism into Finnish art. Their figurehead was the author Olavi Paavolainen and among some of the most prominent members were Uuno Kailas, Katri Vala, Yrjö Jylhä and Mika Waltari.

6. Alanen 2004: 68–9.

7. Ibid.: 68–9.

8. Mika Waltari is internationally best known for his novel *The Egyptian* (*Sinuhe egyptiläinen*, 1945), translated into forty-one languages. Michael Curtiz directed a film adaptation of the novel in 1954.

9. Uusitalo 1972: 7–8.

10. Tulio 2002: 24.

11. Nikula 2000: 49–50.

12. Tulio 2002: 78.

13. See Alanen 1999: 80–3.

14. Talvio 2017: 160. Moreover, Talvio remarks that the actual number of films that include haystack scenes was never very high. The haystack scene evolved into a myth not because it was common but because it condensed conflicts of gender and class, central to the modernising society. Ibid.: 167–9.

15. Kellonsoittaja: 'Tapulista katseen', *Uusi Suomi* 6.1.1938.

16. Koivunen 2003: 273–5.

17. For a discussion on Tulio's *Silja* in the context of the 'cultural crisis' controversy, see Laine 2009.

18. Johannes Linnankoski's *Song of the Blood-Red Flower* has been adapted for the screen five times: Mauritz Stiller (1919), Per-Axel Brenner (1934), Teuvo Tulio (1938), Gustaf Molander (1956) and Mikko Niskanen (1971). For an analysis of the adaptations, see Soila 1994.

19. The Mankala rapids no longer exist as a power company harnessed the river in 1952. Before that, ten films were shot there.

20. There was already a tradition of shooting rapids in Nordic cinema by the time Tulio made his own daring effort. Beginning with Erkki Karu's *The Rapid-Shooter's Wife* (*Koskenlaskijan morsian*, 1923), shooting rapids occurred as the culminating scenes in several Finnish films, although because of technical limitations and the dangers involved, the dramatic action often had to be suggested or rendered verbally rather than shown in its entirety. In *The Rapid-Shooter's Wife*, after exciting footage of rafts coming

down
the rapids and abortive attempts at saving men stranded on a rock, an intertitle reads:
'The raft touched the rocks and in a blinking of an eye the men were saved'. See Seppälä
2017: 65–73. Half a century later, director Mikko Niskanen almost died when he insisted
on doing a rapid-shooting stunt when filming his 1971 version of *Song of the Scarlet
Flower*. Toiviainen 1999: 180.

21. Rkk.: 'Laulu tulipunaisesta kukasta', *Ajan Suunta* 5.12.1938.

22. Tulio 2002: 116.

23. Ibid.: 128.

24. Rajala 2014: 518–19.

25. Tulio and Linnanheimo appear to have had a near lifelong relationship, but they were
never engaged to be married and did not even live together. Linnanheimo was married to
another man between 1948 and 1952, but Tulio never married. Jaana Nikula, in her Regina
Linnanheimo biography, suggests that the degree to which the two withdrew from social
life has been exaggerated. According to Nikula, they renounced their public life but still
kept in touch with a small but close circle of friends. Nikula 2000: 232.

26. Suni 2002: 165.

NEWSPAPERS

Ajan Suunta 1938.
Uusi Suomi 1938.

BIBLIOGRAPHY

Alanen, Antti (1999), 'Born Under the Sign of the Scarlet Flower: Pantheism in Finnish Silent
Cinema', in John Fullerton and Jan Olsson (eds), *Nordic Explorations: Film Before 1930*,
Sydney: John Libbey, 77–85.

Alanen, Antti (2004), 'Nuoren Vaalan kansainvälisiä vaikutteita', in Kimmo Laine, Matti
Lukkarila and Juha Seitajärvi (eds), *Valentin Vaala*, Helsinki: Suomalaisen Kirjallisuuden
Seura, 65–77.

Koivunen, Anu (2003), *Performative Histories, Foundational Fictions. Gender and Sexuality in
Niskavuori Films*, Helsinki: Finnish Literature Society.

Laine, Kimmo (2009), 'Tulio + Sillanpää = kulttuurikriisi', *Kulttuurintutkimus* Vol. 26: 2–3, 5–18.

Nikula, Jaana (2000), *Polttava katse. Regina Linnanheimon elämä ja elokuvat*, Helsinki: Like.

Rajala, Panu (2014), *Tulisoihtu Pimeään. Olavi Paavolaisen elämä*, Helsinki: WSOY.

Seppälä, Jaakko (2017), 'Stumbling on Technology: Erkki Karu's Notion of Rapid Shooting
and the Lack of Telephoto Lenses', in Kimmo Laine et al. (eds), *Noin seitsemännen taiteen
poika. Kirjoituksia elokuvasta ja muista taiteista*, Turku: Faros, 65–73.

Suni, Annikki (2002), 'Fedja, ystävämme', in Sakari Toiviainen (ed.), *Tulio: Levottoman veren
antologia*, Helsinki: Suomalaisen Kirjallisuuden Seura, 157–65.

Talvio, Raija (2017), '"Ihan on ku filmissä!" Suomalaisen elokuvan heinäkasakohtaukset', in
Mari Mäkiranta, Ulla Piela and Eija Timonen (eds), *Näkyväksi sepitetty maa. Näkökulmia
Suomen visualisointiin*, Helsinki: Suomalaisen Kirjallisuuden Seura, 156–71.

Toiviainen, Sakari (1999), *Tuska ja hurmio: Mikko Niskanen ja hänen elokuvansa*, Helsinki:
Suomalaisen Kirjallisuuden Seura.

Toiviainen, Sakari (ed.) (2002), *Tulio: Levottoman veren antologia*, Helsinki: Suomalaisen Kirjallisuuden Seura.

Tulio, Teuvo (2002), 'Elämäni ja elokuvani', in Sakari Toiviainen (ed.), *Tulio: Levottoman veren antologia*, Helsinki: Suomalaisen Kirjallisuuden Seura, 23–157.

Uusitalo, Kari (1972), *Kuusi vuosikymmentä suomalaista elokuvayritteliäisyyttä. Adams-Filmi Osakeyhtiö 1912–1972*, Helsinki: Adams-Filmi.

Uusitalo, Kari et al. (1996), *Suomen kansallisfilmografia 1, 1907–1935*, Helsinki: Edita and Suomen elokuva-arkisto.

CHAPTER 4

Outsider as an Independent Filmmaker

Throughout his career, both as an actor and a director, Teuvo Tulio worked outside of the big studios. Production-wise, this was a decisive factor that affected everything from the choice of subjects, actors and music to editing, distributing and marketing his films. Operating on the fringes of the film industry was, indeed, an essential part of Tulio's status as an outsider.

Finnish film production was, from the 1920s to the 1960s, dominated by a handful of companies, some of which concentrated on producing feature films, while others were fully integrated along the lines of the Hollywood majors. Three of the largest companies, Suomi-Filmi, Suomen Filmiteollisuus and Fennada-Filmi, produced almost 70 per cent of the whole output of domestic feature films between 1920 and 1963.[1] The balance of power of this oligarchy changed during the studio era, but whether the field was dominated by one, two or all three companies at any one time, operating outside the majors was always challenging.

This chapter focuses on Tulio's life and career as an independent filmmaker, by first outlining the general structures of the Finnish studio system, against which Tulio's survival strategies are then discussed. Special attention is paid to the transnational dimensions of Tulio's cinema, especially his dual strategy of addressing national audiences on the one hand, and regional, Nordic markets on the other.

THE FINNISH STUDIO SYSTEM

Tulio is generally characterised as an independent filmmaker. Just what that meant varied from the late 1920s to the early 1970s, and these changes related closely to the general trends in Finnish feature-film production. Therefore, in order to understand the circumstances in which Tulio made his films, it is essential to contextualise them in relation to the ways the major production companies operated during these decades.

When Vaala and Tugai made their first films in the late 1920s, Finnish film production was all but dominated by one diversified company, Suomi-Filmi. There had been a three-year break in feature-film production between 1916 and 1919, first due to the prohibition of filming enacted by the authorities during the last years of the Russian rule, and then, after Finland had gained independence in 1917, due to the economically and politically unstable conditions during and after the harsh civil war of 1918. But by 1919 several new entrepreneurs advertised that they would soon be starting film production, typically on openly nationalistic lines through adaptations of established Finnish literature. Not all of these newcomers managed to get their operations started, and only one of them survived: Suomi-Filmi, which was to become one of the three major companies of the studio years.

The key to Suomi-Filmi's success was that, right from the start, it had diverse areas of operation. During the early 1920s, before film production became profitable, Suomi-Filmi had steady returns from theatrical scene-painting; among the founders of the company were several professional scene painters.[2] In 1926, Suomi-Filmi bought Suomen Biografi, the largest distribution and exhibition company in Finland. From then on, it became a fully integrated company. Being economically superior to its rivals, it was able to outlast companies such as Komedia-Filmi and Aquila-Filmi, let alone the smaller Fennica-Filmi, which saw the beginning of Teuvo Tulio and Valentin Vaala's film careers.

Yet Suomi-Filmi drifted into a crisis in the early 1930s, as a result of a complex series of processes including the general worldwide recession and the uncertainties involved in the coming of synchronised sound, as well as poor management of finances and disputes within the company.[3] While Suomi-Filmi renewed its management and principal modes of operation, for example by separating the task of production manager from that of general manager, the former director of the company, Erkki Karu, set up a new company, Suomen Filmiteollisuus.

Suomen Filmiteollisuus started with very little capital, but with the help of a wealthy and capable financing partner T. J. Särkkä – who soon after Karu's premature death took over the whole company – the company was trading profitably by the mid-1930s. It handled neither distribution nor exhibition; feature-film production remained the bulk of its business to the end of the studio era. However, a mutually profitable contract with Adams-Filmi, a large distribution and exhibition company, compensated for the lack of its own theatres. Around the same time, with the recession over and film attendances on a new rise, the reorganised Suomi-Filmi also got back on its feet. Thus, from the mid-1930s on, Finnish feature-film production was dominated by not one but two companies.

The third major, Fennada-Filmi, was established in 1950 as a merger between the production company Fenno-Filmi and the import and distribution firm Adams-Filmi. With existing facilities for not only producing but also distributing and screening films, Fennada managed to break into the same markets as Suomi-Filmi and Suomen Filmiteollisuus.

For others, especially for independent producers like Tulio, it was always more challenging. The majors had numerous means to secure their oligopoly. On the one hand, they competed with each other, sometimes quite fiercely, but on the other hand, they were capable of cooperating when their mutual interests were under threat. For example, the majors controlled many of the trade organisations, like the Finnish Film Producers Union, for which Särkkä acted as the chairman from 1945 to 1963, with Suomi-Filmi's Risto Orko as the vice-chairman and Fennada's Mauno Mäkelä as his successor. The majors had permanent studios with permanent staff and up-to-date infrastructure – Orko especially was dedicated to updating the filming equipment at Suomi-Filmi from the mid-1930s on – while the independents often had to rely on old cameras, ad hoc studios, small crews and, obviously, overall small budgets. The majors also owned or controlled the best and the most modern film laboratories, which meant that the independents had to either rely on their services or have their films developed abroad. And finally, just as in Hollywood, distributing and exhibiting their films was always more difficult for the independents than it was for the majors, and the deals made with distributors and exhibitors rarely favoured the independent producers.[4]

Yet operating outside the major production companies had its advantages, and for a filmmaker this was not necessarily the second-best choice. Analogous with Hollywood mavericks from D. W. Griffith to Samuel Fuller, who preferred working independently to submitting to the restrictions of major studio filmmaking, Finnish cinema had its non-conformists. A case in point is Matti Kassila, a distinguished studio director who, at different points in his career, worked for all three major production companies. Being a competent, efficient and successful director, he had relative freedom and from time to time managed to convince the producers to indulge his ideas for films (*The Radio Commits a Burglary* [*Radio tekee murron*], Suomen Filmiteollisuus, 1951, *The Harvest Month* [*Elokuu*], Fennada-Filmi, 1956). In exchange, however, he often had to work on more commercial projects commissioned by producers (*It Happened in Ostrobothnia* [*Lakeuksien lukko*], Suomen Filmiteollisuus, 1951, *Scapegoat* [*Syntipukki*], Fennada-Filmi, 1957). Also, in his memoirs Kassila tells of his ambition to improve studio practices and of the memo he handed to Särkkä when working for Suomen Filmiteollisuus in the mid-1950s. In this memo he suggested, for example, that a team comprised of directors and cinematographers should be put together to reconsider the filmmaking process – the length of time needed for scriptwriting, preparation, rehearsing with the actors and so on – and that study trips should be made to larger European production companies. Frustrated with Särkkä's bland response, Kassila resigned and switched to theatre for a time.[5] Several times during his career, he attempted to liberate himself from the limitations of studio work by trying independent filmmaking, most notably with *The Glass Heart* (*Lasisydän*, 1959), but usually with more critical than commercial success.

In spite of the difficulties of working outside the majors, some of the most idiosyncratic films of the studio era – many of which have become established classics of Finnish cinema – were made by either small production companies or independent producer-directors. Films like *The Stolen Death* (*Varastettu kuolema*, Nyrki Tapiovaara, 1938), *The White Reindeer* (*Valkoinen peura*, Erik Blomberg, 1952) or *The Glass Heart* all have a distinctively non-studio look and contain avant-garde or art-house influences, extensive on-location shooting, relatively loose narrative structure and other such elements that, due to their commitment to classical studio realism, would have been unlikely to appear in the films of the majors.

The same applies to Tulio's work: increasingly over the years, his films drew ever further away from mainstream studio expression. In this respect, the careers of Tulio and his early filmmaking partner Valentin Vaala offer interesting comparisons. Whereas Tulio, as far as we know, never aspired to a career in a major studio, Vaala accepted a job offer from Suomi-Filmi in 1935 and became a prolific, reliable and highly professional studio director. At Suomi-Filmi, Vaala had the best studio facilities and film crews at his disposal, and the budgets for his projects were, by domestic standards, usually high. Like Kassila, he had relative freedom in choosing and often also co-writing his scripts, casting and editing his films, as well as negotiating with the composer. This, however, lasted only as long as his films remained successful: during the 1950s his original projects were more and more often replaced by remakes of old successes (*The Foreman at Siltala* [*Siltalan pehtoori*], 1953) or adaptations of classic literary texts (*The Village Shoemakers* [*Nummisuutarit*], 1957), which he was not as invested in as a filmmaker. In 1963 he was finally discharged from Suomi-Filmi after twenty-eight years of service, and though he was soon rehired after a lot of bad publicity for the company, it was no longer for directing feature films, but made-to-order short films.[6]

During his heyday, though, Vaala's working methods at Suomi-Filmi resembled those of Tulio in many ways. Both preferred working with a familiar ensemble cast and crew from film to film. Besides creating an enjoyable working environment, this compensated for the relatively short time reserved for rehearsing. Whereas most studio productions featured actors from the Finnish National Theatre and other major theatres, both Vaala and Tulio favoured amateur or small-stage actors, although partly for almost opposite reasons: the former inclined toward understatement and the latter toward overstatement. Of all the studio directors, Vaala was the best known for his eagerness to 'find' amateur actors for his films; among his star discoveries are Hanna Taini, Ansa Ikonen, Tauno Majuri, Lea Joutseno and, together with Tulio, also Regina Linnanheimo.[7] The aim was to adopt a subtle means of expression that would be detached from the ponderous acting style embraced by, for example, Särkkä.[8] Rauha Rentola, one of the most prolific actors of the studio era, who worked for all the major studios, as well as for Tulio, characterised Särkkä's directing method this way:

> . . . Särkkä told me to give 'one hundred percent more, Miss Rentola' – which I found most unpleasant. Do I have to twist my face again, I thought, must I express so terribly much again? It was embarrassing to overdo it.[9]

In Särkkä's films, especially in the 1930s and early 1940s, such gestural exaggeration usually accompanied declamatory vocal expression. As for the cinema of Tulio, an expressive face was, arguably, more important than refined theatrical articulation: part of his aesthetics was based on static close-ups or extreme close-ups of human faces and on a montage of more or less static shots. Still, Tulio typically also demanded excessively overblown performances, which, as can be seen in Rentola's comment above, might have felt disagreeable to professional actors. According to Rentola, differing attitudes toward acting were reflected in the directing methods Vaala and Tulio adopted:

> . . . while at Tulio's, there was thunder, lightning and storm, Vaala's studio allowed for a gentle summer rain. Such was the difference in studio work. Also, in Vaala's films, you never had to be afraid, whereas Tulio's temper was so fiery that you really were scared of various outbursts.[10]

The differences in working conditions corresponded with the films' aesthetic results. Although Vaala, as a studio director, had to be ready to work within a variety of genres, melodrama – along with sophisticated comedy – remained among his key interests: approximately one-third of his films count as melodramas.[11] The narrative content of his melodramas is often rather similar to those of Tulio – jealousy, passion, blindness, sacrifice – but as Sakari Toiviainen points out, instead of the excess of madness and guilt typical of Tulio, Vaala treats even the sharpest of juxtapositions with subtlety and a certain realism.[12] Furthermore, in contrast to Tulio's idiosyncratic indifference toward continuity editing, Vaala was, arguably, the most inclined to classical Hollywood style of all the Finnish filmmakers of the studio era. Whenever asked, he was willing to reveal that his masters in filmmaking were directors like Frank Capra, Ernst Lubitsch, René Clair and Preston Sturges, all known for their light touch and lively dialogue scenes.[13] In the words of Kassila, who started his film career as Vaala's apprentice:

> [Vaala] had closely observed how scenes are constructed in Hollywood, how découpage, shot scales, framing and continuity are realised, and how information is distributed. In his shooting scripts, Vaala applied exact shot scales (long shot, medium shot, medium close-up, close-up), and he was careful to follow the patterns.[14]

For Vaala, adherence to classical editing and storytelling was not something he adopted after signing with Suomi-Filmi. He tended toward Hollywood-style découpage already in his independent films like *When Father Wants to. . . (Kun isä tahtoo. . .*, 1935).[15] Therefore, it would seem plausible to think that it was precisely because of his inclination to Hollywood storytelling that Suomi-Filmi hired him in the first place; from the point of view of the studio, the Hollywood style meant not only effective storytelling but also regularised, economical and time-saving practices.[16]

As an independent filmmaker, Tulio learned to cut costs even more efficiently than the studio directors but ended up basing his cinematic expression on rather different premises. As the following chapters will demonstrate in detail, over the years his way of constructing cinematic time and space, as well as his persistent repetitiveness, saw him drift ever further from studio storytelling. Had he ever worked for one of the major studios, he would undoubtedly have had to change his aesthetics and filmmaking practices considerably.

FROM FENNICA TO TULIO PRESENTS

Tulio's status as an independent filmmaker varied considerably over the decades. As these changes had an impact not only on the production but also the distribution and exhibition of his films, it is worth taking a close look at the various stages of Tulio's career as an independent filmmaker, starting with his early collaboration with Vaala.

Vaala and Tugai started, in fact, as amateurs rather than independents. In Tulio's words: 'Just like boys decide to make bombs with no idea as how to get hold of powder, we began to write a script, firmly believing that it will turn out fine, even if we had no trace of money nor other necessities.'[17] *Dark Eyes (Mustat silmät,* 1929) was the first of their endeavours that made it to public screenings, but it was not the first they worked on. In his article on Vaala's early years, Lauri Tykkyläinen suggests that they may have shot several 'practice films', the first one possibly with a home-made camera, before completing *Dark Eyes*.[18] If the dividing line between an amateur and an independent filmmaker is that the latter's films premiere in a public film theatre, then from *Dark Eyes* on, Vaala and Tugai would count as independents. *Dark Eyes* was examined by the State Film Censorship Board, which, in practice, was a prerequisite of a public screening,[19] and it premiered in Helsinki in April 1929.

Vaala's and Tugai's early films were financed mainly by private patrons. The first patron was Tugai's mother, who according to some sources provided initial capital for the making of *Dark Eyes*,[20] and at any rate loaned furniture and props for the films.[21] The principal financier was Armas Willamo, a successful businessman and a friend of Tugai's family, who, besides funding the projects, also let Vaala and Tugai use the name of his agency, Fennica Ab.[22] All of Vaala and Tulio's collaborations, as well as the first of Vaala's two solo efforts before joining Suomi-Filmi, were produced under the name of Fennica. According to Tulio's memoirs, Willamo's businesses were hit by the depression, and he was no longer able to finance films.[23] In 1934 Fennica went into liquidation.[24] No data on costs and returns survive, but according to Tulio, Willamo usually got back what he had invested, though no profit.[25]

Besides actual financing, Vaala and Tugai also received other forms of assistance, more or less out of good will. When starting *Dark Eyes*, they asked Oscar Lindelöf, an experienced cinematographer, for filming equipment. Lindelöf, who owned a film-supply store, agreed on the condition that he himself would assume responsibility for the shooting.[26] This, of course, was most convenient for the young filmmakers: not only did they get the equipment on favourable terms, but they also had their first opportunity to learn filmmaking from a true professional.

Since Lindelöf was not available for their next film, *The Gypsy Charmer* (*Mustalaishurmaaja*, 1929), Vaala and Tugai contacted brothers Heikki Aho and Björn Soldan, who ran the production company Aho & Soldan, which specialised in modernist-oriented documentaries. Like Vaala and Tugai, the brothers were close to, if not actual members of, the modernist Tulenkantajat group, and their paths would cross many times in the coming years too: for example, the brothers approached Vaala to direct their first and only attempt at a feature-length fiction film, *Juha* (1937), but since Vaala had already joined Suomi-Filmi, they turned to Nyrki Tapiovaara instead.

There were many advantages in working with Aho & Soldan. First, Björn Soldan was an excellent cinematographer. Second, as experienced documentarists, the brothers had frequently toured around Finland and were able to suggest appropriate shooting locations.[27] And third, Aho & Soldan had its own relatively well-equipped film laboratory, which for Vaala and Tugai was convenient and enabled them to cut costs. Both Vaala and Tugai also worked in the laboratory on and off in the early 1930s,[28] thus not only covering the costs of their films, but also absorbing knowledge about the technical side of the film-making process. Later, this made them stand out as two of the most technically skilled Finnish film directors.

Vaala and Tugai had other ways of cutting costs and making do with a small budget as well. In order to raise money for *The Wide Road* (*Laveata tietä*, 1931), they made a short film, *Ravintolayleisöä kameran silmällä* ('Restaurant patrons seen through the camera lens', 1930), which presents a group of people at a restaurant, including Tugai, introduced in an intertitle as 'the Finnish Valen-tino', as well as a Harold Lloyd lookalike and a party of women, introduced as 'the parade of future film stars'. The main focus of the film is on the products these characters use: the clothes, shoes, coffee, cream, cigarettes and so on, the labels and brand names of which are clearly on display in close-ups or in the intertitles.

Product placement also appeared in some of the feature films by Fennica. In *The Wide Road* this was done explicitly: among the typically sparse opening credits we find out that the settings are provided by the Stockmann Depart-ment Store, the costumes by Maison Augusta and so on. In *The Blue Shadow* (*Sininen varjo*, 1931) the products themselves are openly displayed throughout the film, not only as trade signs or posters, but also in dialogue and songs. According to Vaala's memoirs, the attempt was to embed ads in the dialogue in such a way that the spectators would not quite be aware of the advertising purpose. The income received through product placement was used for buying film stock,[29] which implies that the whole production depended on such, more or less ad hoc, innovations.

Vaala and Tugai used their network of social relations also to overcome the obstacles in distributing their films, obstacles that were typical for independent producers, not to mention amateurs. *Dark Eyes* had its Helsinki premiere in the medium-sized Pallas theatre in the working-class district of Kallio, since Suomi-Filmi was at first reluctant to rent one of its city-centre theatres[30] – perhaps because it was in fear of a potential rival, or because it considered the film too amateurish. For following films, distribution was easier, at least partly thanks to Willamo's connections.

For distributing and screening *The Gypsy Charmer*, Willamo made a con-tract with Suomen Biografi, which at the time was the exhibition arm of Suomi-Filmi. According to the contract, the film would open in the city-centre La Scala theatre in Helsinki, which was a remarkable improvement compared to the previous venue. Fennica would receive 30 per cent of the net proceeds in the cities (which basically meant the cinemas owned by Suomen Biografi) and 50 per cent of the net proceeds in the rural cinemas.[31] For the next two films, *The Wide Road* and *The Blue Shadow*, the deal got still more favourable for the young filmmakers: the films would premiere in Kino-Palatsi, Suomi-Filmi's largest and most prestigious cinema, and for *The Blue Shadow*, Fennica's share would rise to 55 per cent for the opening week and 50 per cent for the rest of the screenings.[32]

If Vaala and Tugai arguably started out as amateurs rather than independents, then Tulio's first films as a director stretch the concept of independent filmmaking to another dimension. He made a deal with Adams-Filmi, which was not an actual production company: it had produced one feature film in 1926 and a series of short documentaries, as well as backed a few productions with, for example, advance payments.[33] However, Adams-Filmi had a remarkable nationwide chain of cinemas (14 theatres in 1938),[34] and as an import and distribution agency it was the largest in 1930s Finland.[35] Thus, even if Adams-Filmi did not produce films on a regular basis, it was a large and wealthy company. Tulio certainly did not have to begin his directorial career from scratch.

In fact, Tulio gives Abel Adams, the managing director of Adams-Filmi, credit for providing him with favourable circumstances for filmmaking:

Old man Abel was most amiable towards me, a young and penniless film buff. He promised me the money I needed, and agreed not to meddle with actual filmmaking. In those days, cinema owners often sponsored filmmakers, and Adams had done that a few times. Once the film was finished, the filmmaker handed it over to the financier and received either a set amount or a percentage of the income as his salary.[36]

The details of the contract between Tulio and Adams remain unclear. According to Tulio, they never actually signed a contract, just sketched a draft on a piece of paper, and after that took each other at their word.[37] It appears that both were quite pleased with the three films they made together, *The Fight over the Heikkilä Mansion* (*Taistelu Heikkilän talosta*, 1936), *Silja – Fallen Asleep when Young* (*Nuorena nukkunut*, 1937) and *Temptation* (*Kiusaus*, 1938). In terms of attendances, *Silja* was especially successful, even by the standards of major companies,[38] and while *Temptation*'s attendances were more modest, Tulio claims that it covered its costs as well.[39] Thus, Adams had no reason to be unhappy. Tulio tells that after the third film, Adams even gave him a considerable bonus.

A telling detail of Adams' generosity is that Tulio was able to lure Erik Blomberg, a young and rising cinematographer, from Suomi-Filmi with a promise of a high salary,[40] 6,000 Finnish marks per month; as a point of comparison, Vaala's monthly salary from Suomi-Filmi at the time was 4,000 marks.[41] Later it turned out that Tulio was not able to pay quite as much as this, and for Blomberg this meant losing his employment at Suomi-Filmi.[42] Yet it is a reminder of the unusual circumstances in which Tulio started his directorial career.

The best aspect of Tulio's contract with Adams concerned distribution and exhibition. According to the estimation by the Finnish National Filmography, between seven and nine exhibition copies were made of each of Tulio's first three films, which was a standard number in the major studios during the period as well.[43] All three also premiered in Bio Rex, a brand-new Adams venue in the centre of Helsinki, and were broadly distributed throughout the country.

It is not quite clear why Tulio's collaboration with Adams ended after three films. Tulio himself recollects that they parted by mutual agreement and simply went their own way.[44] According to the Finnish National Filmography, Adams was disappointed in the lack of box-office success of *Temptation*.[45] Adams died in the summer of 1938, and since Tulio and Adams' cooperation was based on a 'gentlemen's agreement', it could not have lasted after that, even if Adams-Filmi continued as an import and exhibition company after its founder's death. It was not until 1947 that Adams-Filmi restarted producing feature films.

After his deal with Adams-Filmi ended, Tulio had to find yet new ways to keep his auspiciously started career as a film director going. One unrealised project that he does not mention in his memoirs was the attempt to make a film adaptation of *Seven Brothers* (*Seitsemän veljestä*), a classical Finnish novel by Aleksis Kivi from 1870. During the early 1900s, Kivi was gradually canonised as a 'national author', and with the boom of new film-production companies in the early 1920s, a goal was to adapt some of Kivi's works for the screen. Since *Seven Brothers* was Kivi's only novel – the rest of his work consists of plays and poems – as well as his most complex and extensive piece of writing, a film version of it would have been the crowning achievement of any studio. What followed was a virtual competition for adapting Kivi's novel; copyright for his works had expired, as more than fifty years had passed since his death. At least a dozen scripts or drafts for an adaptation of *Seven Brothers* were written in the 1920s and 1930s by well-known authors and scholars, commissioned by several film companies.[46] Among these unrealised plans, Tulio's was, quite possibly, the most peculiar one.

In the autumn of 1938, a non-commercial company, Kansatieteellinen Filmi, announced that it would be making a film version of *Seven Brothers*, based on an adaptation by the distinguished archaeologist and author Sakari Pälsi.[47] Kansatieteellinen Filmi was founded in 1936 with the intention of providing a systematic means for producing ethnographic films, bringing together documentary filmmakers like Aho & Soldan and academic scholars like Pälsi and Esko Aaltonen.[48] As the main objective of Kansatieteellinen Filmi was to document vanishing customs, practices and environments, *Seven Brothers* was to be a one-time exception. The most curious aspect of the endeavour was that it was to be directed by Tulio. This fact was not revealed in the public announcement, but, according to the Kansatieteellinen Filmi company archives, the initiative for the project came from Tulio, who would direct and produce the film, whereas the company would provide ethnographical expertise for 10 per cent of the net proceeds.[49]

While Kivi's novel might nowadays be seen as a multi-layered piece of writing that foregrounds the transgressive behaviour of the seven protagonists and combines and parodies several genres from the ancient epics and Renaissance drama to the nineteenth-century novel, in the 1930s *Seven Brothers* was usually read as a Bildungsroman and a grand narrative of the national awakening. This reading emphasised that after struggling against the rules of society, the brothers learn to read and write and find their places as respectable citizens.[50] In this sense, a filmmaker like Tulio, who specialised in melodrama, would seem an odd choice for directing Kivi's novel. However, his early films like *The Fight over the Heikkilä Mansion*, *Silja – Fallen Asleep when Young* and *The Song of the Scarlet Flower* (*Laulu tulipunaisesta kukasta*, 1938) were rural stories and adaptations of prestigious novels, and, as we shall see, stylistically they were somewhat subtler than his later work. Moreover, a parallel can be found between Kivi's brothers and Olavi of the *Scarlet Flower*: sons of a wealthy farmhouse drift into the 'wilderness' until they return to civilisation and agriculture. From this point of view, *Seven Brothers* might not have been a complete sidetrack in Tulio's career after all.

Production-wise, the Kivi project would have been a logical move for Tulio. After his collaboration with Adams ended, Tulio had to develop a new mode of independent production, with no notable domestic forerunners. As an independent producer-director, he had to play safe and seek subjects and themes that would attract as much public attention as possible. After several publicly debated but unsuccessful attempts to adapt Kivi's novel to the screen, *Seven Brothers* would certainly have been such an outstanding achievement, especially since Tulio would have beaten such noteworthy rivals as Suomi-Filmi in the endeavour. Collaborating with the distinguished scholars of Kansatieteellinen Filmi would have diminished the likely possibility of the conservative cultural elite attacking the project.[51]

Existing sources do not reveal how far the *Seven Brothers* project proceeded. No script has been found, but the archives of the Finnish Literature Society include two handwritten drafts by Sakari Pälsi that most likely relate to this project. What they contain is just what Kansatieteellinen Filmi was supposed to bring to the enterprise: ethnographical instructions as to how to construct and depict the buildings and surroundings, the characters and their costumes, as well as their behaviour and customs. Also included are hand-drawn maps and drawings of buildings. Occasionally the instructions are extremely detailed: precise guidelines are given for how to blow one's nose, load a hunting rifle or skin a cow.[52]

Yet, despite such extreme particularity, Pälsi is careful to remind that there is a flipside to ethnographical accuracy too:

> One should avoid exact and detailed truthfulness in buildings, settings
> and costumes, because that might prove too conspicuous and disturbing,

even ridiculous. Our goal should be a 'Jukola-style' of a sort [Jukola is the name of the brothers' house], simple, approximate, calm, and in terms of history-ethnography, just valid enough to keep critics away.[53]

Even with such concessions, it is easy to assume that Tulio, who at the time was developing his idiosyncratic style based on minimalist settings and an abundance of close-ups, might have disliked Pälsi's detailed ethnographic instructions. In any case, it seems that the project did not proceed past initial preparations. In the summer of 1938, Tulio was already shooting *The Song of the Scarlet Flower*, and as for Kansatieteellinen Filmi, the board members seem to have been divided over the whole project.[54]

From *The Song of the Scarlet Flower* on, Tulio acted mainly as an independent producer-director. The basic preconditions for this were that he had learned to work to a tight budget and with a network of friends and associates from the beginning, and that many of his early films were successful. *The Song of the Scarlet Flower* especially was a massive hit. According to the Finnish National Filmography, it was the most successful domestic film of 1938.[55] Exact attendance figures for Tulio's films are not available, but existing statistics reveal that the most popular films by the majors in 1938 were seen by nearly 800,000 domestic viewers.[56] If the Filmography's estimate is correct, this means that attendances for *The Song of the Scarlet Flower* could have been close to a million, which was a huge figure in a sparsely populated country with 3.5 million inhabitants. The film also appears to have been rather successful in Sweden.

All of Tulio's films until *In the Grip of Passion* (*Intohimon vallassa*, 1947) were at least relatively successful; *The Way You Wanted Me* was among the most-watched films of its year. A four-year break in production during the war years took its toll though, and as a consequence Tulio's career as an independent producer-director never took off as well as it had initially promised. Yet, according to Tulio's memoirs, none of his films were loss-making until *You've Gone into My Blood* (*Olet mennyt minun vereeni*, 1956).[57]

Tulio's first films as an independent were distributed by Suomi-Filmi and premiered in prestigious theatres. Upon completing *The Way You Wanted Me* (*Sellaisena kuin sinä minut halusit*) in 1944, he signed a new contract with Väinän Filmi, a distribution company led by Mauno Mäkelä, who was later to become the managing director of Fennada-Filmi. The theatres managed by Väinän Filmi were somewhat more modest than those of Suomi-Filmi, but good enough to guarantee a success. After signing a contract with Väinän Filmi, Tulio also sold all rights to his previous films. The reason behind this new contract seems to have been an acute lack of money. Tulio says he needed money in order to complete the Swedish version of *The Way You Wanted Me*.[58] Mäkelä, for his part, recalls that Tulio wanted to buy Philips mixing equipment, and needed the money for that. Either way, the contract was more profitable to Väinän Filmi than to Tulio: while the contract price was 2,150,000 Finnish marks, *The Way You Wanted Me* alone made a profit of 4.5 million marks during its first run.[59]

For a few projects during his producer-director years, Tulio made special financial arrangements. *The Rapids of Hell* (*Hornankoski*, 1949) was a co-production between Tulio and Fenno-Filmi that was soon to merge with Adams-Filmi to become Fennada-Filmi. In terms of production, Fenno-Filmi was responsible for the Finnish version and Tulio for the Swedish version. Tulio is credited only for directing the Swedish version, while the Finnish version is credited to Roland af Hällström, who was a contract director at Fenno-Filmi at the time. However, the versions are very similar, and at least according to the cinematographer of the project, Esko Töyri, both films were directed by Tulio.[60] Af Hällström's role was more as an assistant director responsible for dialogue training with the actors.

Once during these years, Tulio tried producing a film made by others. In 1952, Matti Kassila, frustrated with the constant difficulties he encountered at Suomen Filmiteollisuus, approached Tulio for a sequel to his hit adventure comedy *The Radio Commits a Burglary* (*Radio tekee murron*, 1951). The follow-up, *The Radio Goes Mad* (*Radio tulee hulluksi*, 1952), was shot at Tulio's studio with his filming equipment. Tulio offered his help for the production, for example on editing the film, and according to Kassila the cooperation was pleasant and productive until it was time for counting the proceeds of this relatively successful film. In his memoirs, Kassila claims that he and his partners never received any profits and that Tulio avoided his company for a long time.[61]

During the 1950s, the preconditions for acting as an independent producer became evermore challenging as attendances shrank and the general costs of filmmaking increased. For *You've Gone into My Blood*, Tulio made a contract with Alkoholiliike, a state-owned company that had a monopoly for selling alcoholic drinks in Finland. Alkoholiliike backed the production financially, and because of this partnership, Tulio was able to convince the State Film Censorship Board that the film should be freed from taxes. Nonetheless, *You've Gone into My Blood* did so poorly at the box office that Tulio had to close down his business and even discharge Regina Linnanheimo. This turned out to be her last film with Tulio.[62] Soon she started a new career as a translator of film and television dialogue.

After this, Tulio worked on only two more unfortunate productions. *In the Beginning Was an Apple* (*Se alkoi omenasta*, 1962) was a biopic of the socialite Tabe Slioor, played by herself. Tulio worked as a hired director for this project for a while, but he is not mentioned in the opening credits, possibly (and probably) on his own insistence. Even though the star left the project in the middle of shooting, the producers were able to complete a 37-minute film of the material. As an ad hoc solution to the situation, another director, Armand Lohikoski, was hired to write and direct a companion film, *Stardom* (*Taape tähtenä*, 1962), that was shown as a double feature with *In the Beginning Was an Apple*.[63] This is a truly odd double bill: *Stardom* is a parody of the disastrous making of *In the Beginning Was an Apple*.

Tulio's *Sensuela*, even though it was his own production, was almost as unlucky a project as *In the Beginning Was an Apple*. More than a decade in the making, it finally premiered in 1972 with only one exhibition copy, without opening in Helsinki or any other big city, and with only 665 tickets sold. Suomi-Filmi distributed *Sensuela* in principle, but since they suggested that the opening theatre in Helsinki would be the Edison, a small venue that specialised in erotic films, an agreement was never reached. The catastrophe culminated when Tulio once more ran into difficulties with the State Film Censorship Board: *Sensuela* was the first domestic film to receive an X rating, limiting its audience to the minimum age of eighteen, and was given a 'penalty tax' rating of 30 per cent. After negotiating with the head of the Censorship Board, Tulio cut almost five minutes from the film and had the tax percentage reduced.[64] Unlike earlier in his career, he was not able to capitalise on the publicity surrounding the censorship problems. What was to be his final film was buried in silence.

AMATEUR ACTORS AND MAKESHIFT STUDIOS

Tulio has a talent of using scarce settings in a way that still make a varied and lively impression. No large and expensive interiors, two or three corners of a room are enough to create the backdrop that is needed.

T. A. in *Suomen Sosialidemokraatti* 28.4.1946

Among Tulio's survival tactics were the avoidance of large settings, the use of amateur actors, and the recycling of shots and music from his previous films, and even from films made by others, if necessary. All of these tactics contributed to the visual and narrative style of his films, as the reviewer of *Restless Blood* (*Levoton veri*, 1946) aptly remarks in relation to settings in the review cited above.

As we have seen, Tulio favoured amateur actors all through his career; indeed, he started out as an amateur actor himself in his early collaborations with Valentin Vaala. Amateurs were often, if not always, easier to work with than professionals, and much less expensive. Extras were usually roped in without expenses. When lots of cheering crowds were needed for the rapid-shooting scene of *The Song of the Scarlet Flower*, Tulio put an announcement in a local newspaper promising a chance to see daring rapid-shooting 'for free', and 2,000 people showed up.[65]

An additional advantage of using amateur actors was that they were much more flexible and available than professionals. Tight and complex schedules were needed for those professional actors who worked in theatres, since they had rehearsals in the morning and performances in the evening, and so shooting their scenes often had to take place at night. Amateurs, however, could often work any time of the day. This gave Regina Linnanheimo an opportunity to have read-throughs with the amateurs, so that they would be prepared when the shooting started.[66]

As for the settings, Tulio usually made drafts on a cardboard cigarette box. Instead of a professional set designer, he often relied on his trusted friend Kosti Aaltonen, who was a painter and carpenter by profession. Capable of interpreting Tulio's drafts and working economically, Aaltonen was placed in charge of building the sets. In addition, Aaltonen acted, for example, as a props manager and cashier, as he was able to solve whatever problems needed to be solved. Such a jack-of-all-trades was essential for the ad hoc way in which Tulio often operated.

The interiors for Tulio's directorial debut, *The Fight over the Heikkilä Mansion*, were shot in a makeshift studio built in a youth-association house, used by Tulio a few times over the following years. After the success of his first film, however, Tulio convinced Abel Adams to build a well-equipped studio in the Katajanokka district of Helsinki. With technical help from the cinematographer Erik Blomberg, Tulio provided the studio with relatively up-to-date technology. After the collaboration between Tulio and Adams ended in 1930, Blomberg rented the studio for the shooting of Nyrki Tapiovaara's *Stolen Death* and several other films.[67]

After leaving Adams-Filmi, Tulio used whatever makeshift studios were available. Besides relying on the youth-association house, he rented studios from both Suomi-Filmi (*Cross of Love* [*Rakkauden risti*], 1946) and Suomen Filmiteollisuus (*Restless Blood*), as well as using the Fenno Filmi studio for *The Rapids of Hell*. In 1951 Tulio finally established his own studio in the Kulosaari district of Helsinki, in an old tennis-club building, in collaboration with Fennada-Filmi. According to the contract, he was to make two films, and Fennada four films, each year. Curiously, this was at a time when Tulio's career was already in decline in terms of both critical response and popular appeal. Moreover, he was also planning to establish his own film theatre in Helsinki.

According to Mauno Mäkelä's memoirs, Tulio was unable to make the two films a year he had promised, which meant that Fennada had to increase their output in order to keep the studio going. Tulio also ended up owing rent to Fennada, and, according to Mäkelä, in 1962 transferred the property to Regina Linnanheimo in order to avoid paying his debts.[68]

PURSUING SCANDINAVIAN MARKETS

Finnish film production during the studio era presented itself in national, if not nationalist, terms. The major studios were especially eager to emphasise that they were devoted to making Finnish films for Finnish audiences, signalling the producing country in their names. This, however, was never the whole truth. Throughout the decades, the majors sought international markets, though usually with relatively modest results.[69] Furthermore, at the same time as they spoke about the importance of national cinema, the majors, especially Suomi-Filmi and Fennada-Filmi through their distribution branches, were notable importers of foreign films. Thus, whatever the majors may have wanted, Finnish film culture was always thoroughly transnational. Although the market share of domestic films was at times very high,[70] the yearly number of domestic feature films varied between ten and thirty, whereas the typical number of imported films was around 300. Thus, Finnish cinema relied heavily on foreign films.

As internationally inclined and modernist-minded young filmmakers, Tugai and Vaala did not have to rely only on the commercial offerings of the cinema to enhance their film expertise. In the mid-1930s they were active members of the first Finnish cine-club, Projektio. Short-lived though it was, Projektio seems to have had a decisive effect on many young filmmakers and critics. Influenced and inspired by French cine-clubs of the 1920s, Projektio aimed at establishing an intellectual film culture by encouraging the members not only to watch films but also to discuss and write about them. One of the founders was the functionalist architect Alvar Aalto, whose slogan for the club was: 'Good-looking and elegant young people should be flooding in from every door, people who speak of film as if it were their mother tongue'.[71] As might be expected from this statement, Projektio's audience comprised at first mainly people from the upper class. With the involvement of Nyrki Tapiovaara, a prominent figure in the leftist art movements, leftist intellectuals and working-class people started to get involved.[72]

The cine-club's programme was ambitious. The inaugural screening consisted of René Claire's satire on modern business and industry, *Freedom for Us* (*À nous la liberté*, 1931), and László Moholy-Nagy's abstract study on light and movement, *Lightplay: Black-White-Gray* (*Lichtspiel Schwarz-Weiss-Grau*, 1930); the latter probably came about through Aalto's friendship with Moholy-Nagy, who had encouraged him to experiment with a home movie camera.[73] Later, the cine-club's programme comprised three main categories of film:[74] those that had had no commercial success in Finnish cinemas (G. W. Pabst's *Comradeship* [*Kameradschaft*], 1931; Leontine Sagan's *Girls in Uniform* [*Mädchen in Uniform*], 1931), those that were banned by the Finnish Board of Censorship (Josef von Sternberg's *The Blue Angel* [*Der Blaue Engel*], 1930; Georgi and Sergei Vasilyev's

Chapayev [*Chapaev*], 1934), and those that were simply too experimental and/ or controversial for commercial distributors (Luis Buñuel and Salvador Dalí's *An Andalusian Dog* [*Un Chien Andalou*], 1929, Jean Cocteau's *The Blood of a Poet* [*Le sang d'un poète*], 1932). Regardless of the overall liberal/leftist sentiments of the club, Leni Riefenstahl's *Triumph of the Will* (*Triumph des Willens*, 1935) was also among the films screened.

It is not known just what screenings Tulio attended. Yet, in the light of his forthcoming films, the combination of montage cinema, abstract avant-garde, surrealism and Sternbergian melodrama in Projektio's programme appears fundamental. The influence is more obvious in Tapiovaara's films, the eclectic style of which drew inspiration from various avant-garde movements, but Projektio's programme is also a reminder that as idiosyncratic as Tulio's cinematic thinking might seem, it also built upon a filmic tradition, and not only that of silent melodrama.

Even if Projektio was short-lived and may have been somewhat elitist, it reminds us of the dual strategy typical of film-production companies. On the one hand, the major studios and, to a degree, the independents like Tulio, constantly spoke up for self-contained national cinema. On the other hand, such rhetoric did not necessarily match cinematic realities, and imports, exports, foreign influences and international contacts were an essential part of film culture throughout the studio years. In many ways, Tulio exemplified this dual strategy, already in the way he used and changed his name. Starting his career as an actor, he used his Christian name Theodor Tugai, fully exploiting its exotic connotations. However, when he started to direct films he changed his name to the more domesticated sounding Teuvo Tulio. A simple explanation for this is that Theodor Tugai was undoubtedly a phonetically difficult name for many Finns; thus, a practical solution was to adopt an easier name that still alliterated with the original one. Yet, Teuvo Tulio is not just any name. The first name, Teuvo, was an obvious choice: it is a Finnish version of the Greek Teodoros, and thus a 'straight translation' of Theodor. From the 1920s to the 1950s it was a rather common name, and it sounded Finnish enough to erase all connotations to the transnational roots of the name. As for Tulio, it was a made-up name, but it was formed like a typical Finnish surname (Jokio, Talvio and so on), from the root form 'tuli', which means 'fire'. Thus, Theodor Tugai adopted a Finnish name that was at the same time typical and original, a name that connoted 'Finnishness', while also preparing the audiences for the fiery melodramas they were about to experience. It may not have been a mere coincidence that the most popular romantic male actor of the studio era, Tauno Brännes, had just a few years earlier changed his surname to Palo, which also translates as 'fire'.

On a number of occasions during his career, Tulio was drawn into a public debate because of his foreign origins, for the dual strategy he adopted and, indeed, even for his name. The most notable of these debates took place in 1945, during the nationally charged post-war period, when a columnist of the leading social democratic newspaper *Suomen Sosialidemokraatti* – usually not the most obvious advocate of nationalist doctrine – accused Tulio of an inability to understand the mentality of Finnish audiences and for possessing a misleading Finnish-sounding name. Tulio countered the criticism by stating the facts that he had lived in Finland most of his life, that Teuvo Tulio was now his official name and that he had tried to do his duty as a Finnish citizen both during the war and in civil life. In his account of the debate, Harri Kalha sees such attacks against Tulio's foreignness as an attempt to defend the assumed purity of the mythical origins of Finnishness, ironically, in the end, revealing the fragile constructedness of the idea of nation.[75]

What is also of interest is that when approaching Scandinavian markets, Tulio often used his original name. The typical 'Tulio esittää' ('Tulio presents') title in the opening credits of his films changed to the Swedish 'Tugai presenterar'. He first tried making two versions of *Silja – Fallen Asleep when Young*, one in Finnish and one in Swedish. From *The Way You Wanted Me* onward, dual-language versions were almost a rule: with the exception of *In the Beginning Was an Apple* and *Sensuela*, all of Tulio's late films were made both in Finnish and in Swedish, although due to his increasing financing problems the Swedish versions of *A Crooked Woman* (*Rikollinen nainen*, 1952) and *You've Gone into My Blood* were never completed.

Of course, Tulio's idea of shooting his films in two languages was not a novelty. The practice was introduced during the early sound-film period, when film-producing and -exporting companies in Hollywood, Germany and elsewhere looked for ways to overcome the problems of translating films with spoken dialogue; exporting and importing silent films had been easy, since all that needed to be done was to change the intertitles. Using the same script and sets but changing the cast, or sometimes using multilingual actors, two or more versions of the same film were shot in different languages in order to keep international film trade alive. This phenomenon peaked in the late 1920s and early 1930s, until practices of dubbing (mainly in the more widely-spoken language areas) and subtitling (mainly in the less widely-spoken language areas like the Nordic countries) became established as standard ways of translating foreign-language films. The much more expensive multiple-language versions did not disappear altogether, but they became relatively rare.[76]

Thus, when Tulio began to make his dual-language versions, the phenomenon was, in terms of international film business, no longer an obvious choice, either in Scandinavia or in Finland. A few Finnish films were made with Swedish versions over the studio years, but Tulio was by far the most systematic in his efforts to conquer Scandinavian markets with alternative-language versions.[77] In some cases this seems to have been due to survival tactics, typical for Tulio: for instance, in exchange for the Swedish version of *In the Grip of Passion*, Tulio received raw film stock from Sweden.[78] Generally, however, his aim was to widen the potential markets for his films. But what was the rationale behind Tulio's language versions, when most Finnish producers relied on subtitling in trying to export their films?

It seems clear that there was a lot of variation in multiple-language film practices. It was very different making an English-speaking version of a German film, or a Spanish-speaking version of a Hollywood-film, to making a Swedish-speaking version of a Finnish film. The difference was not only in the size of the market, but also in the translating practice adopted in the country importing the film; that is to say, whether dubbing or subtitling was a standard practice in a given area. Generally, it would make sense to assume that the demand for another language version was greater in those cultural areas that, after a transition period, adapted to dubbing foreign films than in those areas that ended up using subtitles. In the national markets that drew upon dubbing, an original, subtitled version of a foreign film was not a lucrative option. As the coming of recorded sound coincided with increasing nationalistic tendencies in many countries, these choices were not always merely economic and aesthetic, but also political. In extreme cases, such as that of Spain after Franco's takeover in 1936, the use of any foreign language in film was banned in order to protect the national language and identity.[79] Alternatively, dubbing had its obvious problems, with erratic lip-syncs and the separation of voice from body, and some time was needed before audiences acclimated to ignore these technical lapses. Therefore, despite the high cost of the process, multiple-language versions competed quite successfully with other processes for some time in the 1930s.

For subtitling cultures such as the Scandinavian countries, the language situation was different. The challenges involved in dubbing didn't arise. However, there were other problems, such as the technical difficulties in printing the subtitles, legal issues over the subtitling patents, and, indeed, challenges in standardising the subtitling practice itself: the translators had to find an ideal balance for the amount of dialogue to be translated. It had to be enough to make the film intelligible, yet not too much, because although literacy was high in Scandinavian countries, audiences were not used to reading quickly while simultaneously watching images.[80] Further challenges arose in bilingual countries like Finland, where both Finnish and Swedish subtitles had to fit on the screen.

Yet despite the challenges involved in subtitling, one would assume that in subtitling cultures the need for language versions was not as high as in dubbing cultures. Why, then, did Tulio and some other filmmakers return to this practice years after the peak of the phenomenon?

Even in dubbing cultures, exporting films from one small film market to another was not always easy. For Finnish films, for example, competing with Hollywood or French films in Nordic markets was a challenge. There was one advantage, though, and that was what Joseph Straubhaar has called cultural proximity, or the tendency of audiences to prefer 'cultural products as similar as possible to one's own language, culture, history, and values'.[81] Finland had been a part of Sweden for centuries, Swedish was the second official language in Finland, and, in general, Nordic cooperation had been a major political and cultural trend at least from the beginning of the First World War. Tulio was clearly well aware of this cultural proximity among the Nordic nations. He dates his own realisation of the close cultural connections between Nordic countries back to 1935, when he acted in a Danish–Swedish co-production directed by George Schnéevoigt, *Outlaw* (*Fredløs*, 1935), that takes place in northern Finland. In his memoirs, he recounts that he got the idea for dual-language versions from this film, which was produced in both Danish and Swedish.[82]

From the beginning of his career as a director, Tulio looked for stories that would meet with interest in other Scandinavian countries too. This was a familiar strategy during the 'golden era' of Swedish Cinema, when Victor Sjöström, Mauritz Stiller and others adapted novels and plays from all Nordic countries and remoulded them into a consistent body of Nordic, if not Swedish, culture.

Tulio started with *The Fight over the Heikkilä Mansion*, adapted from a story by Johannes Linnankoski, whose novel *The Song of a Red-Blood Flower* was well known in Scandinavia. Tulio would have liked to work with the better-known novel, but since it had been filmed twice before in Sweden, the latter version only two years earlier, that was out of the question for the time being.[83] With his second feature, Tulio began his attempts to conquer the Scandinavian markets. He looked for a story that would be already known throughout Scandinavia, and he ended up adapting the novel *The Maid Silja* by Frans Emil Sillanpää. In 1937 there were growing rumours, as well as a great deal of lobbying, that Sillanpää would be the next winner of the Nobel Prize for Literature. It was not until two years later that he was awarded the prize, but there was a lot of debate about Sillanpää in the late 1930s, especially in Scandinavia, since the Nobel Foundation was located in Sweden. This, of course, meant free publicity for the film. Subjects for many of Tulio's later films were picked with cultural proximity in mind. *The Way You Wanted Me*, for example, was inspired by the highly successful Swedish fallen-woman melodrama, *King's Street* (*Kungsgatan*, 1943).[84]

For *Silja – Fallen Asleep when Young*, Tulio adopted the usual way of producing multiple-language versions, the same process he used in most of his later works: the script (translated into Swedish by Regina Linnanheimo), the sets and the staff were the same in both film versions. For each scene, he shot first the Finnish take and then the Swedish take. Whenever possible – if the actors were the same and there was no lip-sync dialogue – he used the same shot in both versions. For the Swedish-language version of *Silja* he used only Finnish actors, many of them amateurs, since it was easier to find bilingual amateurs than professional actors. No doubt, using amateurs was also less expensive. But still, even if most of them spoke Swedish as their mother tongue, the language proved to be a problem: some of those involved in distribution were of the opinion that the Swedish dialect spoken in Finland would not appeal to Swedish audiences. According to Tulio's memoirs, this proved to be a false prediction: Swedish audiences found the dialect somewhat archaic but also exotic and 'melodic'.[85]

Yet for the later Swedish versions Tulio often hired professional Swedish actors for some of the most important roles. They were not big stars but were usually well-enough-known actors to be familiar to Swedish audiences. Whether this decision was made because of the dialect or because he wanted to include actors that would appeal to Swedish audiences is not quite clear – probably both possibilities are correct. In any case, only Regina Linnanheimo, his principal leading lady, was always there for both language versions, and she too, although fully bilingual, took some language lessons later in order to master the Swedish accent.[86]

Generally, Tulio's Finnish- and Swedish-language versions were nearly identical, except that changing the actor naturally changed the role to a degree. In this regard, one remarkable difference is that whereas the Finnish actors were often amateurs, the Swedish actors were professionals. Even if working with amateurs had its advantages, as we have seen, what professional male leads brought to their roles was elegance and sophistication, especially in films like *Restless Blood* and *Cross of Love* that took place among the upper class. According to the biography of Regina Linnanheimo, she was also highly inspired by working with the Swedish actors and was thus able to improve her own expressive skills.[87] Small but noteworthy details were added to some of the Swedish scripts. For example, whereas in the Finnish version of *Restless Blood* there is no mention of the nationality of the characters, the Swedish version tells us that Regina Linnanheimo's character has previously lived in Finland. This not only explains her slight accent, but also adds a touch of exoticism to the character, which was further strengthened in a scene where she tells her fiancé that she learned to read cards from a Finnish fortune teller. While this may have partly been an inside joke, it also implied for Swedish audiences that the Finns were a somewhat archaic and mystical people and not as modern as the Swedes.

Perhaps the most significant difference in these film narratives concerned the depiction of nudity and premarital sex. The after-sex scene, in which the two protagonists of *Restless Blood* lie together naked before they are married, is both longer and more intimate in the Swedish version than in the Finnish one. This is partly explained by the fact that Finnish censorship at the time was relatively strict, whereas Swedish censorship was more tolerant. But this also proved to be a lasting trend in the years to come. From the early 1950s on, Swedish cinema became internationally known for its daring depiction of sexuality, judged by the standards of the period, and Finnish film companies tried to follow suit. In Finland this in some cases meant that a moderate film version was produced for the domestic market, and a version with more explicit nudity for the international markets.[88] In a sense, Tulio's 1940s dual-language versions were early experiments exemplifying such marketing tactics, albeit with relatively modest results: while sensationalism was ever-present in Tulio's work in Finland, Scandinavian versions allowed him to take the film narrative one step further.

NOTES

1. Suomen Filmiteollisuus produced 237 films, Suomi-Filmi 142 films, Fennada-Filmi 53 films and minor companies 187 films, so the total output of Finnish feature films between 1920 and 1963 was 619.
2. Hupaniittu 2016: 33–4.
3. Hupaniittu 2019: 21–31.
4. Hupaniittu 2015.
5. Kassila 2004: 203–4.
6. Uusitalo 2004: 39.
7. Nikula 2000: 34–42.
8. See Laine 2016: 102.
9. Soila 2004: 132.
10. Ibid.: 136.
11. Toiviainen 2004: 177.
12. Ibid.: 172.
13. Kutter 1945.
14. Kassila 2004: 47–8.
15. Laine 2004: 278–82.
16. See Bordwell, Staiger and Thompson 1985: 84, 124–7 and passim.
17. Tulio 2002: 51.
18. Tykkyläinen 2004: 22–5.
19. Sedergren 2006: 15–21.
20. Klemola 2004: 286–7.
21. Tulio 2002: 64.
22. Uusitalo et al. 1996: 405.
23. Tulio 2002: 64.
24. Uusitalo et al. 1996: 622.
25. Tulio 2002: 55.
26. Klemola 2004: 287; Tulio 2002: 52–3.
27. Tulio 2002: 56.
28. Töyri 1978: 57.
29. Klemola 2004: 290.
30. Ibid.: 287.
31. A contract between Suomen Biografi and Fennica, 17 October 1929. Suomi-Filmi Collection, Helsinki: National Audiovisual Archive.
32. A contract between Suomi-Filmi and Fennica, 22 October 1930. Suomi-Filmi Collection, Helsinki: National Audiovisual Archive; a contract between Suomi-Filmi and Fennica, 15

March 1933. Suomi-Filmi Collection, Helsinki: National Audiovisual Archive. Fennica's 50 per cent share was now of the gross proceeds instead of the net proceeds, but since Finnish films had been exempted from taxes in 1930, the deal for *The Blue Shadow* was much better than the previous one.

33. Uusitalo 1972: 20–1, 33.
34. Ibid.: 30.
35. Uusitalo 1965: III.
36. Tulio 2002: 24.
37. Ibid.: 25.
38. Uusitalo et al. 1996: 189–90.
39. Tulio 2002: 97.
40. Toiviainen, Tykkyläinen and von Bagh 1980: 13.
41. Suomi-Filmi's board meeting, 13 May 1936. Suomi-Filmi Collection, Helsinki: National Audiovisual Archive.
42. Toiviainen, Tykkyläinen and von Bagh 1980: 13.
43. Uusitalo et al. 1996: 22, 70, 186, 240.
44. Tulio 2002: 98.
45. Uusitalo et al. 1995: 314.
46. Laine 2020.
47. '"Seitsemän veljestä" filmataan', *Suomen Kinolehti* 10/1938: 416.
48. See Sedergren and Kippola 2009: 264–92. Kansatieteellinen Filmi translates as Ethnographic Film.
49. See Vallisaari 1984: 122.
50. See Lyytikäinen 2004: 236–42.
51. For example, a biopic of the classical nineteenth-century poet J. L. Runeberg, *Runon Kuningas ja Muuttolintu* (initiated in 1937 and completed in 1940 by Suomen Filmiteollisuus), caused a sensation among the national elite. Lehtisalo 2011: 103–4.
52. Pälsi, Sakari, 'Seitsemän veljestä' (1938, 27 p.). Sakari Pälsi archive, Helsinki: The Finnish Literature Society.
53. Pälsi, Sakari, 'Seitsemän veljestä' (1938, 18 p.). Aleksis Kivi Society archive, box 10, KL 11877, Helsinki: The Finnish Literature Society.
54. Vallisaari 1984: 122.
55. Uusitalo et al. 1995: 314.
56. 'SF:n elokuvatilasto', Suomen Filmiteollisuus Collection, Helsinki: National Audiovisual Archive.
57. Tulio 2002: 151.
58. Ibid.: 144.
59. Mäkelä 1996: 84–5.
60. Töyri 1983: 257–8.
61. Kassila 2004: 122–30.
62. Nikula 2000: 205.
63. Lohikoski 1993: 252–3.
64. Uusitalo et al. 1999: 133.
65. Tulio 2002: 106.
66. Nikula 2000: 62–3.
67. Toiviainen, Tykkyläinen and von Bagh 1980: 13–5.
68. Mäkelä 1996: 92–3.
69. Lehtisalo 2016.
70. See Laine 1999: 71.
71. Schildt 1985: 115.

72. Kutter 1955: 43–4.
73. Schildt 1985: 114.
74. See Jäntti 1957: 142–4.
75. Kalha 2009: 138–9.
76. Garncarz 1999: 269.
77. Lehtisalo 2016: 123–4.
78. Ibid.: 124.
79. Sanderson 2010: 49.
80. Honka-Hallila 1996: 469.
81. Straubhaar, LaRose and Davenport 2009: 504.
82. Tulio 2002: 77.
83. Ibid.: 77.
84. Ibid.: 139.
85. Ibid.: 85–7.
86. Nikula 2000: 126–7.
87. Ibid.: 133–4.
88. Römpötti 2019.

NEWSPAPERS AND PERIODICALS

Suomen Kinolehti 1938.

BIBLIOGRAPHY

Bordwell, David, Janet Staiger and Kristin Thompson (1985), *The Classical Hollywood Cinema. Film Style & Mode of Production to 1960*, London, Melbourne and Henley: Routledge & Kegan Paul.

Garncarz, Joseph (1999), 'Made in Germany: Multiple-Language Versions and the Early German Sound Cinema', in Andrew Higson and Richard Maltby (eds), *'Film Europe' and 'Film America'. Cinema, Commerce and Cultural Exchange 1920–1939*, Exeter: University of Exeter Press, 249–73.

Honka-Hallila, Ari (1996), 'Äänielokuva tulee Suomeen', in Kari Uusitalo et al. (eds), *Suomen kansallisfilmografia 1, 1907–1935*, Helsinki: Edita and Suomen elokuva-arkisto, 463–9.

Hupaniittu, Outi (2015), 'Suomalaisen elokuvan pientuottajat 1920–1930-luvuilla', in *Elonet – Kansallisfilmografia*, Helsinki: Kansallinen audiovisuaalinen instituutti, http://www.elonet.fi/fi/kansallisfilmografia/suomalaisen-elokuvan-vuosikymmenet/1919-1929/suomalaisen-elokuvan-pientuottajat-1920-1930-luvuilla (accessed 15 April 2019).

Hupaniittu, Outi (2016), 'The Emergence of Finnish Film Production and its Linkages to Cinema Businesses During the Silent Era', in Henry Bacon (ed.), *Finnish Cinema. A Transnational Enterprise*, London: Palgrave Macmillan, 27–50.

Hupaniittu, Outi (2019), 'Miten mahdoton onnistui? Suomen Filmiteollisuuden synnyn ja toiminnan taloudellinen perusta', in Kimmo Laine, Minna Santakari, Juha Seitajärvi and Outi Hupaniittu (eds), *Unelmatehdas Liisankadulla. Suomen Filmiteollisuus Oy:n tarina*, Helsinki: Suomalaisen Kirjallisuuden Seura, 20–52.

Kalha, Harri (2009), 'The Case of Theodor Tugai: The Filmstar and the Factitious Body', in Tytti Soila (ed.), *Stellar Encounters. Stardom in Popular European Cinema*, New Barnet: John Libbey, 132–42.

Kassila, Matti (2004), *Käsikirjoitus ja ohjaus: Matti Kassila*, Helsinki: WSOY.

Klemola, Pertti (2004), 'Suomalaisen elokuvan kultaiset vuodet. Valentin Vaala muistelee', in Kimmo Laine, Matti Lukkarila and Juha Seitajärvi (eds), *Valentin Vaala*, Helsinki: Suomalaisen Kirjallisuuden Seura, 286–305 (orig. 1965).

Kutter, Hans (1945), 'Vain tekniikalla ei tehdä filmiä – sydämen on oltava mukana. Valentin Vaala puhuu suunsa puhtaaksi', *Elokuva-Aitta* 22/1945, 412–13.

Laine, Kimmo (1999), *'Pääosassa Suomen kansa'. Suomi-Filmi ja Suomen Filmiteollisuus kansallisen elokuvan rakentajina 1933–1939*, Helsinki: Suomalaisen Kirjallisuuden Seura.

Laine, Kimmo (2004), 'Kun isä tahtoo . . . sarjakuvasovituksena eli suomalaisen studioelokuvan kolme perinnettä', in Kimmo Laine, Matti Lukkarila and Juha Seitajärvi (eds), *Valentin Vaala*, Helsinki: Suomalaisen Kirjallisuuden Seura, 271–83.

Laine, Kimmo (2016), 'Conceptions of National Film Style during the Studio Era', in Henry Bacon (ed.), *Finnish Cinema. A Transnational Enterprise*, London: Palgrave Macmillan, 87–114.

Laine, Kimmo (2020), 'Seitsemän veljestä valkokankaalla', forthcoming.

Lehtisalo, Anneli (2011), 'As if Alive before Us: The Pleasures of Verisimilitude in Biographical Fiction Films', *New Readings* Vol. 11, 100–17.

Lehtisalo, Anneli (2016), 'Exporting Finnish Films', in Henry Bacon (ed.), *Finnish Cinema. A Transnational Enterprise*, London: Palgrave Macmillan, 115–38.

Lyytikäinen, Pirjo (2004), *Vimman villityt pojat. Aleksis Kiven Seitsemän veljeksen laji*, Helsinki: Suomalaisen Kirjallisuuden Seura.

Mäkelä, Mauno (1996), *Kerrankin hyvä Kotimainen. Elokuvatuottajan muistelmat*, edited by Kalevi Koukkunen, Porvoo: WSOY.

Nikula, Jaana (2000), *Polttava katse. Regina Linnanheimon elämä ja elokuvat*, Helsinki: Like.

Römpötti, Tommi (2019), 'Kriisi ja nuorisoelokuvan murros SF:n 1960luvun elokuvissa – "Mutta eräänä päivänä joudut kiinni ja vankilaan"', in Kimmo Laine, Minna Santakari, Juha Seitajärvi and Outi Hupaniittu (eds), *Unelmatehdas Liisankadulla. Suomen Filmiteollisuus Oy:n tarina*, Helsinki: Suomalaisen Kirjallisuuden Seura, 307–23.

Sanderson, John D. (2010), 'The Other You. Translating the Hispanic for the Spanish Screen', in Verena Berger and Miya Komori (eds), *Polyglot Cinema. Migration and Transcultural Narration in France, Italy, Portugal and Spain*, Vienna and Berlin: Lit, 49–71.

Sedergren, Jari (2006), *Taistelu elokuvasensuurista. Valtiollisen elokuvatarkastuksen historia 1946–2006*, Helsinki: Suomalaisen Kirjallisuuden Seura.

Sedergren, Jari and Ilkka Kippola (2009), *Dokumentin ytimessä. Suomalaisen dokumentti- ja lyhytelokuvan historia 1904–1944*, Helsinki: Suomalaisen Kirjallisuuden Seura.

Soila, Tytti (1994), 'Five Songs of the Scarlet Flower', *Screen* 35:3, 265–74.

Soila, Tytti (2004), '"Tehtiin miten Vaala haluaa" – Valentin Vaala näyttelijäohjaajana', in Kimmo Laine, Matti Lukkarila and Juha Seitajärvi (eds), *Valentin Vaala*, Helsinki: Suomalaisen Kirjallisuuden Seura, 131–43.

Straubhaar, Joseph, Robert LaRose and Lucinda Davenport (2009), *Media Now: Understanding Media, Culture, and Technology*, Boston: Wadsworth.

Talvio, Raija (2017), '"Ihan on ku filmissä!" Suomalaisen elokuvan heinäkasakohtaukset', in Mari Mäkiranta, Ulla Piela and Eija Timonen (eds), *Näkyväksi sepitetty maa. Näkökulmia Suomen visualisointiin*, Helsinki: Suomalaisen Kirjallisuuden Seura, 156–71.

Toiviainen, Sakari, Lauri Tykkyläinen and Peter von Bagh (1980), 'Kuvaajan matka menneeseen', *Filmihullu* 8/1980, 8–21.

Toiviainen, Sakari (2004), 'Vaala ja melodraama', in Kimmo Laine, Matti Lukkarila and Juha Seitajärvi (eds), *Valentin Vaala*, Helsinki: Suomalaisen Kirjallisuuden Seura, 163–77.

Tulio, Teuvo (2002), 'Elämäni ja elokuvani', in Sakari Toiviainen (ed.), *Tulio: Levottoman veren antologia*, Helsinki: Suomalaisen Kirjallisuuden Seura, 23–157.

Tykkyläinen, Lauri (2004), 'Valentin Vaalan jäljillä', in Kimmo Laine, Matti Lukkarila and Juha Seitajärvi (eds), *Valentin Vaala*, Helsinki: Suomalaisen Kirjallisuuden Seura, 17–31.

Töyri, Esko (1978), *Me mainiot löträäjät. Suomalaisen elokuvan raamikehitysvuodet 1920–1940*, Helsinki: Suomen elokuvasäätiö.

Töyri, Esko (1983), *Vanhat kameramiehet. Suomalaisen elokuvan kameramiehiä 1930–1950*, Helsinki: Suomen elokuvasäätiö.

Uusitalo, Kari (1965), *Suomalaisen elokuvan vuosikymmenet. Johdatus kotimaisen elokuvan ja elokuva-alan historiaan 1896–1963*, Helsinki: Otava.

Uusitalo, Kari (1972), *Kuusi vuosikymmentä suomalaista elokuvayritteliäisyyttä. Adams-Filmi Osakeyhtiö 1912–1972*, Helsinki: Adams-Filmi.

Uusitalo, Kari (2004), 'Valentin Vaala – "Uneksivakatseinen ohjaaja"', in Kimmo Laine, Matti Lukkarila and Juha Seitajärvi (eds), *Valentin Vaala*, Helsinki: Suomalaisen Kirjallisuuden Seura, 33–43.

Uusitalo, Kari et al. (1996), *Suomen kansallisfilmografia 1, 1907–1935*, Helsinki: Edita and Suomen elokuva-arkisto.

Uusitalo, Kari et al. (1995), *Suomen kansallisfilmografia 2, 1936–1941*, Helsinki: Painatuskeskus and Suomen elokuva-arkisto.

Uusitalo, Kari et al. (1999), *Suomen kansallisfilmografia 8, 1971–1980*, Helsinki: Edita and Suomen elokuva-arkisto.

Vallisaari, Hilkka (1984), *Kansatieteellisen elokuvan alkuvaiheet Suomessa*, Helsinki: Helsingin yliopiston kansatieteen laitoksen tutkimuksia 11.

CHAPTER 5

All that Melodrama Allows – Tulio's Films and Principal Obsessions

In this chapter, Tulio's surviving films are discussed in thematic pairs. The themes emerge from his basic obsessions: temptation, loss of innocence, jealousy, passion and female decadence. Finally, Tulio's only comedy and one fragment which he actually disowned are discussed under the heading Anomalous Tulio. Many of these themes appear in most of his films, but this structure allows for the highlighting of Tulio's basic concerns through a thorough treatment of each of the themes in connection with the films that best exemplify them. The structure does not allow for fully chronological treatment of the films, and in some cases the pairs are formed of films of which the latter is a remake or a variation of the former. There is one exception even to this, as the discussion of *Sensuela* (1973), Tulio's last and most extravagant film, although a remake of *Cross of Love* (1946), is left till last. After all, this did provide the outrageous but rather sad finale to his career in filmmaking.

TEMPTATION AND RECONCILIATION

In Tulio's first two surviving melodramas, *The Song of the Scarlet Flower* (*Laulu tulipunaisesta kukasta*, 1938) and *In the Fields of Dreams* (*Unelma karjamajalla*, 1940),[1] the male protagonist is a restless young man at odds with his wealthy family, who expect him soon to assume the responsibility of running their estate.[2] But he is not prepared to settle down, and cannot resist the temptation of taking advantage of a beautiful maid to whom he in turn, handsome and charming as well as wealthy as he is, presents an irresistible temptation. He betrays both the young woman and his family by leaving everything behind as he steps out to make his fortune in the world.

The Song of the Scarlet Flower is based on Johannes Linnankoski's novel of the same name. When it first appeared in 1905 it was immediately recognised as a masterpiece. It became a popular bestseller and was soon translated into several languages. The novel is evocatively sensuous and offers subtle depictions of erotically charged relationships that intertwine with a deeply felt connection with nature. Olavi (Kaarlo Oksanen), the protagonist, is at first innocently minded but fundamentally an inconsiderate and self-centred youth brimming with erotic desire. He appears genuinely sorry when the first girl we see him tempting bursts into tears because of the inappropriateness of his approaches. But the same evening his eyes catch those of another girl, whom he names Gaselli (Nora Mäkinen), in a game where two boys run after a girl, trying to grab her. She is pretty and seductively playful, and as he catches her they end up in an embrace on the ground (figures 5.1–4). In his adaptation, Tulio succeeds well in capturing the joyful eroticism of Linnankoski's novel.

In the film the couple are soon seen in bed together, almost in a state of enrapture. We have no reason to doubt that Olavi is at this stage completely honest: for the time being he utterly believes in his feelings. Although the loving couple have their clothes on, we may presume they have made love – this kind of suggestive prudence appears already in the novel and had to be adhered

Figures 5.1–4

to in films of the era in order to avoid excessive moral reproach. Thus, as they are taken by surprise by Olavi's mother, she is scandalised. The main problem seems to be that Gaselli is merely a maid and that Olavi, in addition to being the future master of the house, is still young and inexperienced. There is a hypocritical trait in this, as the mother herself draws a parallel between her son and husband, who in his time has also fooled around with the maids on the estate. The old father is even more blatantly hypocritical. In a flashback we see him throwing an axe at his wife, furious because of her having surprised him with a maid in the very same place where she found Olavi and Gaselli together. Now he fulminates against his son – effectively for behaving just like he has always done. An archaic sense of morality and the need to keep up distinctions between classes overriding honest human relations was to become a consistent theme in Tulio's films. An integral part of this pattern is that Don Juanism or male promiscuity is accepted as a fact of life, while erotic sensibility leaves women vulnerable to seduction and the consequent fall from grace not only in the social but also in a deeper moral sense.

Olavi has inherited his father's temperament and announces that he will leave the Koskela Manor, even refusing the money his father offers him. As a transition that derives from the tradition of Nordic silent cinema and forebodes many scenes in both this and many subsequent Tulio films, we see an impressive

Figure 5.5

sequence of shots of a rapid, most strikingly one of them upside down. In addition to suggesting the untamed life force that drives Olavi ahead as a log driver, it foreshadows Olavi later on establishing himself as a reckless hero, first by risking his life in order to clear a blockage further downstream, and later on by actually shooting the rapid on a single log in order to make an impression on yet another woman.

On his way roaming round the country, Olavi leaves behind a chain of women whose lives he inadvertently ruins. He may still be assumed to have a moral sense – he appears even to have genuine tender feelings for his conquests. He is not simply hypocritical – his passion just keeps on overwhelming him. The naïve women he encounters succumb to his seductions blind to both the underlying class relationships and the restlessness of his character, either of which could serve as an overwhelming block to a permanent relationship. Thus, the women, given the moralistic attitudes prevalent in their society, are highly likely to be left destitute. Olavi even appears truly sorry when he one by one leaves them behind, even gaining a promise from them of not succumbing to the temptations of other men, unless they really find the one and only man intended for them. The idea that a woman is forever marked by the man to whom she first succumbs was to haunt Tulio's films throughout his career. In the later films the focus is on the victimised women and the seducers are much more inconsiderate scoundrels than Olavi. He even tries to calm down the passion of one the women he encounters, but to no avail, the temptation is irresistible, it is a force of nature. Further transition images of rapids serve as a metaphor of these passions, and suggest that we are following events that are representative of Olavi's stream of life and not just singular events.

Finally, Olavi meets Kyllikki (Raakel Linnanheimo, Regina Linnanheimo's sister), the proud daughter of a substantial landed estate, who is not so easily seduced. They first encounter each other over a fence which marks the border between the rose garden she tends and the world where Olavi roams. Olavi compliments her on the beauty of the roses and asks for one. She replies haughtily: 'In Moisio Mansion it is not a custom to offer flowers to strangers over the fence. Anyone can ask for a flower, but a man must prove himself braver than that.' Her behaviour is simultaneously a rejection and an invitation: she might be interested if Olavi is able to prove his manliness. The flower obviously stands for eroticism, a theme which is even more prevalent in Linnankoski's novel, in which Olavi gives floral pet names to most of the women he falls for – with the exception of Kyllikki, who, tending to her flowers, is in control of her own 'florality'. The pet names are indicative of the genuine tenderness and sensitivity he feels, although in a way which reflects his fundamentally irresponsible attitude toward them. As Pirjo Lyytikäinen has pointed out about the novel, 'Olavi names and fabricates his women, first to satisfy his fantasies, then his desire.'[3] To Gaselli, the only one he refers to with an animal name, he says he wishes she were a flower he could pick up and attach to his shirt. His poetic visions may be genuine, but they also serve as stepping stones toward greater carnal satisfaction, after which he is ready to cast the women away like a withered flower and move on.

Yet, like all his women, Olavi yearns for the kind of wholeness which only perfect love is supposed to deliver. He appears vaguely aware that this is in conflict with his irresistible inclination for restless wandering and womanising, and his consequent inability to commit himself. He may actually accuse those women for not adhering to *his* ideal of everything or nothing, which he argues would enable him to reach that state of bliss. Kyllikki, daughter of the Moisio Manor, is the first who challenges this total lack of emotional logic. In this moral universe the male character may be weak, whereas the woman must be strong enough to serve as an ethical ideal which will eventually save the man.[4] There is also a definite class aspect here: though his father accuses him of having neglected his studies, Olavi has had more education than most of the people he encounters. Olavi also has a talent for words, which is his major asset when flirting with women. Kyllikki in turn is clearly more educated and aware than the women Olavi has his casual affairs with. It is significant that they are offspring of the same class, although Olavi pretends otherwise.

While Tulio has left out of his film many scenes which in the novel serve to emphasise Olavi's near-infantile innocence in dealing with emotional affairs, Raakel Linnanheimo's performance makes Kyllikki appear even stronger than in the novel. She is not above being seduced, but she has the boldness to stand against the folly of this rover, and eventually even the oppressive power of patriarchy. The difference between the novelistic and filmic Kyllikki derives mainly from the way Raakel Linnanheimo reveals her inner uncertainty, perhaps reflecting deeper psychological realism on the one hand, difference in the way of conceiving the role of women in society on the other – the novel appeared in 1905, and the film some thirty years later, when mores and attitudes were already changing. Nevertheless, in both renderings of the story Olavi seems to realise that Kyllikki is much more than he has ever been given to understand to hope for, the question remaining whether he is able to live up to the challenge she presents to him.

But first Olavi decides to win Kyllikki merely by a reckless show of courage. He does this by shooting the fierce rapid on a single log. Kyllikki, as well as a great number of other people, is watching. The man with whom Olavi has made a bet about having the courage to accomplish this feat offers to withdraw the bet, not wanting to be thought responsible for a man's death. Olavi, however, does not even consider resisting the temptation of facing the danger – and winning the heart of a woman who has not immediately fallen for him. The way foolhardy bravery and the desire for this woman connect in his mind is made explicit in a dissolve in which Kyllikki's angel-like image is seen first superimposed against the rapid and then against his own face.

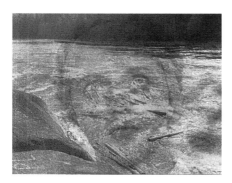

Figures 5.6–7

Through imagery to which Tulio was to return repeatedly throughout his career, Olavi is seen succeeding in this daring exploit. As he reaches the river-bank below the rapid, he receives a hero's welcome from the crowd gathered there – and a bit later on finds a rose waiting for him on the Moisala fence. The rapid sequence is one of the many long wordless sequences of Tulio's oeuvre, and it is followed by another one almost as long in which we see the loving couple swim naked. Here, like in many of his other works, Tulio displays his affinity with the aesthetic of silent cinema.

Perhaps Olavi is now ready for a more stable affair. He is actually prepared to go and ask for Kyllikki's hand, and she is willing to follow him. Her father, however, will not give her to a log driver, and Olavi is too proud to reveal his true ancestry, insisting that he should be appreciated because of what he is as a person. This we see happening in a single shot containing only a single line, the father thundering: 'A Moisio daughter will not be given to a log driver!' echoing what Olavi's mother has told him: 'Never has a maid been married to Koskela house.' Olavi is then seen going away, again riding a single log down the stream, while his fellow workers use a raft. Kyllikki is left behind. Again we see some impressive rapid-shooting, now in a lighter tone to the accompaniment of a popular song, 'Viimeinen lautta' (The Last Raft), based on 'For Me and My Gal' (1917) by George W. Meyer.

Olavi continues his wandering and tries to wash away his love and humiliation with alcohol. Here many of the incidents in Linnankoski's novel have been cut, somewhat reducing the sense of time passing – four years – before Olavi dares to approach Kyllikki again. Left out is a scene where Olavi explains to a married woman he happens to encounter his ideas about love, making the point that true love is free from marriage, sin and all ties that people have invented. He does acknowledge that love is pure only when left unattained, not consumed. The implication is that carnal consummation kills romantic aspirations, leaving behind only the thorns of jealousy. What we do see is Olavi at a brothel in a drunken stupor. He looks at his image in a mirror, horrified, as if for the first time realising how low he really has sunk. The music, supposedly coming from a gramophone player, seems to mock him. This stands for the mirror mocking the already weary man in the novel – Linnankoski's fictional universe is richly animated with different elements of nature and cultural objects commenting on Olavi's actions, as if symptoms of his suppressed bad consciousness and awareness of his destructive way of life.

A re-encounter with Gaselli, now a prostitute, finally brings about a change in Olavi's character. He encounters also other women he has seduced, some of them in reality, others apparently only in his guilt-ridden fantasies. There is a similar slightly dream-like quality in Linnankoski's description of Olavi's re-encounters with some of his conquests. They appear somewhat more forgiving than Gaselli, but nevertheless make Olavi embarrassed and aware of his own depravity. Gaselli, however, delivers a line that was to become a kind of leitmotiv in Tulio's oeuvre, used not only in the dialogue of another film but also in the very title of one his films dedicated to this theme: 'Here I am, just the way you wanted me!'

Olavi returns to his ancestral home and reaches his mother's deathbed just in time to receive some final advice from her: if there has been someone who has been stronger than his desire, that woman is the right one for him. His father having died before this, he is now the master of Koskela Manor, and is able to propose to Kyllikki on the basis of equal social standing. Her stern father, however, still rejects him. As Kyllikki states that she now belongs to Olavi, he retorts that she is free to leave in the same clothing in which she arrived in their house. Defiantly she begins to undress, until the father finally tells her to stop. Reluctantly he gives his permission for the marriage.

Kyllikki's problems with men do not end there. At their wedding a man comes to talk to Olavi and insinuates that Kyllikki is not 'a pure lamb'. Olavi furiously throws the man out for making such an outrageous claim, but then immediately begins to suspect that the accusation might be true. Particularly in the film, Olavi's suspicion appears completely mad. In the novel, Olavi argues to himself that the young man would not have dared to make claims about the spoiled innocence of his bride were they not true. The novel also offers plausibility to his behaviour by repeatedly bringing forth the idea that far from being callous, Olavi actually believes in his ideals, however unable he is to adhere to them in his own behaviour. It is as if he were projecting his own mode of behaviour on Kyllikki, as if he could not genuinely imagine, let alone live up to, a faithful relationship. She affirms her innocence and asks, looking momentarily straight into the camera: 'But how many unwedded wives have you left behind?' Olavi, pathologically full of self-pity, appears at his most immature. He rushes out to quench his rage with his fellow log drivers by the lake. He reaches the shore just as a boat arrives carrying the body of someone who has drowned. It turns out to be one of the women he has seduced and abandoned. This scene is an addition to the story, although something similar happens to an unknown woman according to a rumour told earlier on in the novel. Olavi returns to Kyllikki to say that his life is shattered and that he is going to kill himself. She admonishes him by stating: 'Death is a too easy solution. Wrongs can only be mended by life. You have to live, because of me.' With her hair plaited around her head as if a halo, she has again an angelic appearance, suggesting redemption.

At the end of the film, it is suggested that Olavi will live up to this challenge. This ethos derives from Linnankoski's novel, and it was soon to disappear from Tulio's works. Olavi is seen sowing seeds, followed by images of wavy cornfields. Yet, as if a reminder, one of the women he has seduced, Annikki, appears to Olavi as he is anxiously waiting for news about Kyllikki giving birth. She delivers what anachronistically could be called a feminist diatribe about how men use women, who really only want love. Her sudden appearance at this point and in that place is so improbable that it could be taken as a hallucination, perfectly in accord with Linnankoski's aesthetics. Tulio does not use explicit filmic codes to suggest that Annikki's appearance would be a figment of Olavi's imagination – or bad conscience, rather – except perhaps for Annikki's rather heavy make-up, which seems to suggest her being a woman of pleasure, a creature of the corrupt city rather than the countryside. In Tulio's later films, such characters and such improbable sudden appearances were to abound.

The parallel with her wife giving birth just as Olavi experiences all this, functions quite well in suggesting that Olavi can't expect to live in perfect peace and happiness with himself. Also, the expressions on Olavi's face suggest that his past will continue to haunt him. Yet, in comparison with Tulio's subsequent films, the ending is at least reasonably happy. Olavi and Kyllikki will continue their lives together. Their life will not be as challenging as that Linnankoski chose for his protagonist: Olavi's pride demands that he must make a start on his own by clearing a swamp for agriculture (a persistent motive in Finnish fiction) and the measure of Kyllikki's worth is ultimately that she is willing to join him in this effort, renouncing the comforts of living on an already established estate. Making such a definite new start is only vaguely suggested in Tulio's film.[5]

The Song of the Scarlet Flower opened to mixed reviews. Many critics thought that Tulio had not captured the subtlety of Linnankoski's novel. One critic wrote about 'the robust realism and absence of romantic phantasy and lyrical flights'[6]. Another demonstrated insight into Tulio's artistic character: 'Tulio has a strange way of revelling in people's instinctual life and apparently

Figures 5.8-10 Kyllikki at her most angel-like, Annikki as the fallen woman, and Olavi trying to cope with his feelings of guilt while Kyllikki is giving birth to their child.

he thinks that feeling is merely the wrong kind of possessiveness and nothing else.'[7] In view of Tulio's later films, there is some truth in this observation. Some critics, although otherwise quite critical, approved of Tulio's innovative visual style and praised his boldness in following paths previously left unexplored in Finnish cinema, the cinematographer Fred Runeberg receiving his due share of the praise. One major fault observed by many was the generally rather poor delivery of dialogue, usually ascribed to the inexperience of the actors. It was said to have given rise to some laughter.[8]

Opinions differed about the pace of Tulio's interpretation. Some claimed the film was at times boring, while one at least thought the love scenes moved to their climaxes at a terrific speed. This tendency the critic assigned to Tulio's foreignness, and expressed his hope that if Tulio intended to make more films about the Finnish people – something the critic thought was not desirable – he really should study this topic that was so obviously strange to him.[9] Tulio was not to follow this advice. Instead, he created his own kind of melodramatic aesthetics, which put him in a class of his own, not only in the context of Finnish film culture, but even in terms of world cinema. On the whole, though, the main lines of criticism of Tulio's films were now established.

There are some major differences between Tulio's and Mauritz Stiller's adaptations of Linnankoski's novel. Stiller was a major inspiration for many Finnish filmmakers, Tulio included. He was actually born in Finland, although he made his entire career abroad. His 1919 version of *The Song of the Scarlet Flower* was particularly well received in Finland and served as a model in the pursuit of a national style. His version is understandably even more chaste than Tulio's version, somewhat playing down Olof's, as the protagonist in this version of the story is called, promiscuity. It appears the only major harm he causes is for Gaselli to be dismissed from her job as a maid at the Koskela Manor. But this does lead to her resorting to prostitution, and, after having encountered Olof in a brothel, to her suicide. After Olof learns about the death of his parents, he returns to Moisala to ask for Kyllikki's hand. Only after her father has reluctantly allowed this does he reveal that he is the master of Koskela Manor. Even more than in Tulio's version, there is an unproblematic sense of social order being maintained as a man and a woman of the same social class finally come together, complete with the traditional melodramatic twist of the girl choosing to marry the boy while still under the impression that he is a vagabond. The film ends even without the wedding scene with its unjustified burst of blind jealousy.[10]

In the Fields of Dreams is based on the play *Hälsingar* by the Swedish playwright Henning Olsson. It differs from most of Tulio's other films in that the temptation the main protagonist faces is gambling rather than sex – the only other film in which a similar pattern emerges is *The Rapids of Hell* (1949). Aarne, the younger son of Ylitalo Manor, first appears to be the same kind of rascal as Olavi in *The Song of the Scarlet Flower*, but eventually there is no indication that he would have seduced anyone except the orphan Sirkka (Sirkka Salonen), who becomes his true love.

From the beginning Tulio employs montage as a kind of frivolous shock tactic. Sirkka is seen walking peacefully on a country road. This is cross-cut with Aarne riding recklessly on a small horse-drawn cart (figures 5.11–14). The music – composed by Tapio Ilomäki, who was to work on a number of Tulio's films – provides a somewhat comical effect as the image track alternates between the two. Without much diegetic justification, Tulio imposes an image of a rapid on that of the wildly trotting horse – one could, generously, interpret this as foreshadowing future events. Finally, the two lines of movement clash and Sirkka falls to the ground to avoid being run over by Aarne's horse. He stops and smiling endearingly comes to help Sirkka. If the spectator is already familiar with Tulio's *The Song of the Scarlet Flower*, seeing Kille Oksanen in the role of Aarne makes him appear like another fundamentally inconsiderate seducer, perhaps even an equally innocent one in his narrow self-centredness. In his encounters with Sirkka he appears much like Olavi, particularly when he leaves her,

Figures 5.11–14 Sirkka, knocked down by reckless Aarne, subsequently develops a genuinely tender relationship with him.

promising to return. But we do not see him chase other women, and when he does disappear from Sirkka's as well as everyone else's life, it is to escape his financial difficulties. He is not a rogue, just shamelessly and uncontrollably full of life.

Kirsti (Kirsti Hurme), a dark-haired maid who has been employed at the Ylitalo Manor for some time, assumes Aarne belongs to her and is jealous and cruel toward the blond Sirkka, whom Aarne on a whim employs on their first encounter to serve as a younger maid. The two women stand in obvious opposition to each other, the one blonde and tender, the other dark and nasty.[11] However, it is not exactly a virgin–whore opposition. Although Kirsti, unlike Sirkka, appears to have some experience in life, there is no evidence that she would sleep around – she just desperately wants Aarne for herself and sees some justification for this that no one else is aware of. One notable difference between the two first surviving Tulio melodramas is that, as opposed to the women Olavi seduces in *The Song of the Scarlet Flower*, Sirkka is not ostracised because of her low social status even when an affair develops between her and Aarne. Only Kirsti reminds Sirkka of her inferior background, although she herself does not appear to be much above her. Even Sirkka's pregnancy does not mark her as a woman of loose morals. Instead, both Aarne's mother and his brother Urho (Kyösti Erämaa) insist that he must assume his responsibilities. Urho even protects Sirkka after Aarne has run away. Aarne appears genuinely to love Sirkka and would be willing to marry her, but he has to leave because of the embezzlement he has resorted to in order to cover his gambling debts. Eino Heino's often hauntingly beautiful cinematography wonderfully captures her tender beauty and suggests there is genuine romantic affection between she and Aarne.

Even after Aarne has left her, Sirkka appears able to live a secure life with her baby. But then tragedy strikes. Nowhere else is Tulio so close to nineteenth-century stage melodrama than in the scene in which Sirkka saves a lamb from falling into the rapid. The scene had previously appeared in Ivar Johansson's 1933 film *Hälsingar*, the first sound adaptation made of Ohlson's play and clearly had quite a considerable influence on Tulio. Yet the scene with the lamb is coherently edited in the Swedish film, whereas Tulio takes strange liberties, boldly flaunting the rules of classical continuity.

While Sirkka risks her life saving the lamb, a vagabond steals her baby. Kirsti arrives when Sirkka is crying for God's mercy, and seizes her opportunity to

Figures 5.15–18 Sirkka in desperation, doesn't know what has happened to her baby; Kirsti sees an opportunity to get rid of her rival.

destroy her rival. Seeing the baby's cap, which is lying on the cliff-edge by the rapid, as a sign of what must have happened, she claims to have seen Sirkka throw her baby into the water. Sirkka is unable to provide an alternative explanation. The sequence follows to a considerable extent silent-cinema aesthetics, as the only sound heard for quite some time is the highly dramatic music.

Sirkka is sentenced to two years in prison for infanticide. After her release, she is ostracised. A montage sequence shows children throwing stones at her and adults closing windows as she walks past. A title then reveals rather surprisingly that six years have passed since the supposed crime. Nothing seems to have changed. Kirsti is as nasty toward Sirkka as ever, and Urho still supports her. But then a car arrives and Aarne steps out. He is shamefaced and humbled. He tells Urho that he has worked like a slave in order to earn enough to remedy his wrongdoings. The ever-pure Sirkka is forgiving and assures Aarne that their son must still be alive. Just as Aarne echoes the words 'our son', there is a cut to an old man talking to a little boy. The man is dying and as his attempt at redemption he tells the boy how to get home. This explains why Tulio has had to resort to a rather clumsy way of indicating the passage of time: the kidnapped boy must have reached an age at which to plausibly be able to find his way back to his ancestral home. The little boy's long journey is rendered in a gentle montage sequence. Miraculously, he does reach Ylitalo. Conveniently enough, in good melodramatic fashion, he has a birthmark which reveals his identity to an old farmhand, who has never believed Sirkka to be guilty. As his parents kneel at the altar to be married, the boy steps into the church and the altarpiece depicting Jesus is illuminated by the sun. This is the only real *deus ex machina* plot solution in Tulio's oeuvre, and with that, also of virtue rewarded. The guilty, however, are not punished to any significant degree. Aarne has worked hard by his own accord, and is forgiven; Kirsti leaves the Ylitalo Estate and sends a message to Sirkka begging for forgiveness.

With this film, Tulio's style took a decisive turn toward a more idiosyncratic freedom from the constraints of classical style. Above all, we see him employ a strange devise which was to become one of his trademarks: the impossible point-of-view shot (discussed in chapter 6). We see someone look intently at something that he or she could not possibly see, inasmuch as we are at all capable of making sense of the diegetic space. When Aarne leaves Sirkka to return home, beating once again his horse into a wild trot, it is as if she can see him through the forest, deeply worried about what will happen to him (figure 5.19). She even falls on the ground as if once again knocked down by him. At points Tulio's efforts appear just plain sloppy. As analysed in detail in chapter 6, the scene in which Sirkka goes down the cliff to save the lamb is edited in a way which makes no spatial sense whatsoever. Yet one could argue that this is in perfect accord with the implausible events: the whole episode is quite fantastical, like a bad dream come true.[12]

Figure 5.19

Contemporary critics found a number of faults in the film but were generally quite lenient. Perhaps most interestingly, the reviews in the archive of the National Audiovisual Institute do not mention the way Tulio ignored the norms of continuity of classical film style. Some actually complained that the style is very ordinary. This might connect with the fact that a number of writers complained about the many images of Finnish countryside, which they agreed were beautiful but of the sort that had already been seen in 'tens and tens of Finnish films'.[13] Many critics also complained about the poor quality of the sound recording.

Some writers also wondered why Tulio started the film with the patriotic choral song 'Oi kallis Suomenmaa' (Oh dear Finland). One critic referred to this as 'exploitation of the spectator's feelings'.[14] Indeed, Tulio's use of classical music in this film appears almost whimsical in its heavily overdone seriousness. Later, as Aarne is going through his debt slips and begins to plan his forgery, we hear an orchestral adaptation of Jean Sibelius' song 'Ristilukki' (The Song of a Spider). This makes some sense if we think of the music referring to the salesman who has bought all of Aarne's debts in order to blackmail him, like a spider weaving its web. The next time we see Aarne at this work, we hear a brief extract from Sibelius' *Swan of Tuonela* – presumably, no intertextual reference is intended. When Aarne intends to run away and has a fight with Urho, who tries to stop him, their wrestling is accompanied by Johann Sebastian Bach's 'Toccata in D Minor' (in a rather terrible orchestral adaptation). It is heard again in the scene in which Sirkka tries to rescue the lamb from the cliff and briefly again when Sirkka's trial begins. Finally, after the film has ended at the altar and the image has faded away, Felix Mendelssohn's 'Wedding March' from *A Midsummer Night's Dream* is heard. The original music composed by Tapio Ilomäki is fairly standard film music used in rough leitmotif fashion.

LOSS OF INNOCENCE

According to Linda Williams, '[if] emotional and moral registers are sounded, if a work invites us to feel sympathy for the virtues of beset victims, if the narrative trajectory is ultimately concerned with retrieval and staging of virtue through adversity and suffering, then the operative mode is melodrama'.[15] This certainly applies to Tulio, with one significant exception: though his female protagonists are virtuous, there is no retrieval of their virtue in the eyes of their perversely moralistic society. Once they have been led astray, they are irretrievably stained. This is closely intertwined with Tulio's special brand of melodrama. According to Williams, '[m]elodrama has been viewed either as that which the "classical" has grown up out of, or that to which it sometimes regresses'.[16] It could be argued also that Tulio simply lapsed from the rigours of classical style, to which his 1938 *Song of The Scarlet Flower* still largely adhered. Yet it might be more fruitful to acknowledge that he simply did not aspire to the condition of that kind of stylistic purity. The classical style could not contain his obsessions.

   Loss of innocence was Tulio's most persistent theme. He touches on this in *Song of the Scarlet Flower*, but there the focus is on Olavi's development. His is a story of a loss of innocence of sorts, the development of Olavi from passionately romantic youth through reckless erotic exploits to responsible maturity. His passion overwhelms him again and again, but he blinds himself to the havoc he imposes on the lives of the women he falls for and then leaves behind. In Tulio's next film, *In the Fields of Dreams*, Sirkka falls for Aarne and has a baby with him out of wedlock. This, however, is not represented as a fall from innocence in the tradition of stage melodrama and much of silent cinema. In Tulio's later films, the victim usually is a girl on the threshold of adulthood. She has lived a protected childhood far from the temptations of the big city, or even just the big country house, the owners of which look down on her as a social inferior. She is easily seduced with the promise of love from a man of experience and higher social rank. The inexperienced young girls are too innocent to see any aspect of social climbing in this, but are treated by those who think of themselves as superior as if that was their sole purpose and so are cast down to the bottom of society.

Possibly apart from the first three lost films, loss of innocence emerges for the first time as the fundamental theme in *The Way You Wanted Me* (*Sellaisena kuin sinä minut halusit*, 1944). Maija (Marie-Louise Fock) has lived all her life on an island. However, a frame flashback structure allows us first to see her in the condition to which she has been reduced after the men she has loved have betrayed her, and then in the flashback as an innocent girl. A striking dissolve reveals in reverse the transformation that has taken place.

Figures 5.20–21

In the flashback Maija, daughter of an islander family, is loved by a local young sailor, Aarne (Ture Ara), who is not yet in a position to offer economically secure marriage and who is away at sea for long stretches of time. In addition, their families are for some unexplained reason in permanent state of feud. The character who insists on this is Aarne's stern father, whose only major characteristic and story function the feuding is. Aarne is, if not exactly rounded, at least a character torn by conflicting traits. His jealousy emerges at a barn dance as Maija dances with Erkki, a handsome and sociable young man from the big city. Aarne only calms down as Maija allows him to enter her barn loft.[17] However, he has not got the guts to stand up to his father, who will not allow his sons to have an affair with a member of an 'enemy' family. In one of the most striking scenes the father, having found a sailor's cap near Maija's barn loft, asks his sons one by one, in Maija's presence, if they have been there with her. They all, Aarne included, say no. The father turns to Maija to ask if there was someone with her the previous night. She replies boldly: 'I was there with my fiancé. My ex-fiancé!'

Maija follows Erkki (Kunto Karapää) to the city and is employed as a maid by his mother. Just like Aarne, Erkki cannot resist taking advantage of Maija's

innocence. One evening he tells Maija that because of her purity he is help-
lessly in love with her, that he desperately needs her. On his invitation they
drink a toast to love, and he then makes love with her. Maija appears almost
transported by the idea that someone could actually need her. Tulio uses as a
visual metaphor a burning cigarette on an ashtray, intercutting with the seduction of the still romantically inclined but already doomed woman. By the time
Erkki carries Maija to his bedroom, the cigarette has already burned out.

Maija gets pregnant. Perhaps Erkki would have assumed his responsibilities,
but before he learns about Maija's condition, his mother throws her out of the
household. The old lady argues that because Erkki is, unlike Maija, a civilised
person, he cannot be held responsible. Maija weakly accepts the argument, but
when the lady offers her money in compensation, she contemptuously throws
it in her face. She gives birth to a daughter, but is unable to earn a living. The
montage sequence which shows her trying to reply to one work advertisement
after another is one of Tulio's most pointed social statements. Maija ends up
working as a prostitute in a seedy bar. One night she meets Aarne, who at first
is full of shame when he re-encounters the woman whose life he has ruined. He
offers her money but she refuses it, uttering those fateful words, heard already
in *The Scarlet Flower* and now also the title of this film: 'Here I am, just the way
you wanted me!' 'You whore!' he replies (figures 5.22–23).

A new character appears from nowhere. Henrik, a wealthy elderly gentleman, takes Maija and her daughter Kaarina into his care, treating Kaarina lovingly as his own child. This idyll is soon shattered as Maija's grandmother
without invitation suddenly appears in Henrik's house.[18] She launches a diatribe against Maija, accusing her of living in sin, but is satisfied by Maija's lie
about being married to Henrik – maintaining standards of propriety remained
a theme in Tulio's films throughout his entire oeuvre. Grandma goes away, but
Maija's troubles do not end there. The police enter to arrest Henrik for being a

Figures 5.22–23

spy and he disappears from the story just as unexpectedly as he entered it.[19] By now Tulio has taken full creative freedom from realist motivation: characters come and go merely according to the requirements of the moral scheme, in which they may serve merely a single function. At the plot level, Maija's zigzag fate is Tulio being more melodramatically extravagant than ever before, and the film noir imagery in these scenes shows him at his most expressionist. But more extreme plot twists are to follow.

Again, Maija has to resort to prostitution, and again Aarne happens to find her. Now he is prepared to marry her, but when a drunkard makes approaches to Maija, Aarne in a fit of jealous rage kills him and is taken away by the police. We never see or hear of him again.

Maija tries to protect Kaarina's innocence and brings her up unknowing of how she makes a living. However, in her early teens Kaarina accidentally encounters her mother practising her profession. Totally distraught, she runs into the street and is run over by a car. She is rushed to a hospital where she is operated on by none other than Erkki. When Maija reveals to him that Kaarina is his child, he asks to be allowed to take care of her and Maija. She realises that the only way to protect her daughter's innocence is to fade from Kaarina's life. At the end of the flashback Kaarina receives confirmation in a church. Maija watches, just like Stella Dallas watching her daughter's wedding in King Vidor's film of that name (1937), without revealing herself. The return to the story frame provides a maximal contrast between the already decrepit Maija and the angel-like Kaarina at the alter (figures 5.24–25). Later, Maija sees a man about to take advantage of a young girl and furiously chases him away. She gives the girl some money so that she can make a new start. The girl is not any more likely succeed in this than Maija.

The responsibility for Maija's tragedy lies first of all with the weak Aarne. We may infer that Erkki, given the chance, would perhaps have married Maija against his mother's social prejudice and desire to keep up appearances. However, the real

Figures 5.24–25

Figures 5.26–28

culprits are those who cause the tragedy through their toxic moralising stance: Aarne's father, Erkki's mother and Maija's grandmother. The grandmother, when saying farewell to Maija as she prepares to leave the island, is loving and merely warns Maija about the dangers of sin. But then she appears unfathomably in Henrik's house like a furious monster in a nightmare. We might interpret her appearance as a subjective illusion, in Freudian terms perhaps a symptom of the superego. On the other hand, Aarne's father and Erkki's mother are plain facts of the diegetic world, albeit one of mind-blowing twists of plot and spatio-temporal discontinuities. They are all parts of the rock-hard foundation of Tulio's moralistic universe.

As almost always in connection with Tulio, reviews were mixed, but in this case on average quite positive. There was even uninhibited praise: 'A bold, distinctive, artistically envisaged, powerfully effective film of high quality. One of the best domestic films.'[20] Many writers argued that even with his faults Tulio offered a fresh and bold alternative to other Finnish filmmakers, who preferred to play it safe. Tulio was even referred to as an avant-gardist, whose appearance was a slap on the face of conventionality. There were those who criticised the script and dialogue of *The Way You Wanted Me*, but even they praised the visual realisation. One critic stated:

But if we assess a film as a film, when we focus on how the filmmaker expresses what he has to say, then we have to acknowledge that this work by Tulio is of the highest order that has been produced in this country for quite some time – The director realises his vision by means of camera so beautifully, concisely and tellingly as only a filmmaker who has been endowed by rich imagination, a filmic penetrating eye, undaunting courage and untiring urge of experimentation and technical gifts can achieve.[21]

Many critics pointed out the basic contradictions of Tulio's poetics. One of them thought the dialogue clumsy and long-winded but proceeded immediately to assure readers that 'despite this, the spectator is ready to acknowledge having seen once again a real film that in a specifically filmic sense represents the highest order'.[22] Some thought the cinematography with its abundant use of close-ups and extraordinary camera angles could be compared with French aesthetics,[23] while others specifically denied this, arguing that 'a French director is prepared to relinquish the slightest external effects, if psychological consistency required that. A French director is above all psychologically reliable, Tulio is not.'[24]

The theme of lost innocence is also at the core of *Cross of Love* (*Rakkauden risti*, 1946) and its remake *Sensuela*, both of which tell the story of a young woman who either explicitly or implicitly is defined as a 'child of nature' – this would equally well apply to Maija in *The Way You Wanted Me*. Having lived all her life far from the temptations of the city, her love is pure and she is totally unable to see through the front put up by men who have no inhibitions about exploiting her romantic yearnings. In the tradition of the Don Juan characters of decadent literature, women are 'victims, prey and fruit to be picked'. As Lyytikäinen points out, in this tradition 'the victim is typically an innocent angel, a child virgin, whose heavenly ignorance and self-contained, peaceful life the male demon shatters into death and madness or converts into pitiless torture'.[25] In both films, the male seducer stumbles by accident – literally so – to the remote corner of the world where the girl has lived all her life: in *Cross of Love* he ends up on an island because of a shipwreck, in *Sensuela* a pilot's plane crashes in a remote corner of Lapland. The young woman tends to his wounds and falls quickly for the handsome fellow whose like she has never before encountered. She is a bit like Miranda in Shakespeare's *The Tempest*, but instead of a wise Prospero to protect her, her father is more like an Old Testament avenger intent on killing both sinners and their tarnished victims. This comes about because the cad succeeds in tempting the ingénue to visit the city with him, against her father's explicit warnings. The cad has his way with her, grows eventually tired of her and throws her out, causing her to succumb to prostitution.

Cross of love begins with a credit sequence with images of a sea raging to the accompaniment of an orchestral adaptation of Bach's 'Toccata and Fugue in D Minor'. A strange sequence follows. A cat looks at a clock, then at a parrot climbing a ladder. We see an old man chuckling insanely. Presumably he is cooking food for himself, but, somewhat horror film-like, because of the low camera angle and the expressionist lighting, he looks like a mad wizard brewing a fateful poison. He sees a rat and throws a plate at it. The parrot screams and flaps its wings wildly. The man shouts at it and mumbles something about 'storm and death'. The Bach Toccata continues throughout the scene, sometimes fading out a little. The man climbs to the top of a lighthouse, where the flicker of the light further emphasises the expressionist quality of the scene. He prays for death and asks for his daughter to come and fetch him. Talking to the parrot now on his shoulder, he reminisces how he himself helped the girl into this world, as there was no midwife available. He turns to go downstairs and hears a cry for help. Again he chuckles, and tells the parrot to be quiet. The steps squeak loudly as he continues his descent, further emphasising the horror-film effect. He realises there is someone about to drown and says to himself: 'Again there is a man in the sea, he must not come here.' He gets his rifle and shoots at the helpless victim. Another man appears, takes the rifle away from the old man and goes to pull the man from the sea. With Tulio's typical disregard of spatio-temporal continuity, this does not appear to take any length of time. Meanwhile, the old man grabs a picture of a beautiful young woman and presses it against his chest, saying, 'No one will get you, no one.' As will become apparent at the end of the film, there is a certain weird irony to this.

In the morning the island is bathed in wonderful sunlight and we begin to learn what the situation really is. The rescuer, Pekka (Pentti Viljanen), explains to the man he has saved that the old lighthouse keeper Kalle (Oscar Tengström) goes mad during storms. As he begins to tell why, the story moves into an utterly implausible frame flashback structure. Pekka is needed to furnish the voice-over, although he couldn't possibly know what has actually happened. At the end of the film, it will turn out that the saved man is a painter who has rejected Kalle's daughter Riitta (Regina Linnanheimo) after having discovered that she has been with another man, thus pushing her into suicide. Yet he appears to have been stranded at the lighthouse purely by chance, as if guided by fate, to hear a story in which he himself has played a crucial part. And as if this was not absurdly tight melodramatic storytelling enough, Pekka, although telling Riitta's story sympathetically, appears in his own account as one of her satisfied customers once she has fallen into prostitution. On top of all this, the man who has first seduced Riitta has also ended up on the island because of a shipwreck. This plot twist is needed to explain Kalle's attempt to kill anyone who tries to come onto his island during a storm.

In the flashback we first see Riitta happily frolicking along the clifftops of her island home when she notices a man stranded on the beach. She and Kalle take him into the lighthouse and gradually revive him. She is childishly excited by the idea of the handsome stranger having come from the city, a place her father hates because his wife has escaped there from the solitude of the light-house. When the foreigner is for the first time on his feet again, he sees Riitta go naked for a swim – or so we assume, as the spatial relationships and sight lines in terms of classical syntax do not support this inference.[26] Kalle tells his guest that there will be a boat that could take him back to the mainland within an hour, but the man pretends to be in a worse condition than he really is so as to remain longer with Riitta and further plant ideas about the city in her mind.

Finally he leaves, but only soon to return on his beautiful white sailing boat. It is a wonderful sunny day and he takes Riitta out to sea. She has known only the lighthouse and the island but apparently has for long dreamed about at least visiting the city. Thus it is easy for the man, who it turns out is a Consul (Ville Salminen), to persuade her to go to the city with him, for one evening only. The city is introduced in just one short extreme long shot. It is actually Budapest, possibly pinched from some Hungarian fiction film, as the famous Chain Bridge is easily recognisable, but obviously we are not expected to think that the story has moved to landlocked Hungary. Tulio's story takes place in a seaport.

As Linnanheimo appears to be at least in her late twenties (she was about thirty at the time of shooting), her naïve girl-like behaviour appears embarrass-ingly contrived. The discrepancy is even greater than in D.W. Griffith's films such as *The Birth of a Nation* (1915), when he made adult female characters jump around as if they were still little girls. But clearly we are expected to assume that she is just innocent of what counts as adult, and what counts as childish, behaviour. The Consul at first appears to respect her virginity, but then cannot resist the temptation and goes to the room he has given her. She has discovered a photo album containing pictures of the Consul's previous lovers, but mistakes the pictures to be those of film stars. We should clearly ignore the question of how she could possibly know anything about films, let alone film stars.

After some small talk, he rapes her.[27] There is a cut to Kalle reading Riitta's letter, telling him that she has gone with the Consul but will be back in the morning. Beethoven's *Appassionata* supplies a sense of passionate drama. Then, back to Riitta and the Consul after the violation. She says she can never face her father again. Pekka's voice-over relates that the Consul grew fed up with her within a year, another man followed, and eventually it 'was the same old story'. Pekka himself clearly represents this view, familiar to us mainly from stage melodrama and its successors in silent cinema, in which a fallen woman is stained beyond redemption or even rehabilitation. As we see it, Riitta is trans-formed in an instant from a naïvely innocent girl to a decadent prostitute.

Figures 5.29-30

Yet the melodramatically most extravagant developments in *Cross of Love* are still to come. The first begins when a young painter, Henrik, another innocent, meets Riitta. He wants to use her as a model for a painting depicting the fate of a slave woman in ancient Rome, who is led astray because of her pure love and is punished by crucifixion. The painting is, of course, to be called 'Cross of Love' and the story behind it forms an obvious parallel with the film itself (as discussed in chapter 7). Henrik falls for Riitta, whom he takes to be a pure soul, and does not want to hear about her past. 'For me, love is beautiful and pure', he exclaims. Again, we see Linnanheimo at her most innocent. We are clearly supposed to accept her as such, in contradistinction to all the moralising characters, including Henrik, who should know better, given his interest in the story of the ancient slave woman. But for the time being, the two are hopelessly in love, intent on maintaining faith in the purity of love. Linnanheimo (or in some shots at least, probably a stand-in) provides the most sacrilegious image in Tulio's entire oeuvre. He probably was not challenging religious sentiment per se, but rather simply sought to create a shocking effect. His occasional use of religious imagery in his films merely served story functions, usually in a rather sentimental way.

Riitta returns to see her fellow prostitutes at their common lodgings. Most of them scorn her dream of being able to start anew. Briefly, Riitta's prospects look hopeful as she gets a job as a seamstress. But then the situation turns into a complete mess because of Kalle. Riitta has been sending her father letters, trying to convince him that she is living a decent life with the Consul. Kalle is even more naïve than Riitta, rejoicing in the idea that after marrying the Consul his daughter will become a fine lady attended by obliging, demure maids. Even the parrot appears wiser, screaming scornfully when Kalle goes on about how well things have turned out. Kalle boasts about the marriage to Pekka and another sailor, but then overhears them making disparaging remarks about Riikka as a 'complete whore'. Kalle storms into the city to find out for

Figures 5.31-34

himself. When he is convinced that he has discovered the true state of affairs, he announces that he is going to kill both Riitta and the Consul. Riitta finds out what her father is up to, but is more worried about what her father will do to himself than what he is about to do to her. She persuades the Consul to put on an act so as to calm Kalle down. The Consul is not entirely callous, and even agrees to stage a mock wedding when Kalle comes to accuse him for having made his daughter a whore.

The mock wedding is accompanied by a raucous adaptation of Mendelssohn's 'Wedding March'. The irony grows almost unbearable at the reception as Kalle goes on about the purity of love. Then he makes an abortive attempt to tell Riitta things that a young bride should know about what happens between a man and a woman on their wedding night. The scene is simultaneously both outrageously ridiculous and heart-rending. Kalle's moralistic madness is like a force of nature, and, just like certain fathers in earlier melodramatic traditions, he would no doubt kill Riitta if he gained evidence his daughter had become, in his terms, the most despicable kind of person he could imagine. However, the most fatal twist of the drama emerges from Henrik's innocence. For him, moral collapse comes in the guise of success: his painting has won a major prize and with inevitable melodramatic logic it has been bought by the Consul. It is not clear whether or not he recognises Riitta in the picture. Things go downhill when Henrik appears at the mock wedding to collect the last instalment for the painting. He appears at first amused when the Consul tells him what is going on, but becomes furious when he discovers that the mock bride is none other than Riitta. His life is shattered when he realises that his pure beloved is, as he sees it, a woman of the streets – despite having first encountered her on a street with the unmistakable appearance of a melodrama prostitute. He renounces his love and rushes out. Between what appears like a purifying legend and hopelessly sordid reality, he chooses to see only the sordid reality, and thus both he and Riitta are crushed by Tulio's melodramatic machinery.

Riitta escorts Kalle to a boat that is to take him back to the lighthouse. Bidding farewell, Riitta grows hysterical, alternatively begging him to go away and to stay. She herself has internalised the moral code so thoroughly that she sees fault only in herself and desperately wants to protect her father from sorrow as much as she still can. Finally, the boat takes Kalle away, for ever. Riitta and the Consul go to a bar where Henrik happens to be drowning his sorrow in alcohol along with the favours of the kind of women he so despises. He goes to Riitta's and the Consul's table and behaves so aggressively that finally the Consul punches him in the face. The Consul appears genuinely willing to start anew with Riitta, but back at his apartment Riitta shoots herself. She whispers to him: 'Don't tell my father, say that I died as your wife, accidentally.' She dies and the Consul raises his eyes to the painting of another innocent victim of love gone awry. As we return to the frame story, Kalle is seen praying at Riitta's grave, asking for death to come and collect him.

In the opening credits the story is claimed to have been freely inspired by Alexander Pushkin. This is assumed to be a reference to his short story *Stationmaster*. This might be just an attempt to give the film a cultural prestige it does not deserve or need. In the short story a young woman named Dunia is seduced by a Hussar who takes her with him to St Petersburg. A couple of minor details apart, this is where the similarities end. The father does follow them, but with no intention to kill, simply to see his beloved Dunia again. The Hussar cruelly throws him out of his house, and the father returns to his post where he eventually dies a poor, lonely man. It is the father's tragedy, not the daughter's. There is a reference to women who come to the city with high hopes and end up as prostitutes, but toward the end Dunia is said to have come to visit her father's grave as a fine woman. Somewhat strangely, whereas the English title is *Stationmaster*, a true translation of the original (Станционный смотритель), the Finnish title translates as *The Stationmaster and his Daughter* (Postimestari ja hänen tyttärensä).

There is an intermediary text between Pushkin's short story and Tulio's film, namely Gustav Ucicky's film *Der Postmeister* (1940).[28] This begins as a quite straightforward adaptation of the novel, set amid the desolate steppes, but then moves to St Petersburg. At this point the screenwriter is given scope to display his creativity, as is the set designer: we see a German version of Russian aristocratic decadent splendour, with Romani musicians and dancers creating an exuberant atmosphere of mock-Russian revelry. Dunja, who even as the supposedly modest postmaster's daughter already appears more like an elegant and self-conscious woman of the higher levels of society, does not look in the least bit out of place here. But she has to struggle to maintain her moral integrity: the Hussar, with whom she has eloped, apparently has no intention of marrying her and has given her as a lover to an older officer. By now she has fallen in love with a young officer and chooses to support herself as a seamstress rather than continue a life of decadence among the aristocracy. This passage is slightly difficult to interpret from a contemporary point of view, as it might be that a more considerable fall from moral standards might be implied than is immediately apparent in terms of our modern sensibilities. This might be an instance of what Richard Maltby in connection with Hollywood cinema has referred to as a '"deniable" mode of narrative construction', meaning something that might be considered unacceptable for a larger audience is merely suggested in such a way as to give enough scope for the filmmakers to argue that nothing morally dubious is taking place.[29] Tulio, at this point in his career, was above (or below, depending on one's moral point of view) such niceties and in his own film made the more salacious aspects of the story much more evident.

Ucicky's main addition to Pushkin's story is a mock marriage, which Dunja stages with her still-obliging Hussar in order to calm down her father. He has come to St Petersburg with the intention of killing his daughter whom he, on the basis of rumours, considers to have become a whore. The ploy seems to work and the old postmaster is overjoyed, but then the marriage feast is interrupted by the young officer, with whom Dunja has started an affair. He grows furious, thinking that he has been betrayed by a woman of low virtue, and almost succeeds in making the old man see the deception. Dunja becomes near-hysterical and, soon after seeing her father off on a train, commits suicide. It is this storyline, rather than the one Pushkin supplied, that Tulio adapted. The main difference is that in Ucicky's film Dunja, played by Hilde Krahl, who at this stage of her career was already something of a film star, is quite a strong character, while in Tulio's film Riitta appears naïve and helpless.

There is an even more substantial difference between Ucicky's and Tulio's films in that the latter harks back to the moralism of nineteenth-century melodrama. Once again, we may speculate about Tulio's intentions. Whereas Ucicky's postmaster is a serious, even a touching character, in our contemporary eyes at least, Kalle seems not only silly but plain ridiculous. Yet it is not clear that Tulio intended Kalle to be a comic character. The spectator is not likely to feel particularly sorry for him, as it is he more than anyone else who drives his own daughter to destruction. If he would not divide women strictly into whores and virgins – motherhood being conspicuously absent from this story, as it is from most of Tulio's films[30] – Riitta could return home, chastised, but able to continue her life on her desolate home island. Another strange inversion is that the Consul, the seducer, appears as the only level-headed person in the story. While Henrik is just as mentally limited as regards women as Kalle, the Consul is actually prepared to do all he can to protect Riitta when Kalle and Henrik are intent on killing her because of her having become, against her will, a prostitute. Refraining from psychological speculation, we have to be content simply with the fact that Tulio used the notion of 'whore', or rather, the notion of men obsessed with the notion of a whore, to the point of blinding themselves to the tragedy of innocence lost, a tragedy in which they are the main culprits.

Critical reception of *Cross of Love* followed the already established line: condemnation of the lack of psychological depth and even plausibility, and lots of praise for the filmic quality. One critic at least noticed that the film was 'a rough copy of his previous film . . . brewed together from roughly the same materials and according to the same recipe, but lacking the right touch that would make it into a work by an artist'.[31] Another writer pointed out: 'Tulio does not care about psychological consistency, for him it suffices to have an excuse to disperse here and there images of naked or half-naked girls and a few images of Christ, all in happy accord with one another, to the extent that a woman is hanging on the cross (and what a horrible painting it is).'[32] Other writers agreed that Tulio was exploiting sensational materials to achieve maximum effect, but only succeeding in producing something inauthentic and artificial.[33] Yet at least one writer tried to express a balanced view:

> None of our directors creates such pure, expressive assured film as does Tulio . . . His pictorial effects are exuberantly powerful. He produces concentrated, crystallised and suggestive film art. His films are full of visual imagination, accuracy of visual language, suavely moving rhythms, his manner of telling is masterful. But the topic of the story is appalling – the script of Cross of Love is technically good, but in terms of psychology, depiction of characters and story logic it is of the poorest quality, inauthentic, false – This whole story is horrible, on the level of the worst pulp fiction, and it is presented crassly, clumsily underlined.[34]

MAD JEALOUSY

Many of Tulio's characters are haunted by jealousy, not only of those with whom they have formed a permanent relationship, but of those they have rejected. Olavi in *The Song of the Scarlet Flower* is an extreme case as he, having seduced an entire chain of women, grows madly and unreasonably jealous of his newly married wife Kyllikki, merely on the basis of what he has heard another man jealous of Kyllikki say at their wedding about her past. However, jealousy does not loom large in *In the Fields of Dreams*, except that Kirsti is jealous of Aarne, and this motivates her to give false evidence against Sirkka, thus causing Sirkka to be imprisoned for having killed her baby. In the 'loss of innocence' films jealousy appears only briefly when the woman's new lover, a pure soul, mistakes the mock marriage ceremony for a real one and denounces his love for her. In a sense, the pathological need to protect the innocence of a young woman is also a form of possessiveness that could be thought of as a form of jealousy. But in some of the films Tulio made after the Second World War, the story circles round the obsessive need to have exclusive rights to one's beloved, to the point of being prepared to mutilate and kill not only the beloved or the competitor for his or her love, but also oneself.

Restless Blood (*Levoton veri*, 1946) depicts intense rivalry between two sisters, Sylvi (Regina Linnanheimo) and Outi (Toini Vartiainen), who both fall at a fairly early age for the same man, Valter (Eino Katajavuori). Valter is a doctor, and at the beginning of the film we see him tending to the crippled Outi's foot. He tells her that the foot could be operated on in Central Europe, and that after that she will be able not only to walk but to dance around. She's still underage, and again Tulio has the actress, this time twenty-three years old, put on a rather contrived act of being a much younger, immature girl. The discrepancy is made even more pointed by Outi wanting to pose as older than she really is, an adult woman. Sylvi, genuinely a young adult, although sad about causing disappointment to her beloved sister, admits to being in love with Valter herself. Uselessly, she tries to convince Outi that her love is still immature, while Sylvi's own love is that of a mature woman.

On a beautiful summer evening, Sylvi and Valter go for a walk. A sad Outi watches them go. Again, according to the little we know about the villa in which the young women live, this seems like an impossible point of view. But as such settings are repeated, it develops almost into a leitmotiv which is in counterpoint with Sylvi's later blindness/fake-blindness. This applies also to sound. Outi realises what is happening between Sylvie and Valter and alarms their prudish aunt. Indeed aunt, rather than parents: apparently the sisters are orphans. Nothing is explicitly made of this point, but not having a moralising Old Testament-type father around does help in shifting the thematic point from the loss of innocence to jealousy. And so Outi tells the aunt that Sylvi has gone out with Valter, causing the aunt to discover Sylvi and Valter in a bed in what we may assume is a sauna or a hut by the beach. The flickering of light suggests they are in a place warmed by a fire.

Valter immediately announces that he will assume his responsibilities and marry Sylvi. Outi is seen to react to this, although she could not possibly have heard his words. But then again, perhaps Outi reacts to this when hearing about it later on, as things now move very quickly: immediately after the reaction shot of Outi, we see the wedding take place. This is followed by an image of a raging sea, and one of Outi presumably on board a boat, still with her crutches. Presumably she is on her way to Central Europe to be operated on. Next we see Valter as a paediatrician and it turns out that he and Sylvi already have a baby. Suddenly the boy is a few years old. This sequence is a clear indication that Tulio has grown even more elliptical than in his two preceding 'innocence' films. Such rapid storytelling has seldom been seen on screen (or anywhere else) for other than comic purposes. Whereas Henrik-the-spy's unexpected appearance in *Cross of Love* can hardly fail to appear as a rather clumsy piece of storytelling, this sequence is quite ingenious, even masterly.

From the married couple's conversation we learn that Outi has been in Germany for years and that in addition to her foot having been treated, she has also studied music. But by now it is high time for tragedy to strike, and it does so with vengeance.

Sylvi goes with her son to a millinery shop in the city centre. While she is trying on new hats, the boy goes out and is run over by a bus. It appears that he has walked some way before this happens, yet when the crash happens, Sylvi hears it and only has to walk across the street to find him. She brings the body to Valter who diagnoses him dead, and hearing how the accident has happened, immediately announces that he will never forgive Sylvi. We are informed in passing that Sylvi is not able to have another baby. Valter is then seen in his laboratory with a decrepit-looking woman.[35] Suddenly he grows angry at her and furiously throws her out and down a staircase. He also throws money after her, which she, unlike the heroines of the 'innocence dramas', is not too proud to accept. Completely drunk, Valter returns home and goes to the bedside of the family maid. Nothing happens between them, but Sylvi overhears them, draws the wrong conclusion and takes poison. It does not kill her but makes her blind. Valter's love is to some extent rekindled as he takes

Figures 5.35–36

care of her. The new situation appears to save their marriage, and Valter finds a foreign doctor who might be able to provide a cure. Valter leaves for his laboratory and in a strange repetition of some earlier set-ups, Sylvi counts the time Valter needs to reach a certain spot on the street and goes to the window to wave him goodbye. Weirdly foreshadowing later plot twists, he responds as if she could see him.

Immediately after Valter has left, Outi unexpectedly returns home. Nothing has been heard of her, and Sylvi at first addresses the person who she has heard entering the room as if Valter had returned. Outi is shocked to discover that Sylvi is blind, but appears so happy with life that she could dance – which she does a bit, with Valter when he returns. She clearly has not entirely got over her love for him, and in the new situation he quickly begins to fall for her. He cannot resist flirting with her, taking advantage of his wife's blindness. In a striking scene, Outi uses as her love-call Chopin's A Minor Waltz, playing it on the piano. Long ago she has heard Valter whistle its sweetly melancholy tune when coming to a romantic encounter with Sylvi, and a rather heavily orchestrated version of this piece is heard repeatedly as background music. At the turning point of the drama Sylvi asks Outi to play something on the piano and Valter adds: 'Play then something that even I can understand.' And what else could that be than the Chopin waltz, soon taken over by an otherworldly orchestra. Without Sylvi realising it, Valter goes to stand by Outi. After a while he can't restrain himself anymore and passionately kisses her, interrupting her playing. Sylvi asks why Outi has stopped and encourages her to continue. Outi does so, and now the music broadens into a furious variation of the tender waltz. Finally, Outi can't bear it anymore and rushes out. Only when Sylvi asks what has happened to Outi and Valter responds, does she realise that her husband has moved to the side of her younger sister.

On his visit to Finland, a Swiss doctor examines Sylvi and comes to the conclusion that her sight might be restored in an operation at his clinic. The risks are great, and she might lose all hope of recovering her sight. She decides to take the risk and travels to Switzerland. The operation is successful, but the doctor warns that Sylvi must be careful: too much light might make her go mad. She returns home and immediately realises that her husband and sister have become lovers. She decides to hide the fact that she has recovered her sight and begins spying on the lovers with the intention of making them eventually feel all the more guilty. She is driven mad by her jealousy, and not without good reason: Valter and Outi seem to go through the same process of forming a relationship as Sylvi and Valter years before, even for the first time consummating their love on the very same spot. Sylvie sees this, although again it is not clear where her point of observation is exactly. She starts cruelly tormenting the lovers, quickly descending into madness, indicated by Linnanheimo's distorted facial expressions and raucous, hysterical laugher.

Figures 5.37–44 Sylvi and Valter listen to Outi play. He moves next to Outi. They embrace passionately. Sylvie wonders why Outi has stopped playing. The lovers are as if taken by surprise. Each character reacts.

Regina Linnanheimo's extraordinary range of facial expressions in *Restless Blood*.

Valter has taught Sylvi to read braille and so she is able to read – or pretend to read – to he and Outi a terrifying story about betrayal which parallels their own situation.

Outi visits Valter's laboratory to tell him she is pregnant. He is happy to hear this and they have a very brief romantic moment together. Throughout this scene there is a flickering light, probably an attempt to create a sense of city lights but looking more as if the lab was located next to the lighthouse of the *Cross of Love*. But Sylvi has overheard them and steps in, finally revealing that she has been able to see everything ever since her return. She first threatens to drive them to suicide, then demands that Valter perform an abortion on Outi. She writes a letter in which she repeats this demand, threatening to reveal embarrassing facts about Valter's career and suggesting that a gun might provide a way out of the situation (figures 5.45–46). Superimposed images give the impression that the guilty lovers have already internalised her accusations (figures 5.47–48). Sylvie leaves the house and the familiar street-window shot-counter-shot pattern is repeated. In a mad rage she drives away, crashes and dies. But just before this, in a whispered voice-over, she seems to turn her accusation against herself. At the end of the film, Outi and Valter read a letter of reconciliation. It is far from clear at what point Sylvie might have written it. Did she have second thoughts before the mad drive? Was the first letter, revealed only in a voice-over, merely what she first intended to write? Here

Figures 5.45–46

Figures 5.47–48

again Tulio displays his disregard for virtues such as spatio-temporal continuity, diegetic consistency or psychological plausibility. All that matters is the stormy drama of love, guilt and jealousy.

Reviews were more polarised than ever. One critic condemned *Restless Blood* because of its 'incredible lack of logic and psychological plausibility'.[36] But another stated:

I would not be at all surprised, if he [Tulio] would one day become a universal film director. He sees the whole thing completely in images, genuinely, full bloodedly – he does not relate to this story in a literary fashion, like so many of our other filmmakers. He has a wonderful pictorial fantasy, but no literary sense whatsoever. And at times this seems like a fatal lack. Filmic visions capture Tulio to the extent that he entirely forgets about all human description, psychological veracity.[37]

The writer has captured an important point. Many of Tulio's colleagues, adhering to the classical film style, approached their topics and above all their dialogue in a very literary fashion. This could provide at least the modicum of psychological plausibility that most Tulio films lack, but it can hardly be denied that their films in turn often were slow-paced and cinematically unadventurous. Some spectators at least, tolerant of the absence of psychological plausibility and story coherence, still preferred Tulio's cinematic extravagance.

At least one critic noticed the importance of Linnanheimo's contribution to Tulio's aesthetics:

> It is a great victory for the director that in this film Regina Linnanheimo appears as a mature class actress, who both knows how to and dares. There is in her something new, genuine and warm, and in her huge display of power toward the end she approaches in her shocking hysteria the effectiveness of an actress such as Bette Davis.[38]

Another writer was of the opinion that Linnanheimo's contorted facial expressions in the madness scene were over the top, but blamed the director for that.[39] Yet another critic made a similar observation and thought that, as inappropriate as the habit of a certain part of the audience to laugh at dramatic moments is, in this case it was justified, taking into consideration how forced the acting was.[40] The increasing number of observations about laughter, as well as indulgence toward such expression, in critical reviews can in retrospect be seen as a symptom of a gradually changing attitude toward Tulio's art. There is something almost heroic in the director relentlessly pursuing his own line, despite such signs of losing his grip on his audience.

Jealousy (*Mustasukkaisuus*, 1953) is in many ways a remake of *Restless Blood*, but with some elements borrowed from Tulio's other films, mainly *The Rapids of Hell*. It tells the story of two sisters, Riitta Linnanheimo and Anja (Assi Raine), who fall in love with the same man, Jyri (Eero Paganus). This time the story is set in rural Finland, and once again, a rapid serves as a major plot device as well as a thematic element. Almost as a sign of this being another Tulio film, we first see rapid-shooting and galloping-horse images, but at least this time the music is different and the horse-drawn cart is driven by two exuberant young women instead of a reckless young man. Another standard scene follows, this time one that appears in great many Finnish rural melodramas – a barn dance.[41] Two men fight over a woman, a knife is drawn, but eventually the conflict is settled in more a gentleman-like fashion with bare fists. The cart reaches a river ferry, but during the crossing the cable preventing the ferry from being carried away toward the rapid and a waterfall, for no apparent reason unravels, thread by thread, and suddenly everyone on the ferry is in mortal danger. A man, who is assumed to be a log driver but turns out to be Jyri Maras, a respectable forest owner, bravely saves the women, who both immediately fall for him. The opening sequence lasts over ten minutes without a word being spoken. A little later there are still more images of the rapid-shooting, now with the familiar 'For Me and My Gal' tune. It is as if Tulio just couldn't show his rapid footage without it.

This time the role of the naïve younger sister with a wounded foot, known as Anja in this film, is given to the little-known actress Assi Raine, whereas the older sister Riitta is once again played by Linnanheimo. The major difference with respect to *Restless Blood*, one of only two instances in Tulio's entire output and quite rare even in the history of cinema as a whole, is a first-person stream-of-consciousness voice-over revealing Riitta's scheming mind. Jyri is easy prey for her. They go night-fishing. She is flirtatious and he suddenly grabs her in a passionate embrace. It lasts only a second or two, as Riitta realises the boat has been caught in the stream. Jyri is not worried and even appears to be amused by Riitta's near panic. He saves the situation, but they get wet. This has the advantage of them having to get to a sauna to dry their clothes, which allows for a bit of flirtatious fooling around, with Riitta covering herself only with a towel. The scene contains some of the most subtly erotic images in Tulio's oeuvre so far. Most of the time it has been a calm summer night, but suddenly it appears sufficiently stormy to wake up Riitta's grandmother, who, perhaps prompted by Anja, surprises the frolicking couple. At first Riitta looks horrified but the expression on her face changes almost immediately. Her voice-over explains: 'Horrible! Or, perhaps not. I can almost hear the wedding bells ringing.' No more explaining is needed, as with very Tulio-like rapid storytelling, just as in *Restless Blood*, we see images of a church, the church bells, Riitta and Jyri at the altar, Anja travelling away, Riitta in a bed with a baby and the happy father joining her. In a further brief montage sequence the boy quickly ages a couple of years.

Then the accident happens. While Jyri is at work and Riitta is trying on a new dress, their son goes out alone on the narrow suspension bridge over the rapid. This comes as something of a surprise, as the family appears to be living in an urban- rather than a rural-looking home, with a grand piano and other indications of a comfortable city life. At this point in Tulio's career a rapid with merry log drivers is there whenever it is time for something tragic to happen. But in this film, so is Jyri, and again he jumps into the rapid to save a life. But he is too late, and the boy drowns. This time we only hear Jyri's accusation of the accident having happened because of the boy's mother's vanity through Riitta's interior monologue. When we see them together, he refuses to talk to her. To a rather amusing effect we suddenly hear the merry 'For Me and My Gal' tune. So does Jyri, who goes to the window and sees the log drivers shooting the rapid. Jyri rushes upstairs to change clothes and then, perhaps in order to escape his sorrow, goes out to shoot the rapids himself. But there is a blockage in the river at some point, and the log drivers are about to dynamite it. Riitta follows Jyri and arrives at the blockage as the explosion happens.

Figures 5.49–54 In a rapid sequence, Riitta's horror at having been caught in the act changes to a mischievous realisation as to what this will mean for her. As soon as she thinks of wedding bells we see and hear them, followed by images of her at the altar with Jyri, Anja travelling away, and Jyri by Riitta's bedside after she has given birth.

Now there is a totally unexpected cut to winter images of the felling of trees and men in a sauna – stock footage Tulio had already used a few years earlier in *The Rapids of Hell*. Jyri is there and ends up in a fight with someone still angry with him for having married Riitta despite being a foreigner in the region. He then receives a letter informing him that things have gone bad at home. Jyri returns and is reconciled with Riitta. A spectator who has seen *Restless Blood* is likely to guess that she has gone blind because of the explosion, but to Jyri this comes as a shock. Suddenly there is a cut to a woman jumping into water and enjoying a swim. The tone for this scene is given by the music, an adaptation of the merry folk festival theme from Carl Maria von Weber's *Der Freischütz*. The swimmer is Anja, who has returned home to take care of Riitta. Still in her swimming costume, she arrives just as Jyri has just discovered that Riitta is blind. Again, narrative coherence is stretched to breaking point, but to intriguing effect: the rapid succession of contrasting narrative elements is truly astonishing.

Riitta soon realises that Anja and Jyri are spending time together. Jyri does not seem to register her suggestions that Anja should be allowed to move away to pursue her art studies. Riitta calls for him, and all of a sudden we see Anja, again just about to jump into the water. Jyri joins her from behind and together they jump in. They appear to be swimming in a calm lake, but then we see Riitta by the rapid. In terms of real-life geography the waters would have to be quite far apart, but when Riitta calls for Jyri, he appears to be swimming just by her in perfectly calm water. Riitta asks where Anja is, and Jyri claims that she has already gone away. Somewhat ridiculously, she dives as if to hide from the blind Riitta. Riitta has only turned to leave when Anja and Jyri start talking about her. How could they not realise she is still within a hearing distance? It is as if she was supposed to be deaf rather than blind, or as if they rather than she were blind. Tulio is not always clear about which perceptual or mental faculty of which person is defective. Melodramatic rather than real-life logic reigns; once again everything is organised solely in terms of evoking immediate sensations.

Riitta contacts a doctor who might be able to restore her sight. Medical services having improved in Finland since the making of *Restless Blood*, she only has to go to Helsinki for the operation. It helps that it just so happens that there is an international medical conference taking place there. The operation is successful, but when she takes off her dark glasses the doctor sternly tells her not to do so, as too much light might not only make her permanently blind, it might also make her mentally sick. As she is released from the hospital, we hear Bach's 'Toccata and Fugue in D Minor'. And as often before in Tulio's films, this music accompanies another stormy night. Guided by her dog, Riitta goes to the sauna where her own relationship with Jyri began and discovers Anja and Jyri naked. When they all meet later, she pretends that the operation on her eyes has failed. She decides to kill Anja, and tries to accomplish this by dropping a large vase on her sister's head. She misses and apologises for her carelessness.

Later, Anja, having observed Jyri momentarily about to fall prey to Riitta's seduction, decides to go away. But to do that she still has to cross once more the suspension bridge. This gives Riitta her second chance, as she finds some tools at the other end of the bridge. She saws a cable, which splits thread by thread as Anja is crossing (the images of the cable breaking are probably the same as those used at the beginning of the film). In an exciting sequence, the cable finally snaps and the bridge falls into the rapid. This is probably just another instance of Tulio recycling his materials in order to economise, but it could be seen as a metaphor of fate preying on the characters. This time, Anja succeeds in holding on to the remains of the bridge, but soon loses her grip and is carried away by the stream. Meanwhile, Jyri once again runs to her rescue, finds a boat and rows to pick her up. We do not get to see this last-moment rescue – suddenly Anja is in the boat.

When Riitta hears that the collapse of the bridge is assumed to have been caused deliberately, she attempts to escape in Jyri's car, but is unable to get it started. Anja appears and first discovers that her sister can see, then further realises the extent of her deception and finally that she has gone completely mad. Anja takes a gun from the glove compartment, but somehow the weapon changes hands and Riitta shoots at Anja. Riitta then escapes up a tower which is part of a sawmill, an impressive structure which allows for some extremely striking imagery. Jyri, who Anja has told about Riitta's state of mind, follows her and tries to calm her down, almost succeeding in this. But as the siren of a police car is heard, Riitta jumps to her death. As if to make sure that no one misses the metaphor, Jyri remarks that in every one of us there is something restless and wild and that Riitta was as wild and uncontrollable as the rapid.

Figures 5.55–58

Critical reception of *Jealousy* was rather bland, and as the film was not widely distributed (it was not screened in Helsinki at all) the number of reviews was much smaller than previously. Most critics who did write about it were becoming increasingly aware of how much Tulio recycled his earlier material. One even wrote that 'Tulio roughly repeats the same mistakes he made twenty years ago with his first attempts at filmmaking'.[42] There was one reviewer, though, who appreciated having recognised new actors and new ideas 'in this interesting depiction of love life'.[43] Opinions differed more on Linnanheimo's performance. Some still thought her a fine actress, who could almost save Tulio's efforts, while others thought that the rolling of her eyes did not constitute effective acting. One critic pointed out that the director's insistence on close-ups only revealed the weakness of her acting skills,[44] while another was of the opinion that close-ups, although Tulio tended to overuse them, brought out well Linnanheimo's 'bold mimicry and strong facial features'.[45] Later, Linnanheimo was to reach even further in expressing extreme emotions, but that would not save either her's or Tulio's careers.

DESTRUCTIVE PASSIONS

After the two 'tarnished innocence' films there was in some respects a significant change in Tulio's works. This may have been a return to the themes of his first film, *The Fight over the Heikkilä Mansion*, as already in that film Regina Linnanheimo had taken the role of a very strong woman. Also, in *Restless Blood* and later in *Jealousy*, Linnanheimo's character is an adult woman able to make things work out the way she wants them to – until things go wrong. But even after blinding herself, she does not become just a helpless victim, not at least of the desire of reckless men. Instead, she finds a way to exact her revenge on her husband, who has betrayed her with her own younger sister. In the two films following *Restless Blood* Linnanheimo had the role of a strong woman who may be emotionally the victim of a relentless code of honour or the manipulation of men, but who is not ostracised and who is able to take care of herself.

In his *In the Grip of Passion* (*Intohimon vallassa*, 1947) Tulio returned to the milieu of the rural melodrama. The film is a remake of his first film, *The Fight over the Heikkilä Mansion*, which was lost in a fire together with his second and third films. Like his first surviving film, *The Song of the Scarlet Flower*, it is based on a novel by Johannes Linnankoski. The theme of innocence is left out of the picture, and jealousy and sexual temptation are no longer the main issues. Regina Linnanheimo plays a woman of character, giving arguably her best performance in one of Tulio's films. The story begins almost in the manner of a gothic horror film – if not comedy horror, as it is difficult to say how seriously Tulio may have intended this sequence to be taken. As with the beginning of *Cross of Love*, it is a stormy night, but the camera shows a grisly, humpbacked old man digging a grave and growling madly in the moonlight. A young couple visits the graveyard. The young man talks about a curse on his family, promising to fight against it and maintain the family estate at Ylitalo. An older man appears from the dark, expresses his admiration for strong women and promises to tell the story of the young man's mother. The story is then told in flashback.

A village dance is interrupted by the song of merry log drivers, once again to the accompaniment of the 'For Me and My Gal' theme, and the all-too-familiar rapid-shooting images – this had almost become Tulio's signature sequence which he employed several times, often without much narrative significance. In this case it is not even made explicit that the male protagonist is the man shooting the rapid, the feat serving simply to introduce the merry-heroic ambiance that Tulio seemed to think his films needed to balance the excessiveness of their melodramatic elements.[46] A man is seen approaching a fence against which a beautiful blonde is leaning (Linnanheimo). The set-up is reminiscent of *The Song of the Scarlet Flower* and at first it appears that this encounter is taking place later than the village dance or the shooting of the rapid we have just seen. But then the young man asks the band to play a popular piece, the 'Vagabond's Waltz', and the dance continues. This is just another instance of Tulio simply ignoring the strangeness of the spatio-temporal effect that his deployment of unprepared narrative devices creates.

The boy and girl, Olavi and Aino, fall quickly in love. He decides to quit log-driving and settle down, despite Aino's father having promised her to the son of another estate. Olavi becomes an apprentice to a blacksmith, and acquires immediately the skills of a craftsman. But this is not enough for the stern old father. A standard figure in Tulio's works, he is a man obsessed with social hierarchy and the honour of the house. The situation is almost exactly the same as in *The Song of the Scarlet Flower*, but the way things develop is very different. Both Olavi and Aino are firmly dedicated to one another and he appears to be a reliable fellow, but she is so committed to the values of the rural world that she decides their affair must come to an end. The fatality of it all is repeatedly emphasised with heavy, emphatic chords as the manor house, the symbol of the unalterable social hierarchy, is seen. Again, without any delay in storytelling, Aino is married to Paavo, her father's choice for her. Before this, he has only been seen in a few random shots, angrily observing the loving couple from some unspecified point. The bride is clearly unhappy and faints when being presented to the crowd attending the wedding. Life continues, but everyone is unhappy. Aino visits Olavi, who is building a house for himself. She isn't able to hide being jealous because of a rumour she has heard about Olavi marrying a maid from a nearby estate. Suggestively, Olavi is the first to hear that Aino is pregnant.

Aino gives birth to a son, Niilo. Paavo, however, is a hopeless, violent drunkard and is about to wreck their joint heritage. He drives a cart in a drunken fury. The imagery of the fast-trotting horse resembles that of Tulio's older films (as discussed in chapter 7). Later, two similar rides occur, both with the same imagery of a trotting horse. Repetition may be seen both as an index of Paavo's and as a symptom of the director's obsessions. In each instance, Paavo lashes the horse violently and continues this even after having arrived home. After the first ride we see Aino sternly chastising him about hurting the animal, and he responds by lashing her also. Olavi sees this – quite impossibly, but in full accordance with melodramatic

Figures 5.59–64

metaphysics – and rushes in. He even draws his knife, but Aino tells him he has no business at Ylitalo. At this point Olavi appears almost like Wagner's Siegfried, interrupted in the process of forging his sword (figures 5.59–64).

Olavi goes away, and soon after leaves the village entirely. Years later, Aino sees him at a village fair, drunk, behaving even worse than Paavo. She chastises him, but her real problems are back at home. Her husband and the farmhands have become useless drunks. Aino assumes control, and, in one of the most striking scenes in Tulio's entire oeuvre, lashes Paavo into submission in front of the maids and farmhands.

Paavo, a deceiving weakling, is forced to accept the situation, but clearly wishes to have his revenge. In a mainly silent and partly obscure sequence, Aino appears to prepare a bottle of booze for Paavo, perhaps with the intention of pouring something out before handing it to him and thus controlling his drinking.[47] She hands the bottle to Paavo through a door, but he forces himself in and attempts to rape her. She hits him on the head with the bottle, and he retreats. He is then seen resisting the temptation of the bottle and taking out a knife, obviously contemplating the possibility of killing his wife.

Olavi returns to the village and after witnessing Niilo having an accident, carries the boy home. Aino, who is in bed, says she will take the boy into the

Figures 5.65–68

town to see a doctor, but Paavo, who strangely appears perfectly decent in this scene, including talking calmly with Olavi, argues that she should stay in bed because of her heart condition. This mention is another plot device that Tulio just inserts for immediate narrative purposes without any preparation. While Paavo is away, Aino's and Olavi's mutual love is rekindled, but Aino says she is already old whereas he is still young. This is rather strange in view of there not having been any indication of her being any older than him. But the main point here is that Aino's sense of honour and virtue curb her love. This marks her as a truly unique Tulio character.

Paavo's trip turns into another drinking bout, and he even offers drink to Niilo, still a minor. But he also finds a way to restore his position: he buys some rat poison and back home mixes it into a cup of coffee Aino is about to drink. The plot works and Aino dies. Paavo succeeds in convincing people of his own account about his wife's death having occurred because of heart failure. He continues his mad drinking and starts hallucinating about Aino returning to chastise him. Here the film resorts to horror-film conventions. Olavi appears, but it is not possible to determine whether he really is there or is what we see only a figment of Paavo's imagination. Finally, Paavo hangs himself. He is discovered by the same hunchback we first encountered digging a grave at the beginning of the film, and who has been seen at the manor every now and then, without serving any apparent purpose. The story returns to the framing narrative in which the elderly man who came to tell his story to the young couple reveals himself to be Olavi, the true father of Niilo. Aino kept the secret to the end of her life in order to retain the honour of the house. The sun rises, and the loving couple look with new hope to the future.

In the Grip of Passion differs markedly from most of the films Tulio directed after the war, not only in that the female protagonist is a very strong, self-willed character, but in that it shows that woman accepting and eventually even embodying the social order that stands in the way of her romantic passion.[48] Inasmuch as it could be said that she is punished for her sexuality, she herself is the instrument of her chastisement. Her father having died, she herself becomes the moralising agent, but for no better result than that at least she dies as a respected, perhaps even feared, member of the society, instead of as an outcast in misery, like the Linnanheimo character in *Cross of Love*. Subsequently Linnanheimo was to have roles with a difference in Tulio's films, but never again was she to have a part of such an authoritative woman as Aino. Much of this comes from Linnankoski's novella *Taistelu Heikkilän talosta*, which had also served as the source of the first film Tulio directed. The little surviving material suggests that for the most part the first adaptation did not differ significantly from the second adaptation. And, of course, both films feature Linnanheimo in the principal role of the stern mistress absolutely dedicated to making her family heritage flourish. Judging by the still images and contemporary reviews, she was truly imposing in this role, at only twenty years of age.

Figure 5.69

At least in *In the Grip of Passion*, and in all likelihood also in *The Fight over the Heikkilä Mansion*, Tulio changed Linnankoski's narrative structure quite drastically. This is partly because of the necessities imposed by the difference between the two mediums, and partly because of Tulio not having had the courage to adopt Linnankoski's non-linear narrative structure. The novella has a distinct literary character. The essential narrative feature of the first part of the novella is the non-omniscient third-person narration, telling the story of the Heikkilä Mansion and its young mistress, as observed, or rather surmised, by people from outside. The narrator has no access to her interiority, leaving her as much a mystery for the reader as she is for the people in the vicinity who try to understand her and what is going on inside Heikkilä. In this first part the mistress has no lover. As if to emphasise her enigmatic nature, her first name is mentioned only once. Her son turns out very serious-minded at an early age and then disappears from the house after his father has made him drunk on that visit to see the doctor. No one really knows why, but the reader may assume that his mother has removed him from the corrupting influence of his father.

The second part of the novella focuses on a man named Matti, who, once introduced, is mainly referred to simply as 'he'. We first encounter him recollecting falling in love at the age of eighteen with a girl, the only offspring of the Heikkilä Mansion. She has apparently been in love with him, but there is no way her parents would allow her to marry a farmhand (not a merry log driver, nor a master blacksmith, as in Tulio's second adaptation). She agrees, and so he goes away. He continues hearing rumours about what is going at Heikkilä, but is in the end left guessing just like everyone else. They meet only once on a road. Earlier, he has boasted about doing bold things even when not under the influence of alcohol, but he has begun to lose control and now he happens to be drunk. He is ashamed, pulls his hat lower and tries to pass unnoticed. But she stops to say just: 'Matti . . . did you too have to become such a lout – like everyone else?' Linnankoski describes masterfully his extremely mixed feelings, of humiliation and sense of pride, of love and hate he feels for the woman who he feels has destroyed his life. The second part reaches the point where the first ended: the proud mistress has died and her widower has fallen again to drinking and is behaving as if with the deliberate intention of wrecking the family heritage. Matti sees a vision of his one-time beloved, but now with a strange hairpin . . . or is it too big to be a hairpin, is it something bigger? He talks with the local vicar, who, having had his own suspicions about the mistress' sudden death, finally agrees to a request for her grave to be opened. A nail is found to have been hammered into her head. The widower is arrested, and eventually Heikkilä is taken over by the son of its former enigmatic mistress and her indomitable spirit. He employs Matti as a farmhand for the rest of his life. There is nothing to suggest he is the boy's real father.

It is understandable that Tulio rejected Linnankoski's intricate narrative structure. It would not have yielded easily to adaptation in terms of classical cinema, not even with all the liberties Tulio had become accustomed to taking. That kind of storytelling simply was not in him, nor was it in hardly any other filmmaker before the cinematic modernism of the 1960s. On the other hand, at least by the time of *In the Grip of Passion*, he had no compunction in adding material to his liking, such as shooting the rapids, which he had shot for his adaptation of another Linnankoski story, *The Song of the Scarlet Flower*. One aspect which he completely missed was the sense of mystery surrounding the mistress. This was near unavoidable, as the filmmaker had to visualise almost everything, thus making things more explicit. On the other hand, there are certain features in the novella that might actually have had a role in the way Tulio's own style developed. Linnankoski's novella runs to only sixty pages, yet a lot happens: there are no extensive passages in which characters go through their emotions and relationships, and so events move forward quickly. But whereas Linnankoski keeps a narrative distance from his characters, to the point of hardly referring to them by name, Tulio develops the story into a fierce drama between characters driven by raging passions. To do this he had to combine the two chapters of the novella, told from different perspectives, into a single linear narrative and boost the love story to the extent that Aino and Olavi have apparently consummated their relationship. This slightly undermines the consistent treatment of Aino's character. In the novel, Matti wonders how this woman he loves has the strength to lash her

good-for-nothing husband into obedience, yet did not have the courage to challenge her parents when her love for Olavi was at issue. Olavi in the film might add
the question of why the honour of the house is so important to Aino that she even
denies her child the knowledge of his true father. Again, we must remember that
Tulio's melodramatic poetics is not at all about psychological realism.

According to contemporary critics, *In the Grip of Passion* was in many ways
considerably weaker than Tulio's first film, of which they saw it as a copy.
They did not fail to notice that the director was recycling narrative elements
and using familiar imagery. One critic even speculated whether he should call
the film an epigraph or a film parody. But some critics still had faith in this
exceptional director. One of them wrote:

> The thing that really indicates the power of Tulio's extraordinary vision
> is that although the style alternates between naturalistic everyday real-
> ism to unreal log-driver operetta, from romantic yearning to the most
> chilling horror-film effects, and from folk-play stock characters to
> expressionist visions, there is nevertheless a sense of wholeness, which
> is truly astonishing.[49]

The Rapids of Hell (Hornankoski, 1949) is another rural melodrama with extreme
passions and blind jealousy serving as its driving force. The story is set in the
Yli-Koskela Manor, the grounds of which are somewhat implausibly divided by a
fierce rapid. The local council and most neighbours would like to tame the rapid
by building a power plant across it. Those who live at Yli-Koskela, however,
are no more willing to let this happen than they are inclined to curb the fury of
their passions. The danger of being washed away by the rapid serves as an obvious metaphor for the danger of being carried away to destruction by the force
of uncontrollable emotions and enmities. Like *In the Fields of Dreams*, this is a
story of male sibling rivalry, with Artturi (Åke Lindman) as the more mature son,
ready to assume responsibility for the family inheritance, and Aarne (William
Markus) as the restless, womanising vagabond. Both fall for the next-farm girl
Lea (Linnanheimo).

In the manner of *Cross of Love*, the story begins on a stormy night. An
old woman's attention is caught by a fierce knocking at the door. She wakes
her son Artturi, who goes to open the door. A man, a neighbour, comes in to
discuss the prospect of selling the rapid to a power company. No reason is
given for the urgency of discussing the matter at such a time in such adverse
weather conditions. Nor does it help discussing the matter there and then:
Artturi and the old lady (Annie Mörk) , the matriarch of the estate, angrily
refuse any such infringement of their sense of independence. Morning reveals
a pastoral landscape. Artturi timidly woos Lea. At the mention of Aarne and

his reckless way of life, there is a dramatic cut to their mother looking out of a window with an angry expression on her face. It is as if she were able to see not just the farmyard bathed in wonderful summer light, but all the bad things Aarne is up to. As this image is repeated throughout the film, always without any reasonable prospect of her actually being able to see what is going on, her furious gaze functions as that of a moralising overseer, the stern guardian of the honour of the estate.

The rapid serves as an excuse to recycle the impressive shots of log drivers shooting the rapid, to the same merry musical accompaniment as in Tulio's earlier films. Soon after, there is another familiar pattern, those beautiful, bold images of a trotting horse, now with Aarne holding the reins. Again, the reckless horseman knocks down a pretty blonde, Lea. Aarne stops and offers her a lift, and the journey continues. Tulio does not hesitate to use the same images as just a moment before, now with an added shot of Lea sitting next to Aarne, captivated by his exuberance and the excitement of the wild ride. They arrive at Yli-Koskela, and Aarne suggests to his mother employing Lea. Artturi has suggested this possibility to Lea on their first encounter that we have witnessed, but apparently he has not yet got as far as talking about it with his mother. Clearly, he is bitter because of Aarne having succeeded in taking the initiative.

Tulio now takes yet another bold step in developing his style. In some ways he returns once again to silent melodrama, but now boosted with bold sound effects. One day Aarne comes to the barn where Lea is working. There is a cut to a spade, accompanied by a heavy, ominous musical chord. A hand grabs the spade. We may assume it is Artturi's hand, as we have just seen him approaching. The next cut is to Aarne, approaching Lea from behind so as to surprise her. The ominous music continues as he lifts her up and she smiles radiantly. But then she appears to notice something further away and the expression on her face changes. Aarne lowers her down, and, again with an emphatic chord, there is a cut to Artturi with the spade in his hand. He pushes it forward, as if to indicate that it is time for work, not for play. A cut to the matriarch looking out of her window, made evermore emphatic by a track-in and dramatic music – another of Tulio's impossible point-of-view shots, now aspiring to the level of metaphysical moralism. Back to the barn, where Aarne takes the spade from Artturi and goes away. The music becomes a bit more relaxed, but there is still tension between Lea and Artturi. He does not seem to have a way with women, and only after a heavy silence is able to ask whether she would come to the barn dance with him. With a complete lack of enthusiasm, she responds: 'Why not?' Until this exchange, the sequence has been totally wordless (figures 5.70–77).

There is a second plot line of jealousy in operation too, as if borrowed from *In the Fields of Dreams*, involving a brunette maid, Irma, who would like to have Aarne for herself. And like the rascal brother in the earlier film, Aarne has a problem with losing money at cards. Artturi chastises him, and again there's

Figures 5.70–77

an image of the old woman at the window telling them to stop quarrelling. Again, the set-up is emphatically spatially impossible as the brothers and their mother must be in different buildings some distance away from one another.

However, Tulio is certainly not simply repeating his earlier efforts. There is a sequence in which Aarne watches Lea go naked for a swim from a sauna. As she returns, he suggests that he could come and wash her back – a standard folksy way of discreetly suggesting an erotic encounter. An important difference emerges in respect of Tulio's earlier films. Lea is not a helpless ingénue – she knows very well what faces her if she succumbs to Aarne's temptations, however much she might be infatuated with him. She holds her own even when the frustrated Aarne accuses her of 'preferring a wedding ring to love'. She is clearly aware that in such an expression 'love' stands for sex, and that a poor, fatherless maid who has got herself pregnant would not be accepted as the matriarch of Yli-Koskela. Aarne, perhaps quite sincerely, argues that his mother would accept her because she has already proven herself to be a good worker.

Meanwhile, at the barn dance the frustrated Artturi succumbs to drink, very much to the chagrin of Irma. Apparently she would be happy with either Artturi or Aarne, who both ignore her in favour of Lea. Next morning the brothers meet, somewhat ironically both seething with sexual frustration because of not having had their way with the woman they both desire to the exclusion of everyone else. As they depart Tulio makes explicit the rapid metaphor by a dissolve from a close-up of Artturi to the rapid.

The old woman really does appreciate Lea and, unaware of the underlying conflict, hands the keys of the storehouses to her. Having thus achieved a certain status in Yli-Koskela, Lea is more prepared to let her relationship with Aarne develop. Artturi notices this and seethes with jealousy. He seems to be watching the loving couple although it appears he is at a completely different location. Furthermore, although we see the couple in the middle of a field, they suddenly hear the 'For Me and My Gal' theme announcing that merry log drivers are shooting the rapid again. In this film more than in any other of Tulio's works, seeing and even hearing function purely in terms of character subjectivity at the expense of spatial logic. The spectator must learn not to expect the level of realistic motivation that may be expected when watching classical cinema, but he or she is obviously free to be terrifically amused by such bold freedom of expression.

Hearing the log drivers' song, Aarne immediately goes to meet them, leaving Lea looking unhappy. We then see Aarne gambling with the log drivers. One of them turns out to be a cheater, and Aarne starts a fight with him. The cheater tries to escape and, with the cheater's knife pulled, they end up fighting on the suspension bridge over the rapid. This is the most exciting action scene in Tulio's entire output. It ends with the dishonest log driver falling into the rapid. Artturi has witnessed the event and persuades Aarne to run away lest he be accused of manslaughter and thus bring shame on the family. Artturi goes downstream, finds the log driver, pulls him out from the stream and then tells him to disappear. From the other side of the rapid Lea observes this, but apparently does not quite understand the significance of what she sees. Aarne escapes, daringly shooting the rapid on a single log. The terrified Lea watches this, again quite impossibly, as most of the time she is just standing still while he is moving away at a terrific speed. Much of the scene repeats the rapid-shooting shots from *The Song of the Scarlet Flower*, although the situation of the characters is very different. But what is even more remarkable is that the entire aesthetics of this film is based on characters seeing things going on far beyond their physical position.

Artturi tells his mother and Lea that Aarne is guilty of murder. He argues with his mother that he should marry Lea so as to take her into the family and keep her quiet, thus protecting the reputation of the house. Even more important from the point of view of the old woman is that it turns out that Lea is pregnant. The matriarch is furious and forces Lea to marry Artturi, despite knowing that the child is Aarne's and that Lea loves him: 'That will be your punishment.' The Matron is stern but understanding and forgiving: instead of disparaging Lea, she persuades her to do what is best for her and her child. Thus, in contradistinction to the 'innocence films', Lea is not thrown out to survive as well as she can but forced to remain and marry a supposedly respectable man she doesn't love.

Suddenly it is winter and we see men felling trees and then rolling in the snow as part of their sauna bathing – this clip is apparently from some documentary footage Tulio happened to get hold of. Aarne is there, talking openly about his situation with other men. Most of them agree that he should give himself up and have the matter settled. He would like to do that, but is inhibited by having accepted Artturi's claim that their mother has a weak heart and would not survive the shame of her son being convicted as a murderer. When the child is born, Artturi proudly and in good faith introduces him as his own. But now the other pattern of jealousy emerges. Irma, still entertaining hopes about Aarne, points out that the baby has appeared rather too soon after the marriage.

The spring comes and together with the log drivers Aarne reappears. As Artturi boasts about 'his' child, Aarne misunderstands the situation and is furious because of what he sees as Lea's betrayal. He goes out with Irma to another barn dance, thus provoking Lea's jealousy. Artturi would like to go there too with Lea, presumably to boast about his beautiful wife, but she refuses, arguing proudly that it is not proper for a matriarch of Yli-Koskela go out with log drivers. She sees Aarne and Irma go to a barn and follows them, arrogantly announcing that maids are not employed at Yli-Koskela for love-making. An argument ensues and Lea reveals to Aarne that he is the father of her son. By now just about everyone is mad at everybody else.

Finally, Aarne comes to talk to Lea, and at last she begins to understand how they both have been deceived. But so has Artturi, who has remained naïvely convinced that he is the father of Lea's child. Only gradually do Irma's insinuations begin to gnaw at his mind. In a fight, Artturi wounds Aarne's arm with an axe. Soon after, mad with jealousy, having finally realised that Aarne is really the father of the little boy, he tries to kill Lea by releasing the ropes of the bridge as she is crossing the rapid. At the last moment he changes his mind and desperately tries to hold onto the ropes which are now pulling him into the rapid. Meanwhile, Aarne has noticed what is happening and succeeds in saving Lea just as the bridge falls down with Artturi entangled in the ropes. Aarne saves him too, but Artturi has broken his leg and is thus unable to take care of his responsibilities as the master of the estate. Because of this, his mother furiously argues that Aarne must not give himself up to the police because there is too much work to be done at the farm. 'Yes', she tells Aarne, 'the estate means more to me than do people!'

Artturi sees Lea follow Aarne upstairs and, dragging his wounded leg, follows her with a knife in his hand. He is restrained by the screaming of his mother as she, horrified at everything that she sees going on, falls down the staircase and dies. A funeral follows, in which the priest talks about how the old woman, although widowed even before giving birth to her second child, brought up two fine men in domestic harmony. Artturi, vexed by the hypocrisy of it, storms out. At the sight of the man he claimed had been murdered by Aarne, he jumps on a horse-drawn cart. Lea jumps in too, finally having realised that the man she saw Artturi pull out of the rapid must be the one of whose murder Aarne has been accused. Now she wants to extort from Artturi the final confirmation that he has lied all along. Again we see the familiar images of the fiercely trotting horse. In his drunken rage, Artturi pushes Lea off the cart and drives into the rapid. A shot of the rapid dissolves into an image of a power plant. The film ends showing Lea, Aarne and their son gazing at the fields that are now only theirs.

In *The Rapids of Hell* Tulio plunges into the tradition of action melodrama. The film is still essentially about sexual passion and the problems of maintaining family unity, but these considerations give rise to more fast-paced action than in any of his other films. It could also be seen stylistically as a major step forward in Tulio's career, although opinions may differ as to whether this was to his advantage or not. Whereas in some of the earlier films continuity disruptions may have appeared like mistakes, now they, particularly the impossible point-of-view shots, are so systematically employed that, intentionally or not, they function like a stylistic feature giving rise to an almost mysterious sense of characters seeing what the others are up to even when they are somewhere else – with the significant exception of Artturi's fatal lie. As has been pointed out, for the most part there is no point in speculating about Tulio's intentions, we just have to accept his films as he happened to complete them. And while the plot twists are even more contorted than in his earlier films, the fading away of the 'innocence tarnished' theme allows Linnanheimo again to develop a much stronger, more mature and interesting character.

The film's Finnish version was credited to Roland af Hällström and only the Swedish version to Tulio himself. However, according to the cinematographer Esko Töyri, af Hällström served merely as an assistant director in charge of coaching the dialogue.[50] Tulio himself also did much of the editing of both versions, adding material from films also by other directors. Some of it would reappear in his subsequent films. His editing is often striking, but at times rather sloppy in that there are fairly obvious continuity errors, as when the number of the log drivers on the raft oscillates between six and eight.

Quite surprisingly, some critics thought the film was too ordinary, referring to what we would call stock characters and conventional scenes such as shooting rapids, dancing, drinking and gambling. One of them wrote that the film 'in no way differs from the familiar ways of domestic serious films'. The writer clearly focused only on the subject matter, which he thought had 'the right sense of drama', and stated the film came close to real life.[51] Some others observed the absurdity of the lands of the estate being split by a rapid, as well as many other incongruities. Perhaps most scathingly, one critic wrote that the film was a compilation of all the features that had been criticised previously in Finnish cinema – 'a parody, but not intentionally so'.[52] But at least one spectator in a readers' column protested that the film had been unjustly blamed as it quite clearly was intended as a parody of all the 'clumsiness and tastelessness that Finnish cinema has been blamed of'.[53] Thus it appears that already Tulio's contemporaries had problems in figuring out how intentional some of the weirder aspects of his films were.

FEMALE DECADENCE

In *A Crooked Woman* (*Rikollinen nainen*, 1952), jealousy serves as the cause of misunderstandings, but soon the plot moves beyond such normalities in human affairs. Instead of shooting rapids and driving madly a horse-drawn cart, this film begins with three motorboats racing. One of them is driven by Eeva (Linnanheimo), a young woman full of the joys of life, the other two by the judge Lauri (Tauno Majuri) and the doctor Kristian (Kurt Ingvall). She wins the race, while both men end up in water. Eeva toys with their feelings, but finally accepts Lauri's proposal. She phones Kristian to invite him to a meeting concerning matters of her heart. He is too impetuous to listen to what Eeva has to say and is thus encouraged to buy an engagement ring, only to discover on the spot that he has been invited to Eva's and Lauri's engagement party.

After the brief wedding scene, some slapstick follows demonstrating Eeva's inability to take care of the household. Lauri appears a bit hard on her, not allowing her to hire a maid. This forces her to scrub the floors, a job for which she does not appear particularly suited, all the more so because she is pregnant. Kristian still attends to her in a friendly manner. There is a suggestion of jealousy when Lauri observes this. Soon a baby is born and, in a montage sequence, he grows to a few years old. Later we learn his name is Kari. Kristian comes once again to see Eeva while Lauri is away. Eeva hurts her foot on the veranda and Kristian carries her inside. As a doctor, he is tending to her foot when Lauri comes in. They appear to be having more fun than would be appropriate, and in a fit of jealousy Lauri throws Kristian out and quarrels with Eeva, calling her a slut. She announces she will go to visit her grandmother and we see her board a train. Soon after, Lauri is invited to a police station. He is shown items which belong to his wife. On the basis of the clothes, he identifies a mutilated body as being that of his wife. He and Lauri are reconciled in their mutual sorrow.

On a peaceful boating trip, Lauri is followed by a swimmer who grasps a rope tied to the boat and asks the oarsman to row faster. Then she disappears. Strangely, we do not see her face, and even more weirdly, Lauri is seen against a black background, although it is supposed to be a beautiful summer's evening. The episode is strangely but gently expressionistic.

Lauri, now in charge of a women's prison, is informed about the arrival of new prisoners. One of them, a woman referred to as Veera, is a particularly notorious criminal who has come to serve a life sentence. She is thought to be mad, as she does not talk and has a tendency to have fits. Some of her fellow inmates suggest that this is just a way of trying to avoid responsibility for her crimes. We do not get to see her face before Lauri gives a reception speech to the new inmates. With rolling eyes and distorted expressions, she certainly appears like a stereotypical madwoman.

Figures 5.78–79

Veera is struck by the sight of Lauri, conveyed by film negatives which invert the black-and-white image. She collapses and is carried away. The spectator may or may not recognise the face of Regina Linnanheimo. A little later Kristian brings Kari to the prison. Lauri is not too happy about seeing his son there and guides the visitors out through a corridor which Veera is scrubbing. Kari runs and knocks over the water bucket Veera is using. Somewhat cruelly, none of them notice Veera, let alone recognise that she is actually Eeva. But having seen a glimpse of her son, she has a vision of him, conveyed to us by means of multiple superimposition. Her facial expressions suggest that something is happening in the depths of her mind.

Between these scenes, Lauri has met in a forest the woman he first encountered on the lake. She has sprained her ankle and Lauri carries her into a nearby cottage where they spend the night together. They appear to do so with their clothes on. Later, Kristian is called to attend to the woman's foot, a situation forming a curious parallel with the similar event with Eeva. The relationship between Lauri and the woman, Riitta, develops rapidly, and Kari likes her too. Riitta is a painter, and she asks for a permission to paint the boy's portrait. Thus, she discreetly gets into Lauri's household. Kari only appears a little

Figures 5.80–83 Veera/Eeva scrubs a prison corridor and sees her husband and son as if in a vision.

unhappy about the idea that Riitta will become his new mother. He clearly still misses his real mother, whose photograph he has by his bedside. He also regularly visits her grave.

Eeva's memory seems to be returning very slowly, causing visions and strange behaviour. Because of this, she is sent to do hard labour in a swamp. Riitta is saddened by the sight of prisoners working there. Lauri agrees and says he only accepted the job of prison manager because the job was offered to him when he was going through a particularly dark phase in his life. He says that he intends to leave his position soon. It does not seem to occur to him that conditions at the prison could be improved. Tulio is not in the business of making social commentaries, and the sad state of the prison and its inmates appears like a fact of life that serves conveniently as a plot device.

One day Riitta's eye catches Veera working in the swamp. She asks Lauri for permission to use her as a model. He accepts, and so Veera enters what had once been her own home. Memories start coming back to her, particularly when she sees Kari's portrait. When the boy himself runs in, she hysterically embraces him, calling him by his name, thus frightening the boy. She is taken away, but Kari is left wondering how the strange woman could know his name. Later, he compares Riitta's sketch of Veera with the photograph of his mother. He goes to the prison and gets all the way to the cells before anyone notices. We are not shown exactly how, but he gets hold of the prison keys and helps Veera to escape. He hides her in the cellar of his home, and only when seeing the woman there does Lauri recognise her as Eeva. Not having a clue as to how it is possible, he faces the daunting task of explaining the situation to his new wife. While he is doing this, Eeva takes Lauri's car and without any obvious purpose drives erratically through the countryside, taking a shortcut through fields and almost getting smashed by a train. She is followed by the prison guards, the police and Kristian. The sequence is somewhat reminiscent of some of the most impressive action melodrama chases. The audience, familiar with *Restless Blood*, might expect Eeva to crash and die, but there are more plot twists to come.

Finally, Eeva is captured and again Kristian takes her into his care. He performs an operation on her head, removing a piece of her fractured skull which has caused her amnesia. The operation brings back her memory, but she does not understand what has happened between the original incident and her recovery. Kristian emphasises that it is dangerous for her to realise the truth of the new situation too soon. A slightly farcical situation emerges as an attempt is made to solve the complex situation by pretending to her that Riitta has been hired to serve as a housekeeper. The pattern is further complicated by Kristian insisting that he join the household so as to be able to follow Eeva's recuperation. Obviously, the masquerade is doomed to fail, partly because of Lauri's total inability to show affection to his first, legal, wife. Eeva's suspicions are confirmed when she sees Lauri and Riitta kiss and Kari blurts out the true

situation to her. She storms off and boards a train, with Kari and Kristian following her. Being on the train restores her memory about the accident: she has
been knocked down by the real Veera, who has taken her clothes and posses-
sions and then perished as they have struggled together on the moving train.
The film ends with Kari and Kristian consoling Eeva. It is left for the audience
to imagine how the situation is resolved.

A Crooked Woman differs from Tulio's earlier films in that here he does not
recycle any visual material. Also, the entire story is very different from his earlier efforts. The one element that is familiar is of course Linnanheimo. Already
in earlier Tulio films, she had shattered the image of a fragile beauty that had
been her trademark in the films she made for bigger studios. Prompted by
Tulio, she had tried a truly excessive acting style in the madness scenes of *Restless Blood*, which she later on repeated in its remake, *Jealousy*. In *A Crooked
Woman*, she further explored her abilities in this respect, replacing crazed
madness with the anxiety of a woman who has lost her memory and with that
her entire orientation in life. One reason why Linnanheimo left a salaried position at the Suomi-Filmi studios was that she wanted more challenging roles.
With Tulio she participated in scriptwriting and could start to develop the
kinds of characters that suited her ambitions, giving plenty of scope to put her
unusual acting talents to good use.

One critic described his cinematic experience as the most 'embarrassing
and agonising for a long time'.[54] This and many other critics regarded Linnanheimo's script and her facial distortions the film's foundational weakness.
Another point of criticism was the artificiality and implausibility of the chain
of events.[55] As usual with Tulio's films, the cinematography earned praise,
as did Tauno Marttinen's music. It was predicted that the film would attract
audiences only on account of Tulio's previous merits.[56] Yet, even that was not
enough: attendance figures were clearly below average.

Figures 5.84–85 Linnanheimo as the exuberant Eeva, who beats her suitors in a boat race, and
as the imprisoned, anguished Veera, having totally lost her identity.

You've Gone into My Blood (*Olet mennyt minun vereeni*, 1956) has a partial frame flashback structure which narratively harks back to the 'tarnished innocence' films. We first see Rea (Linnanheimo) reminiscing about her youth, imagining people from her past seated round a dinner table. This serves as a way of introducing the other main characters and suggests that she may be losing her sense of the real world. She is lonely, but still a beautiful woman. We enter a flashback, in which we see her as a factory worker bored with her life. Her friend Eeva (Rauha Rentola) criticises her for seeking romance in the cinema rather than in real life. The scene soon changes to a dance restaurant, a type of place Rea is visiting for the first time in her life.[57] In a shot reminiscent of silent cinema, we see hands descending on a woman's lap. She is clearly enjoying the attention. A female voice sings: 'I am just an ordinary girl, who would like to have a friend'. This little sequence is not connected to the storyline – it merely serves to indicate what kind of sordidness may take place in a dance restaurant, contrasting Rea's innocence with that of a highly experienced woman. A little later the contrast is made explicit, not only by the facial expressions of the two women, but by the hand of one of the men Rea has met descending on hers.

Rea explains in a voice-over that this was the decisive moment in her life. She meets two men, composer Tauno (Ami Runnas) and his friend Erkki

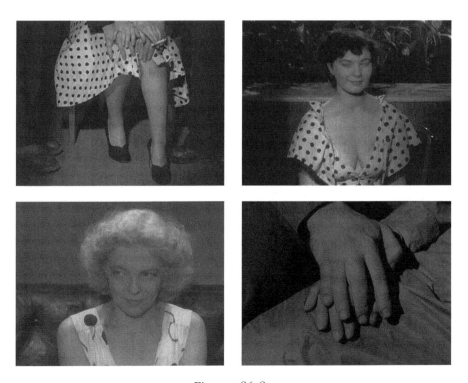

Figures 5.86–89

(Åke Lindman), a sea captain. She ends up with both of them in Tauno's apartment but, having her first experiences with alcohol, gets so drunk that although she immediately falls for Tauno, apart from a bit of kissing, nothing happens. Both men seem to desire her but are too gentlemanly to exploit her condition. Erkki might be the more romantically attached. He takes her home, but departs at the gate.

Next morning Rea wakes up with the first hangover of her life. Her mother – the only mother of an adult female character to appear in Tulio's entire oeuvre – chastises her for succumbing to alcohol, as if her alcoholic father wasting the family fortune and drinking himself to death would not have been a sufficient warning. Suddenly Rea realises that she must have left her handbag at Tauno's apartment. She rushes there and as she arrives her voice-over tells us that the door to the apartment was to signify her fate. He offers her a drink, another, and so on. The situation develops without dialogue, with only Rea's voice-over explaining her confused feelings. The two are getting intimate when Erkki suddenly appears in order to bid farewell as his boat is leaving. Rea at first hides, but Erkki realises that he has interrupted an intimate encounter. Tauno asks Rea to show herself. Erkki is clearly upset seeing Rea there, but hides his feelings. Instead, noticing the glasses, he warns Rea about the dangers of alcohol: it can be good but also dangerous, and might lead to inappropriate company. Tauno overhears this and jokingly acknowledges that Erkki's comment might be a reference to him.

While Erkki is away, Rea's and Tauno's relationship develops. According to her voice-over, she is happy for being loved more than she ever thought possible. The story proceeds by means of Rea's voice-over and the images that alternately are in accord with and contradict what she says. In one shot we see their faces with hers above, kissing him gently, he lying below with a blank expression on his face. She talks about her tender feelings and the power of love, and he suddenly embraces her with sexual passion. We also see a fire burning, then extinguished.

Figures 5.90–91

Soon Rea is pregnant. Tauno is not at all willing to have a child with her and in a letter gives her the address of an abortionist. Rea's anguish is expressed in another lengthy sequence carried forward only by images and her voice-over. The distraught Rea goes to Tauno's apartment, where the 'fateful door', as she describes it, is opened by a woman who presents herself as Tauno's wife. She quickly turns away, and in an almost surreal fashion we see also Erkki at the door. He follows her through the crowds on the streets, losing sight of her as she goes to the abortionist. We then see her go to a restaurant for a drink, where Erkki finds her. Possibly this takes place sometime after the abortion, but once again temporal relationships are obscure. Only in another voice-over do we learn that Erkki explains to her Tauno's situation: he has only been able to pursue a career as a composer by means of his wife's fortune. At this point, the story appears to return to the frame level, and so apart from the fact that we still hear the voice-over, we must assume that the rest of the film takes place in a narrative present of sorts.

Rea and Erkki marry, but on their wedding night she finds herself reluctant to go to their marriage bed as she is still in love with Tauno. Before she is able to go to their bedroom, it turns out that Erkki has already left to go back to sea. She rushes to the harbour and insists on sailing with him on what becomes a sort of working honeymoon. But after the first journey she has to get used to the more traditional role of a sailor's wife: waiting at home for him to return. After a brief period of happiness, things take a turn for the worse. Erkki's constant absence due to his work leaves Rea lonely and unhappy. Her voice-over insists on her yearning for love, but she also chastises herself, above all for her weakness to alcohol. She starts going to restaurants and on one occasion happens to meet Tauno. Not a word is uttered, she simply goes away. Rea meets Eeva, the old friend from her days at the factory. There is a montage sequence during which they visit a circus and watch a trapeze show. The only point about this appears to be to serve as a metaphor of her life swinging from one extreme to another. Rea and Tauno meet again, and he exploits her weakness for alcohol, eventually getting her into his bed. When she wakes up in the morning, she feels ashamed. As opposed to the 'lost innocence' films, Rea accuses herself rather than being the victim of moralising pillars of the society. She decides to change her life and starts spending more time with her daughter – the girl has suddenly appeared in the story already a few years old. Rea has a bad conscience, uncertain whether to confess to Erkki what has happened.

One day Rea receives a phone call. In a short silent sequence, we see that the callers are Tauno and Eeva. How the two have come together is left unexplained, and their invitation creates the paranoid sense of people round Rea conspiring against her. Rea is, after all, the narrator, and to some extent we may assume that also the visuals are part of her narration, or her subjective experience – possibly even her distorted recollections. This becomes apparent in a hallucination scene, in which her 'bad self' successfully encourages her to resort to drinking. Tempting her to drink ever more is also what Tauno and Eeva are doing, although we could also assume that they do so to a significant degree simply because of thoughtlessness.

When Tauno phones again, Rea, drunk and lonely, first refuses to join him. But then Eeva comes in and, to the accompaniment of merry music, they leave together to Tauno's farewell party – he is leaving for abroad. Rea entirely forgets about her daughter, who wanders after her and is locked outside: it is winter and she is in her pyjamas. Erkki happens to return and finds the girl alone in the cold. He also finds an invitation card to Tauno's party and drives there to tell his wife that their daughter is ill. She is so drunk that at first the message just does not go through. When she finally realises the situation, despite Erkki's efforts to stop her, she jumps in the driver's seat of their car and starts off. Erkki barely succeeds in getting in, and as they struggle, rather implausibly she pushes him out of the car and he is left lying on the snowy road. This shot cuts to one of Rea lying on a floor. When she wakes up it turns out that she is in prison. Erkki has died and she has received a two-year prison sentence. No one comes to see her or even sends a message, so when she is released she does not know what the situation is with her family. She finally finds her sick mother in an old people's home and hears that Tauno and his wife have adopted her daughter. She visits them and it turns out that the girl no longer recognises her. She realises that Tauno's wife and the girl have developed an affectionate relationship and so, Stella Dallas-like, Rea decides that the adoptive parents can offer her daughter a better life than she herself can.

Rea tries to start life anew, but very much like in the 'innocence lost' films, social conditions do not allow for this. Soon she succumbs once again to alcohol. One night she literally falls into the gutter, where she is seen in a typical Tulio-like melodramatic coincidence by Tauno and his wife. As she is released after a period of rehabilitation, she meets Tauno again, and he offers her a couple of drinks at a restaurant. We might wonder whether he is deliberately wrecking her life so as to get totally rid of her, or whether this is merely another instance of thoughtlessness on his part – or that of the screenwriter/director, mindful of the film being sponsored by the state alcohol company Alko as part of its campaign against alcoholism. Tauno asks why Rea never comes to see her daughter. Apparently it does not occur to him that this might not be such a good idea, considering how much Rea has become alienated from the girl, and in what poor condition she is. She points out the irony of Tauno not having wanted to have a child with her, but then adopting the child she has had with another man. On the street, Tauno watches her walk into the distance.

You've Gone into My Blood is the second and last of Tulio's films in which the narration is dominated by Regina Linnanheimo's very subjective voice-over.

She was once again the principal screenwriter, this time hidden behind the acronym Arel (her complete name was Aska Regina Elisabeth Linnanheimo). There are elements from the 'innocence lost' as well as the 'jealousy' films, in which the negligence of a mother puts her child in jeopardy, only this time it is the father rather than the child who gets killed. But despite the narrative potential, apart from a couple of wry remarks by Erkki, the jealousy theme is not developed.

The film was not widely distributed and thus received only a handful of reviews. Most of those that did appear were condescending, emphasising how old-fashioned Tulio now appeared, even at his best. A couple of critics mentioned there was laughter in the auditorium because 'The film trick and narrative style – inasmuch as one can talk about style in connection with this film – are from the 1920s'[58] . . . 'Tulio's inflated style is, even at its most serious, comical.'[59] Linnanheimo did receive some praise for depicting convincingly a woman who has lost everything in her life. The Board of Film Classification at first imposed a 15 per cent tax on the film, but Tulio succeeded in getting this repealed as he could prove that Alko, the company which had the monopoly on selling alcohol in Finland, had supervised the making of the film and considered that more than any other domestic film *You've Gone into My Blood* depicted convincingly the real nature of alcoholism.

ANOMALOUS TULIO

Whereas there is a certain consistency to Tulio's melodramas, to a great extent because of the obsessive recycling of subject matter and materials, two of the films he made are quite exceptional. These are the farce *Jiggs and Maggie* (*Vihtori ja Klaara*, 1939) and the fragment *In the Beginning Was an Apple* (*Se alkoi omenasta*, 1962). In his autobiography, Tulio relates having come to the conclusion that, despite the fair success of *Jiggs and Maggie*, he realised that farce was not really his line. The latter film, because of him having lost control of the failed production, Tulio disowned. Regrettably, in the autobiography Tulio does not reflect on the late phase of his career at all.

Jiggs and Maggie is based on George McManus' comic strip *Bringing Up Father*. It had already inspired Tatu Pekkarinen to write a theatrical farce based on it (1931) and this in turn inspired Nyrki Tapiovaara to direct the film *Two Henpecked Husbands* (*Kaksi Vihtoria*, 1939). Eino Jurkka had become celebrated for his roles as Vihtori (Jiggs) and he proposed that a third film should be made based on the same characters. The second had been a comedy directed by Tulio's old friend Valentin Vaala, *When Father Wants . . .* (*Kun isä tahtoo . . .* 1935), based on *Bringing Up Father*, although this is not acknowledged in the credits. At the time Tulio had already invested in a project which fell through because of copyright issues. He was in desperation about what to do with the equipment he had rented and the staff he had hired, so accepting this project saved him financially.

The film begins with the sound of crockery breaking. We then see Maggie throwing dishes at Jiggs, who is trying to take cover behind a table. The quarrel is about going to the opera, an idea that does not appeal to Jiggs, who has more popular tastes. The children are in principle on his side. His daughter Vappu argues: 'I prefer to sleep at home.' The kids, having watched their parents all their lives, do not have a very high opinion of relationships between men and women. Their son Nisse observes: 'Love is blind, and marriage is the best optician.'

The story continues in episodic fashion, with Jiggs first going out to walk the dog and having a horde of kids jeering at him because of his puny dog. He next goes to a bar to watch a series of quite impressive variety numbers, and then to play billiards with three friends who afterwards follow him to his family apartment to listen to an account of a boxing match on the radio. Maggie returns home and immediately throws all the men out. In slapstick fashion, they are seen rolling down the stairs.

A plot begins to develop when it starts to appear that Jiggs has a lover called Ritva. He talks with her on the phone, but then receives on another phone a call from Maggie, telling him that she intends to buy a beauty parlour. Fairly amusingly, Jiggs mixes up the two phone calls. Next Vappu comes to tell him that she intends to marry. Jiggs is exasperated and complains about the fact that humanity never develops: 'My grandfather married. My father married. I am more married than anyone else. And now my daughter comes and tells me with a blank face that she's going to marry!' Maggie is equally dismissive until she hears that the bridegroom-to-be's name is Peter von Schaslick. 'A real "von"! Why didn't you say that straight away?'

Ritva does not seem to take her affair with Jiggs too seriously, and appears to prefer Klaus, the manager of a garage. But she also flirts with Peter, who is completing his engineering degree training at the garage. He responds and does not seem to object to Ritva taking advantage of Jiggs' folly, such as having him buy her an expensive piece of jewellery. Klaus only has to appear with an even more expensive item, and she leaves with him.

The film jumps fairly incoherently from one brief storyline to another. For example, Jiggs as well as Vappu and Peter end up being taken into custody at the same police station, the former because of having been caught climbing down a rope made of sheets as he tries to escape from Maggie, the latter because of speeding – another completely pointless episode. Only slightly more coherently, confusion emerges from Jiggs buying a beauty parlour for Ritva. A visit to such a venue that happens to be for sale frees him of all his inhibitions about spending money as he shamelessly relishes the sight of young women in a variety of gymnastic activities.

Another farcical plot line develops when Peter visits Ritva to explain how the jewellery Jiggs intended for her finally ended up in the possession of Maggie, who thought it was intended for her as her second name is Ritva. As Jiggs unexpectedly arrives, Peter hides under the bed, and when Maggie even more unexpectedly appears, Jiggs joins him. In between, Peter succeeds in getting hold of the deed to the beauty parlour. This he uses later on to blackmail Jiggs to give him the hand of his daughter. But as Maggie catches a glimpse of him, still under the bed, she immediately decides she is against the marriage and succeeds in turning Vappu against Peter. Surprisingly, Ritva rescues Peter's reputation by offering quite an implausible explanation about a dog having taken the papers of the beauty salon from under her bed and Peter having crawled there to collect them. She also offers to sell the beauty parlour to Jiggs and Maggie – Jiggs has paid the original owner for the beauty parlour and a second time to Ritva, to whom Maggie has given it as a gift. But Ritva will now marry Klaus, who she perhaps genuinely loves. Thus everyone gets the partner he or she wants, and Maggie can start her own beauty parlour. Ritva sends a letter to Jiggs which ends up in Maggie's hands.

The film has some quite amusing scenes, thanks to a great extent to Eino Jurkka's merrily over-the-top performance as Jiggs. Also, some of Nisse's comically cynical rejoinders hit the mark precisely. Huge amounts of dishes being smashed by Maggie is in its excessiveness clearly supposed to be a major comic draw, but perhaps the story behind the logistics of getting all that crockery to be smashed is funnier than the actual activity of breaking them in the film. Tulio succeeded in getting free a huge amount of crockery from the Arabia tableware company because of minor faults. But as company rules forbade selling or even giving away this material, all the pieces had to be collected, weighed and returned to the factory to ensure that not a single fragment was missing.

The cinematically most ambitious scene takes place when Jiggs dreams of trying to escape Maggie's fury over the roofs of the city. This was done partly on a real roof with the ridge broadened on the other side and stand-ins dressed as Jiggs and Maggie. The result was praised in the otherwise rather lukewarm, when not actually dismissive, contemporary reviews. When Tulio's films were re-released in the 1980s, some commentators opined that in terms of visuals and cinematic storytelling, 'Tulio was decades ahead of other Finnish filmmakers.'[60] While with a number of reservations this statement may be accepted about Tulio as a whole, this is one of the films in which this distinction is least obvious.

In the Beginning Was an Apple (*Se alkoi omenasta*, 1962) is another anomaly in Tulio's oeuvre. The film was to be based on the revelations of a jet-set beauty, Tabe Slioor, about her relationship with Erik von Frenckell, the one-time Mayor of Helsinki. She was a celebrity at the time, having even gained the reputation of being the first woman in Finland to be allowed into a restaurant alone.

Slioor herself had the leading role. At least three other major directors were approached before the project was offered to Tulio. The project was interrupted when less than half of the script had been shot: Slioor turned out to be too much of a diva to be controlled. The producer shot some extra material using a stand-in and edited a 36 minute-long film that eventually was exhibited together with a parody about Slioor and the film project, directed by Armand Lohikoski and titled *Stardom* (*Taape tähtenä*, 1962). This farce tells the story of a celebrity who is supposed to star in a film but as she couldn't care less about the shooting schedule she is replaced by the script girl.

In the Beginning Was an Apple . . . is dominated by Tabe's voice-over (actually provided by Tuija Halonen, the actress who also served as Tabe's stand-in and as the star in *Stardom*). The film begins with an old man by a fireside. Tabe comes to him with a photo album of pictures of herself and starts telling her life story. The rest of the film is seen as a flashback. Her father was a Persian prince who had to escape to Finland because of a revolution. Her parents separated and she spent her childhood in a children's home. Because of her 'dark beauty', other children envied and bullied her, calling her a gypsy. The matron of the children's home in which she was placed was equally cruel, forcing her to do hard work while the other kids were playing. When the little girl says her father will come and fetch her, the matron tells her not to expect ever to see her father again because he is dead.

The story jumps to the wartime, when Tabe is already a young woman. She meets a soldier in a bomb shelter and they fall immediately in love. He might look very ordinary to us, but for her he is 'the prince of her dreams'. He has to go back to the front – we briefly see stock footage of the war – and she joins the home front forces. However, she has to resign because she is a foreigner and ends up having to do hard manual labour. But at least after the war she meets her prince again and they marry.

Tabe Slioor plays herself, and the voice-over is at times shamelessly narcissistic. It turns out that her husband is a painter. When they finally succeed in finding a decent flat to rent, they are happy for a while. But his artistic ambitions soon become a problem. 'My husband explored every aspect of my beauty. I stood for hours on end as his model, as he tried to eternalise my exotic beauty and my wonderful figure. I bravely swallowed my tears as I watched how difficult it was for my husband to capture my beauty on the canvas. But what would a loving woman not sacrifice for her love?'

Eventually it turns out that the husband is a loser, who thinks it does not befit him as an artist to try to find a real job. The two of his paintings we see do not suggest he has any talent. Tabe even has to assume the task of trying to sell her husband's works, but to no avail. She finds it humiliating, but at least she does not have to succumb to prostitution. They have a child, but their affair sours because of his apparently unfounded jealousy. Soon he leaves her alone with the baby. The girl grows up quickly and Tabe has to work hard to support them both. One day a middle-aged woman storms in. She insults Tabe, introduces herself as the sister of Tabe's husband and demands custody of the child. Tabe of course refuses this, but the child nevertheless inexplicably disappears from the film. Possibly a fragment explaining what happens to her had not been shot at the time production was interrupted.

An elderly soldier appears out of nowhere to help Tabe and her daughter. He arranges for Tabe to go to a mannequin school. After he has served this function, he too disappears from the film. Without any training, Tabe excels as a mannequin because of her natural talent – or so she claims. She intends to establish her own mannequin school, but before she gets that started she meets another elderly man and they fall in love. He is rich and even takes her to Stockholm. This gives her a new direction in life: 'We visited several art museums, churches and art galleries, and these awakened my hidden artistic talents, that later on have bloomed so wonderfully in my literary works and in the field of art photography.' There is a problem, though. The old man's wife knows what her husband is like, nags at him and tries to convince him that everyone is laughing at him. But the affair continues, and Tabe claims to have been unhappy only when he tries to buy her presents: 'I only wanted his love.' Perhaps this is because, while he is prepared to buy her a golden bracelet, he does not offer her a wedding ring. He even 'betrays' Tabe by continuing to live and even travel together with his wife! The lovers have a quarrel, but soon he and Tabe are together again, lovingly enjoying a beautiful summer night. The film ends with a picture of the fireplace we saw at the beginning of the film, as if some kind of conclusion has been reached.

It would not be fair to criticise a film which is recognised as a fragment for a lack of narrative coherence. On the other hand, it is quite Tulio-like that characters come and go from a film serving only a single narrative function. Whether

Figures 5.92–93 Tabe has chased her lover and his wife in her car and blocks the road. The wife blowing the horn does not help. Why the married couple have been shot in such a blatantly staged manner is a matter of conjecture.

these disappearances are due to problems of production or not, together with the fact that we are never informed about the names of Tabe's men and her excessively self-indulgent voice-over, they serve well to emphasise her impeccably narcissistic character. Being absolutely self-assured, she is not a typical Tulio female protagonist any more than Slioor is a typical Tulio actress. Perhaps he could only handle properly the ever-indulgent Regina Linnanheimo, and was just incredibly lucky to have such a faithful friend and collaborator.

The film was first banned because it was thought to be indecent to make a scandalising film about a still-living person – this despite the fact that none of the men Tabe has an affair with is even given a name and that the real affair had been publicly known for a long time. It was further argued that the character of the protagonist could serve as a bad role model for young women. Tulio in turn was offended by the film being distributed at all, as it had been advertised as his film, yet he had lost control of the entire production. But as his name did not appear in the opening credits, the courts concluded that his reputation as a director had not been compromised. The real irony is that Tabe Slioor's life would have contained material for a much more substantial film. She was acquainted even with President Urho Kekkonen, and rumour has it they had an affair. She lived for sixteen years in the United States, and succeeded in capturing a fair amount of media attention there. Her daughter Aulikki Slioor-Knight, far from disappearing from her life, followed her and pursued a colourful and successful career as a cow breeder, pilot, freelance writer, radio hostess and gallerist.

THE OUTRAGEOUS FINALE

The making of Tulio's last film, *Sensuela,* began in 1964, but because of financial difficulties most of the shooting took place in 1967–8. The film was finally released in 1973. Even more absurdly than in connection with the *Cross of Love,* the opening credits announce that the story is based on a novel by Alexander Pushkin. *Sensuela* makes a fair bid to being one of the craziest films ever made with, presumably, any degree of serious intention. One film that can challenge it in this respect is Edward Wood's *Plan 9 from Outer Space* (1959), which is now considered 'simply too amusing to be considered the worst film ever made',[61] with its peculiar charm emerging from its very ineptitude. Both films may well be considered to be beyond any form of serious criticism.

In terms of its main storyline, *Sensuela* is a remake of *Cross of Love,* although with major differences. Above all, it is Tulio's one and only colour film, and quite extravagantly so, with prominent, highly saturated primary colours dominating. This prevented Tulio from recycling his earlier, black-and-white, visual materials, but it did not hinder him in any other way. The setting is modernised and it

Figures 5.94–95 Hans' profession as a fashion photographer serves as an excuse for introducing elements of pop culture.

borrows much more nudity than any previous Tulio film, probably in an effort to take advantage of the much-spoken-of sexual liberation of the 1960s. He could be seen trying to do something similar to what Bigas Luna, for example, was doing in Spain in the 1970s: making soft porn a respectable form of cinema.

Yet, just like its predecessor, *Sensuela* contains one of the most awkward of plot devices in nineteenth-century stage melodrama, the mock marriage staged to fool the girl's father, another innocent of the ways of the world, but embittered and crazed enough to perform extremely violent actions against the man who in his view has despoiled his daughter. As in *Cross of Love*, the father figure can be seen as a kind of perversion of innocence, a moralistic force, who in his avenging fury completes the destruction not only of the perpetrator but also the victim. Such melodramatic aspects go over the top to the extent that one cannot help wondering whether Tulio was actually indulging in self-parody. In view of his earlier films it might seem nearly impossible, but Tulio succeeds in excelling himself in bringing together a great variety of mutually incompatible materials. Totally artificial-looking fictional storytelling is intercut with pseudo-documentary about the lives of Sami people. Later on, there are sequences which resemble travel advertisements and which may well have been appropriated from such material.

The beginning of the film takes place during the Second World War. We see shots of impressive snow-capped mountains, unknown to the natives of Finland before foreign travel.[62] The first images of the characters are of the crew of an aeroplane about to crash-land. Crew members are seen collapsing puppet-like before the plane hits the ground, and only the pilot is able to jump clear and parachute to safety. The images from inside the plane immediately reveal this as a truly low-budget film, in which a mere suggestion of a setting is supposed to evoke the impression of an environment such as the cockpit of an aeroplane (a clear parallel with *Plan 9 from Outer Space*).

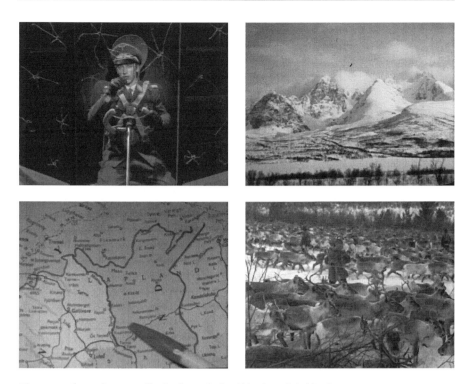

Figures 5.96–99 German pilot in the cockpit of his aircraft (with what we must assume are bullet holes in the windscreen), falling into an alpine-looking terrain. So as to locate his story geographically, Tulio inserts here mock-ethnographic material about the Sami people. The images of reindeer herds have probably been appropriated from genuine material.

A young woman in Sami dress observes the falling aircraft and comes to the rescue with a reindeer-drawn sledge. To totally absurd effect, Tulio intercuts between the pilot being pulled by the wind along the ground and the woman following him on the sledge, hilariously to the accompaniment of Pyotr Tchaikovsky's *Swan Lake*. A variety of excerpts from this ballet will form the background music for the rest of the film, irrespective of how incompatible they may seem with whatever happens or what is seen. But incompatibility or implausibility had never disturbed Tulio very much, and in his final film he abandoned such ponderous concerns completely. We see this again as, together with the handsome German pilot Hans (Mauritz Åkerman), we watch with astonishment Sami life as depicted – perhaps we should say parodied – by Tulio. In a scene which a few decades after the film's release would have been deemed politically unforgivably incorrect, we see mock-Sami people drinking and hollering. As an example of supposedly ethnic customs, Aslak (Ossi Elstelä), the father of the young woman, castrates a reindeer with his bare teeth, spitting the testicles into the snow. The reindeer – and later on, wolves – are seen howling. It is blatantly obvious that the images are of stuffed animals and that the howling has been faked by humans.

As a German officer Hans is at the time of the crash fighting on the same side as the Finns. However, unknown to him or the Sami people who extend their hospitality to him, Finland switches sides and so Hans becomes technically an enemy.[63] When a ski patrol comes to check that the area is free of German fighters, Aslak, following his people's code of honour, protects and hides his guest. He does this even though he correctly suspects that Hans is after his precious daughter Laila (Marianen Mardi). Soon afterwards, Hans leaves disguised in a Sami costume, but after peace has been restored he returns to Lapland, having resumed his profession as a photographer. It is easy for him to persuade Laila to come with him to Helsinki. Then occurs the most astonishing time jump in Tulio's entire oeuvre: judging by the plane in which Hans and Laila travel to Helsinki (Finnair DC 8, in reality only used for transatlantic flights) and the settings in which the film continues, the characters have been transported into the late 1960s. Yet none of them appear to have aged in the slightest.

In Helsinki, Hans and Laila are at first happy together and pursue a joint career with Laila as Hans' photographic model. We see them make love in some quite beautiful close-up soft-porn imagery weirdly intercut with images of a sulking Aslak and Lapland landscapes – all this to the accompaniment of Tchaikovsky. A voice-over relates how happy Laila is and how much she has learned from Hans. However, in the city moral corruption appears to be everywhere. Tulio makes this point by staging a party with uninhibited females dancing topless, if not naked, and couples making love (figures 5.100-101). This spirit of sexual liberation is in stark contrast to the underlying attitudes of the story that are exactly the same as in *Cross of Love*, anachronistic already then. A charitable reading might see this as an instance of self-parody on Tulio's side, or perhaps an attempt to measure his old materials against the new trends and mores of the 1960s.[64] A more likely interpretation is that Tulio is once again using whatever material is available for his own, outmoded, purposes.

Hans belongs in this world of licentiousness. He soon becomes tired of Laila and even tries to pimp her out to his friends. But unlike her predecessors in Tulio's earlier films, she remains strong and refuses to be prostituted. Despite not having any education or training, she is able to find employment and make a living – the film was made during an economic boom. Her only problem is that she is again and again subject to sexual harassment. She does not allow this to continue and prefers to leave these jobs. However, she nevertheless lives with Greta (Marja Pertamo), a woman making a living by prostitution.

Laila gets to know a workmate, Pekka (Ismo Saario), and gradually develops a romantic relationship with him. Tulio is at pains to perform a balancing act between depicting their relationship as a chaste affair and keeping up the erotic appeal of his film. For no narrative or thematic point whatsoever, Pekka

Figures 5.100–101

is an athlete and is shown winning a race at the Helsinki Olympic Stadium. An image of this impressive landmark together with an attempt to appeal to the popular tendency to celebrate successful athletes appear to be the only motivations for this episode. In a sequence in which Tulio simultaneously exploits notions of sexual liberation and the sense of moralism that he was never able to shake off, we see the couple swim and go to a sauna. Somewhat implausibly in terms of 1960s Finnish working-class norms, the young couple at first take turns in going naked to the sauna. Finally, as they gain the confidence to get more intimate, we see a genuinely erotic scene, quite discreetly and exquisitely photographed.

Laila has continued to send letters to her father, giving him the impression that everything is going well in her life. Now she writes to tell him she intends to marry. Aslak is seen reading the letter in a shop and being extremely happy about it. But then his eyes catch a calendar hanging on the wall with a photograph of the naked Laila. He is infuriated and, in his full Sami costume, travels immediately to Helsinki with the firm intention of killing both Laila and Hans. He goes first to Laila's flat and meets her flatmate Greta, whom he immediately recognises as a prostitute –something completely different from what Laila has led him to expect. Threatening her life, he tries to force her to tell him whether his daughter is a prostitute. They depart and each tries to reach Laila before the other. Greta finds her first and warns her about her father's homicidal fury. Laila gets to Hans before Aslak and they agree about how to calm Aslak: they will pretend to be lovers about to get married. Aslak almost believes them, but then sees on the wall the same calendar that first incited his fury. The shrewd and suave Hans resolves the conflict with a short lecture on photomontage. He explains how he has combined a picture of Laila's beautiful face with that of the body of a suitable model. Aslak is terrifically amused by this and accepts the explanation, which in his mind cleanses his daughter's reputation and restores the family's honour. He is so happy about Laila's marriage that he allows Hans to kiss his bride already, explaining that he is really 'not all that old-fashioned'.

Hans organises a mock marriage ceremony. Luckily, the prudish Aslak does not wonder why the wedding does not take place in a church. One of Hans' friends passes as a priest, despite hardly being able to hide his own desire for Laila. Meanwhile, Pekka has grown suspicious and somehow finds his way to Hans' apartment. He is furious when he sees Laila in a wedding dress, accusing her for having betrayed him. Hans, determined to play his role through in this charade, confronts him. They have a fist fight, with Tchaikovsky providing an impressive if incompatible accompaniment. Hans is beaten and his new girl-friend exposes the whole masquerade. Pekka storms out, but now it is Aslak's turn to manhandle Hans – with a vengeance! He castrates Hans as if he were one of his reindeer. So as not to make the act too explicit, Tulio cuts to the earlier images of Aslak working on his herd, spitting the testicles on the snow. Having completed the job, he announces that he will never again come to the south and that he no longer has a daughter.

One of the most tender passages from *Swan Lake* is heard as Laila is seen on a bridge, preparing to throw herself into the water. A young man, Joni (Matti Nurminen), appears and takes her under his wing, but only to prostitute her at Hamburg's Reperbahn (or so it is vaguely suggested).[65] The plot is mov-ing very fast now, and hardly has the scene been set when Pekka comes in with his new girlfriend. Laila is naked on the stage, just having finished her part in a sadomasochistic show. Pekka is astonished to see her but pretends he doesn't know her. Immediately afterwards, it is Hans' turn to visit the brothel. Apparently, castration has not lessened his appetite for sex, as he pays for a private show which just happens to feature his ex-girlfriend. She resorts to the emblematic Tulio line: 'Here I am, just the way you wanted me!' and continues with a feminist tirade, pointing out that women only want love and that it is the gentlemen who turn women into whores and then discard them. Throughout this sordid episode, Tchaikovsky provides the musical background.

Figures 5.102–103 The 'child of nature' of the narrator's description ends up as a stripper and a prostitute on Hamburg's Reperbahn.

Joni comes out of a building. Somehow the story has returned to Finland. Greta is seen with a young man in Sami costume, whom we first saw briefly at the beginning of the film. Joni kills Greta as she tries to distract him so that the young man can save Laila from Joni's clutches. Just for the effect, we hear a steam engine puffing, and after Joni has stabbed Greta, there is a shot of a train crossing a railway bridge (pulled by a diesel engine). There is not the slightest attempt at explaining how the train and the killing might be spatially related, but this is only a particularly blatant example of how Tulio's taste for big effects may at any time override the need to adhere to a spatio-temporal logic of any kind. There is a cut back to the young man telling Laila that Aslak has died and that, having inherited his reindeer herd, she is now a rich woman. In the final images we see Laila and the young man at Aslak's lonely grave. According to the voice-over, Laila has realised that she does not belong in the civilised world, as her home is Lapland.

At the time of its release *Sensuela* did not receive a single critical review. When Tulio's films were reissued at the turn of the century after an almost complete break of half a century, some critics were only able to relate to his late films, *Sensuela* in particular, as camp. However, as far as we know, Tulio was deeply offended when he realised audiences were laughing at his film, and forbade further screenings until the very end of his life. For a retrospective of Tulio's films on television in 2017, Harto Hänninen wrote:

> Tulio's last film always surprises with its tastelessness. It is bad and clumsy, but it is also turgidly sexist, overwhelmingly strange and repellently carnal. Put together, these features add up to more than their sum as *Sensuela* is one of the funniest domestic films ever. It is a pure delight for all those who know what camp is and a basic lesson for those who don't.[66]

Who could have expected that Tulio could actually overreach himself at the very end of his career – sadly, in terms of his most remarkable weaknesses rather than his very real strengths?

NOTES

1. Between these two productions Tulio made the film *Jiggs and Maggie* (*Vihtori ja Klaara*, 1939). This comedy, based on the George McManus comic strip originally titled *Bringing Up Father*, is untypical of his oeuvre and will be discussed below under the heading 'Anomalous Tulio'.
2. Being an owner of a significant farmhouse in rural Finland was a mark of high social prestige and financial security, particularly as opposed to being a tenant farmer (*torppari*), who would have to undertake a prescribed amount of labour for the landowner or pay

for the right to cultivate a piece of land by handing over to the landowner an agreed amount of the produce. In some subsequent fiction, most significantly in Väinö Linna's *Under the Northern Star I-III* (*Täällä Pohjantähden alla I-III*, 1959–62), the severe and uncertain circumstances in which tenant farmers and their families lived were criticised. Linna's work was a powerful social commentary, giving rise to much debate. Tulio uses the social standing of the tenant farmers as a dramaturgical device but does not criticise the prevailing social order in any way.

3. Lyytikäinen 1997: 184.

4. Ibid.: 194.

5. This may be partly because of narrative economy. In the novel Olavi has an elder brother, Heikki, who will run the Koskela farm, although earlier the more talented Olavi was supposed to assume this task. In most filmic adaptations, Heikki is omitted from the story.

6. Svenska Pressen 8.12. 1938.

7. T.: 'Linnankosken Laulu tulipunaisesta kukasta', *Karjalan Suunta* 8.12.1938.

8. Esko: 'Elokuvakatsaus', *Satakunnan Kansa* 21.12.1938.

9. –rkk–: 'Laulu tulipunaisesta kukasta', *Ajan Suunta* 5.12.1938.

10. *The Song of the Scarlet Flower* has been adapted for the big screen on three other occasions: in Sweden by Per Axel Branner in 1934 and Gustav Molander in 1956, and by Mikko Niskanen in Finland in 1971. Tytti Soila has discussed the reception of all five versions in her article 'Five Songs of the Scarlet Flower' (Soila 1994). An interesting observation she makes is that some members of the audience giggled when seeing the 1934 Branner film. The director shared this fate with Tulio.

11. Sirkka Salonen's hair was dyed for her role in this, her only film. She was actually a brunette. A more serious issue, as many critics pointed out, was that she had had no voice training. But she did have the advantage of having been Miss Europe 1938, an accolade that entitled her name to be displayed on the posters more prominently than those of her fellow actors.

12. Romani people stealing children is an age-old fear in Europe. Even today, children with a relatively fair complexion have been taken away from their Romani parents by officials because of the suspicion of abduction – until DNA examination has proved otherwise (see Walker 2013). Romani people or sub-proletarian folk stealing middle-class babies was a standard theme in nineteenth-century melodrama and appeared also in early cinema, such as in Lewin Fitzhamon's *Rescued by Rover* (1905).

13. Parras: 'Unelma karjamajalla', *Aamulehti* 20.1.1941.

14. T.A.: 'Unelma Karjamajalla', *Suomen Sosialidemokraatti* 2.10.1940.

15. Williams 2001: 15.

16. Ibid.: 17.

17. The word used here, *aitta*, does not translate easily into English. The basic meaning is a barn for agricultural products, but it could also be used for sleeping. In Finnish fiction with a rural setting, a young unmarried woman might in the summer stay in an *aitta*. If she lets a man in at night she risks her reputation and, depending on her social status, even her livelihood.

18. Maija calls her *muori*, a word usually used for any old woman, but here presumably meaning that she is Maija's grandmother.

19. Henrik turning out to be a spy could be seen as the film's single reference to the war, which had ended just before the film was released.

20. E. L.: 'Sellaisena kuin sinä minut halusit', *Sosialisti* 23.10.1944.

21. P.Ta–vi: 'Sellaisena kuin sinä minut halusit', *Helsingin Sanomat* 19.10.1944.

22. S. S.: 'Sellaisena kuin sinä minut halusit', *Uusi Suomi* 16.10.1944.

23. Ibid.

24. Antti Halonen: 'Kotimainen elokuva voisi vähentää virheitään', *Elokuvateatteri* 9/1944.

25. Lyytikäinen 1997: 179.

26. A beautiful young woman swimming naked was a fairly standard way for Nordic cinemas to sell films abroad with discreet eroticism – often quite successfully. Some of the most famous Finnish examples are Toivo Särkkä's *Hilja – the Milk Maid* (*Hilja – maitotyttö*, 1953) and *Preludes to Ecstasy* (*Kuu on vaarallinen*, 1961) (see Lehtisalo 2019: 262). Although Tulio was often criticised for showing naked women, he does not offer anything more titillating than these films. None of these swimming scenes appear particularly sensational to contemporary eyes.

27. At least to contemporary eyes the act can be seen as rape. Possibly, at the time of the film's making, it could be seen as seduction, for which the naïvely defenceless woman falls.

28. Ucicky made his film while the Molotov–Ribbentrop Pact between the Soviet Union and Nazi Germany was still in force. The film was imported to Finland almost immediately after its release. After Germany attacked the Soviet Union in June 1941, the film was withdrawn from circulation. Finland joined the attack against the Soviet Union in the hope of regaining the territory lost in the Winter War (1939–40).

29. Maltby 1996: 447.

30. More precisely, the mothers of all but one female character are absent from the films, and most female characters who have a child during a film, lose them in one way or other. A dearth of biographical information does not allow much scope for psychological speculation about the reasons for this.

31. Paula Talaskivi: 'Tukistusta Tuliolle', *Taiteen Maailma* 3–4/1946.

32. T. A.: 'Rakkauden risti', *Suomen Sosialidemokraatti* 14.3.1946.

33. L. A.: 'Rakkauden risti', *Työkansan Sanomat* 30.3.1946.

34. R. H–m.: 'Elokuvapalsta', *Uusi Suomi* 10.3.1946.

35. The actress is Nora Mäkinen, who played the part of Gaselli in *The Song of the Scarlet Flower*.

36. O.V–hl: 'Valkokankaalta', *Aamulehti* 26.4.1946.

37. R.H–m: 'Elokuvapalsta', *Uusi Suomi* 28.4.1946.

38. P. Ta–vi: 'Viikon filmejä', *Helsingin Sanomat* 29.4.1946.

39. T. A.: 'Levoton veri', *Suomen Sosialidemokraatti* 28.4.1946.

40. T. J:nen: 'Levoton veri', *Kansan Lehti* 28.3.1946.

41. Some shots are appropriated from Nyrki Tapiovaara's film *One Man's Fate* (*Miehen tie*, 1940).

42. Camera: 'Elokuvakatsaus', *Satakunnan Kansa* 19.8.1953.

43. - nen: 'Mustasukkaisuus', *Turun Päivälehti* 15.3.1953.

44. H-O K.: 'Mustasukkaisuutta', *Uusi Aura* 15.3.1953.

45. Camera: 'Elokuvakatsaus', *Satakunnan Kansa* 19.8.1953.

46. Log driving has served as an integral element of many Finnish films. It typically has the function of providing restless young men unprepared to assume their social responsibilities a chance to enjoy their freedom before settling down. From this derives log driving's other narrative function, suggesting erotic licentiousness. When the log drivers first arrive after the winter, the village girls run to the riverbank to welcome them. Log drivers are presented as irresponsible, lacking moral codes and thus a threat to stable rural society. Yet, though most of them are simply boisterous and lacking in respect, they appear to have a good work morale. (Koivunen & Laine 1993: 138–9.)

47. In Linnankoski's novel this is presented as a matter of communal speculation. After the mistress has assumed control of the farm, the master is not seen drinking anymore, but is at times observed to be reeking of alcohol. No one has ever seen the mistress handle alcohol, but people guess that she controls the master by administering to him just as much alcohol as is needed to keep him content.

48. There was a small tradition of films set in rural mansions in which the matriarch was the dominating figure and the married man jeopardised the family honour by falling for another woman. Among the major works were adaptations of a series of plays by

Hella Wuolijoki – *The Women of Niskavuori* (*Niskavuoren naiset*, 1938), *Loviisa* (*Loviisa, Niskavuoren nuori emäntä*, 1946), *Heta Niskavuori* (*Niskavuoren Heta*, 1952), *Aarne Niskavuori* (*Niskavuoren Aarne*, 1954), *Niskavuori Fights* (*Niskavuori taistelee*, 1957), *The Women of Niskavuori* (*Niskavuoren naiset*, 1958), *Niskavuori* (1984) – as well as a number of films such as *The Farmer's Wife* (*Riihalan valtias*, 1956) and *The Widow and Her Daughter* (*Sillankorven emäntä*, 1953).

49. H.M.: 'Intohimon vallassa', *Kauppalehti* 26.3.1947.

50. Töyri 1983: 257–8.

51. Pta.: 'Hornankoski', *Keskisuomalainen* 19.4.1949.

52. Juha Nevalainen: 'Elokuvan vaiheilta', *Ilta-Sanomat* 19.3.1949.

53. Jouko Hytönen: 'Arv. T.A.', *Suomen Sosialidemokraatti* 13.3.1949.

54. T.P.: 'Elokuvat', *Savon Sanomat* 25.3.1952.

55. O.V–jä: 'Epäaitoa ja teennäistä', *Aamulehti* 18.3.1952.

56. Martti Savo, 'Kaksi kotimaista', *Työkansan Sanomat* 3.2.1952.

57. There is a twentieth-century Finnish tradition of going to a restaurant not only to dine but also to drink and dance. The restaurant thus served as a venue for men and women to meet one another in a relaxing environment. The only talents required were minimal dancing and small talk abilities. Alcohol helped men to overcome their anxieties. Until the 1970s many restaurants refused entry to single women.

58. Martti Savo: 'Olet mennyt minun vereeni', *Työkansan Sanomat* 23.9.1956.

59. Olavi Veistäjä, *Aamulehti* 24.9.1956.

60. Antti Lindqvist: 'Vihtori ja Klaara', *Katso* 35/1983.

61. Wikipedia, sv. *Plan 9 from Outer Space*.

62. There have been at least two other films depicting Finland as an alpine country. One is the American film *Ski Patrol* (Lew Landers, 1940), set at the time of the Winter War and Finland's struggle against the Soviet Union; the other is the Finnish film *Big Game* (Jalmari Helander, 2014), in which Air Force One is shot down while flying over Finnish territory and the US president is saved by a young Lappish boy. In terms of real-world geography, the highest point in Finland is the gently sloping Halti Fell (1324 m) near to the Norwegian border.

63. The Finnish Continuation War ended on 4 September 1944. In the peace treaty with the Soviet Union, Finland committed to expel German troops from its territory. The Germans regrouped in the north and this phase is known as the Lapland War. It ended as the last remaining German troops moved to Norway by the end of April 1945.

64. Jussi Karjalainen speculates on the possibility of Tulio having made *Sensuela* tongue-in-check ('!Sensuela', *TV-maailma* 24/2011: 29).

65. This is how the place is defined in the decision of the Finnish Film Board to withdraw its decision to impose an exorbitant punitive tax of 30 per cent once this scene was deleted. The scenes cut at this stage were restored in the DVD version.

66. Hänninen 2017. https://yle.fi/aihe/artikkeli/2017/04/26/sensuela-uskomattoman-camp-pornon-leikkaamaton-versio-ensi-kerran-tvssa.

NEWSPAPERS AND PERIODICALS

Aamulehti 1941, 1946, 1952.
Ajan Suunta 1938.
Elokuvateatteri 1944.
Helsingin Sanomat 1944, 1946.

Ilta-Sanomat 1949.
Kansan Lehti 1946.
Karjalan Suunta 1938.
Katso 1983.
Kauppalehti 1947.
Keskisuomalainen 1949.
Satakunnan Kansa 1938, 1953.
Savon Sanomat 1952.
Sosialisti 1944.
Suomen Sosialidemokraatti 1940, 1946, 1949.
Svenska Pressen 1938
Taiteen Maailma 1946.
Turun Päivälehti 1953.
TV-maailma 2011.
Työkansan Sanomat 1946, 1952, 1956.
Uusi Aura 1953.
Uusi Suomi 1944, 1946.

BIBLIOGRAPHY

Grodal, Torben (2009), *Embodied Visions – Evolution, Emotion, Culture, and Film*, New York: Oxford University Press.

Hänninen, Harto (2017), '*Sensuela* – uskomattoman camp-pornon leikkaamaton versio ensi kerran tv:ssä!', https://yle.fi/aihe/artikkeli/2017/04/26/sensuela-uskomattoman-camp-pornon-leikkaamaton-versio-ensi-kerran-tvssa (accessed 26 September 2019).

Koivunen, Anu and Kimmo Laine (1993), 'Metsästä pellon kautta kaupunkiin (ja takaisin) – Jätkyys suomalaisessa elokuvassa', in Pirjo Ahokas, Martti Lahti and Jukka Sihvonen (eds), *Mieheyden tiellä – Maskuliinisuus ja kulttuuri*, Jyväskylä: Jyväskylän yliopisto, 136–54.

Lehtisalo, Anneli (2019), 'Maitotyttö maailmalla – SF:n elokuvien ulkomaanlevitys', in Kimmo Laine et al. (eds), *Unelmatehdas Liisankadulla – Suomen Filmiteollisuus Oy:n tarina*, Helsinki: Suomalaisen Kirjallisuuden Seura, 254–69.

Lyytikäinen, Pirjo (1997), *Narkissos ja sfinksi – Minä ja Toinen vuosisadanvaihteen kirjallisuudessa*, Helsinki: Suomalaisen Kirjallisuuden Seura.

Maltby, Richard (1996), '"A Brief Romantic Interlude": Dick and Jean Go to 3 1/2 Seconds of the Classical Hollywood Cinema', in David Bordwell and Noël Carroll (eds), *Post Theory. Reconstructing Film Studies*, Wisconsin: University of Wisconsin Press, 434–59.

Soila, Tytti (1994), 'Five Songs of the Scarlet Flower', *Screen* 35:3, 265–74.

Toiviainen, Sakari (2002): *Tulio – Levottoman veren antologia*. Helsinki: Suomalaisen Kirjallisuuden Seura.

Töyri, Esko (1983), *Vanhat kameramiehet. Suomalaisen elokuvan kameramiehiä 1930–1950*, Helsinki: Suomen elokuvasäätiö.

Walker, Jesse (2013), 'The Legend of the Child-Snatching Gypsies. An old fear rears its head again', *Reason* 30 October 2013, https://reason.com/2013/10/30/the-legend-of-the-child-snatching/ (accessed 24 September 2019).

CHAPTER 6

Exploring a Style of Passion

Teuvo Tulio has been discussed as a studio-era auteur since the 1980s, when his films were being rediscovered. His fame peaked at the turn of the millennium, as his films became widely available. Tulio's passionate films, most of which were independent productions, are often experienced as more personal and idiosyncratic than those of his colleagues working on more conventional lines for the big studios Suomi-Filmi and Suomen Filmiteollisuus, Valentin Vaala and Hannu Leminen being good examples.[1] In the 1930s and 1940s, which were Tulio's heyday, critics discussed him as an inimitable filmmaker whose film style was exceedingly cinematic. 'One is always accustomed to expect something special from Teuvo Tulio. He is a man of audacious deeds who has walked his own path as an artist,' one reviewer argued.[2] In the 1950s he was either forgotten or scorned, as passionate melodramas relying on old genre conventions came to be seen as clunky and old-fashioned. Another strand of the contemporary auteur discussion concerns the stylistic and thematic coherence of Tulio's works. It has even been argued that his oeuvre is homogeneous to the extent that it is internationally unique.[3] Today Tulio is celebrated in Finland for both the idiosyncrasy and the coherence of his oeuvre. However, the quality of his films remains a matter of debate.

Remarkably, as celebrated as Tulio's style was and is, it remains largely unstudied; what we have at best are impressionistic observations, not a systematic examination. By providing a quantitative and contextualised analysis of shot lengths in Tulio's cinema, this chapter will enhance our understanding of his use of stylistic means. The analysis will reveal whether there are significant changes in Tulio's style and whether these amount to discernible trends over his career. The results will be compared to film historical data with the purpose of examining how Tulio's style relates to cinematic styles of the past and those of his contemporaries. What follows is not a comprehensive analysis of Tulio's film style, but one that provides insights into its nature and development.

In his autobiography, Tulio mentions that *The Fight over the Heikkilä Mansion*, the now-lost film that was his directorial debut, 'contained lots of short flashes instead of long scenes shot from one side'.[4] The film premiered in 1936; that is, in the early sound era of Finnish cinema, the transition to sound taking place in the early 1930s, a few years later than in Hollywood. Tulio's statement is probably accurate, as film reviewers celebrated *The Fight over the Heikkilä Mansion* as 'a film and not a mere tableau or collection of scenes'.[5] The implicit assumption here is that Finnish cinema of the mid-1930s was slow and theatrical. The mainstream of Finnish silent cinema of the 1920s is best discussed in terms of cinematic theatricality, which means a fusion of tableau aesthetics and Hollywood conventions.[6] In the late 1920s, Vaala as a director and Tulio as his actor, audacious young filmmakers as they were, created faster-paced films by borrowing more heavily from the classical Hollywood style than their colleagues did. Their efforts were celebrated as something new and cinematic. But as the sound era began, filmmakers were forced to use long takes and sequence shots – or 'scenes shot from one side', as Tulio put it – as sound had to be recorded live. This was the situation in other countries as well. Against this background it was possible to consider Tulio's use of 'short flashes' as cinematic, which set him apart from his competitors and reminded critics of the dynamics of the best silent films.

To understand better the trends in Finnish cinema and the uniqueness of Tulio's debut, we need to explore average shot lengths (ASL). ASL signifies the length of a film divided by the number of shots in it. The figure tends to correlate with the tempo of the storytelling: it indicates how often a filmmaker cuts and how long his shots last. In the late silent era, the most common ASL in Hollywood was 5 seconds,[7] which entailed quite fast editing. The figure increased to 10.8 seconds in the 1928–33 period, as Hollywood filmmakers turned to synchronised sound cinema. There was a notable slowing down. Little by little, the sound technology became more flexible in Hollywood, as a result of which the ASL decreased to 9 seconds in the 1934–9 period.[8] Nurtured by rapidly edited Hollywood cinema of the silent era,[9] Tulio followed its aesthetics and by using short takes differentiated *The Fight over the Heikkilä Mansion* from the mainstream of Finnish cinema. Tulio's connection to silent cinema was stronger than that of most Finnish filmmakers.

It is possible that the ASL of *The Fight over the Heikkilä Mansion* was faster than that of the typical Hollywood film of its day, because unlike his Hollywood colleagues (and most Finns, for that matter), Tulio shot many of his sequences silent. By doing so he was not as restricted by the inflexible sound technology as those on both sides of the Atlantic creating so-called 'full talkies'. The argument is best supported by an analysis of *The Song of the Scarlet Flower*, which is Tulio's oldest surviving film. It was released in 1938, only two years after *The Fight over the Heikkilä Mansion*, which had been followed by *Silja – Fallen Asleep When Young* and *Temptation* in 1937 and 1938 respectively. *The Song of the Scarlet Flower* contains numerous scenes that were shot without direct sound. During these the audience can hear music that was added to the soundtrack in post-production, but no dialogue or sound effects. Such sequences are common in all of Tulio's surviving films. While such scenes were common in most Finnish films of the early sound era, Tulio used them systematically throughout his career. In *You've Gone into My Blood* (*Olet mennyt minun vereeni*), which Tulio directed in 1956, the vast majority of scenes were shot silent. Tulio never fully embraced the possibilities of synchronised sound cinema, like his colleagues in Hollywood and Finland did, as he was unwilling to let go of silent cinema conventions. There were, of course, aesthetic reasons for this. Like all filmmakers of the era, Tulio had grown up watching silent films, but unlike most others, he was unwilling to adapt major stylistic influences from classical sound cinema or modernist cinemas that followed neorealism in the 1950s. One also needs to acknowledge the economic side of the matter. As Tulio produced *The Song of the Scarlet Flower*, he avoided the use of direct sound, as the technology was not only cumbersome to use but also expensive. Toward the end of his career, he worked with smaller and smaller budgets.

Tulio's first three films had been produced by Adams-Filmi, a small production company operating in the shadows of the big studios Suomi-Filmi and Suomen Filmiteollisuus. The main activity of the company was distribution. Considering that Adams-Filmi was a lesser production company and Tulio an inexperienced filmmaker, it is unlikely that the production budgets of the early works were significantly higher than that of *The Song of the Scarlet Flower*. Tulio remarks in his autobiography that the company granted him full artistic freedom.[10] It is thus reasonable to suppose that an analysis of *The Song of the Scarlet Flower*, which he produced as mentioned, can shed light on the style of the earlier films. Furthermore, it has been suggested that *The Song of the Scarlet Flower* belongs to the same film cycle as the three lost films.[11]

The central discrepancy in Tulio's film style is his reliance on both silent cinema aesthetics and those of synchronised sound film of the 1930s. This can be illustrated through an analysis of two sequences in *The Song of the Scarlet Flower*. As the opening credits roll, the protagonist, Olavi, is shown ploughing a field. In the first shot following the credit sequence, Annikki (Mirjami Kuosmanen), a young woman holding a milk churn, walks across the field towards Olavi. Noticing her, he stops ploughing. As Olavi and Annikki meet, they smile, as she offers him the milk churn, from which he drinks voraciously while she coyly admires his strong figure. Having slaked his thirst, Olavi drops the empty milk churn, lifts Annikki into his arms and they passionately gaze into each other's eyes. Olavi carries Annikki away, while a horse watches them go. This minute-long sequence is told without any dialogue or sound effects, but is accompanied by background music. Consisting of eleven shots, the ASL of the sequence is 5.6 seconds. *The Wide Road*, a silent film with synchronised music that Vaala and Tulio made in 1931, has exactly the same ASL.[12] Keeping in mind that the most common ASL in Hollywood in the late 1920s was 5 seconds, it is clear that these sequences shot without sound are akin to silent cinema. Some contemporary reviewers were aware of Tulio's dislike of the slow style of early sound-era films and his attempt to create films similar to those of the silent era in which images 'speak'.[13] In *The Song of the Scarlet Flower*, Tulio uses dialogue and sound effects when he has to, particularly in sequences in which characters have key discussions. The opening sequence analysed above is followed by a scene in which Olavi and Annikki hug each other while sitting in a field talking about their relationship. It is a good example of Tulio's use of direct sound. In a roundabout way, Olavi asks for sex, but Annikki refuses and runs away, soon turning round and playfully asking him to join her for a dance in the evening. This sequence, too, is approximately one minute long. But as it consists of only four shots, its ASL is 23 seconds. In other words, the direct sound sequence is four times as slow as the silent cinema sequence. Stylistically, it is not dynamic and compelling like the opening sequence. This demonstrates that Tulio did not only use 'short flashes', as he writes in his autobiography, but also long takes typical of the early sound era. With bigger budgets and better technology, he probably would have quickened the tempo of his dialogue scenes.

Tulio employed 'short flashes' in silent sequences, which are akin to the aesthetics of mature silent cinema, and long takes in sound sequences that could not be avoided, which are typical of the early sound era. Contemporary reviewers found Tulio's silent sequences particularly cinematic, as they differed from the mainstream of Finnish cinema in their dynamism and fast pace. This issue is explored in more detail below.

One anonymous reviewer praised *The Song of the Scarlet Flower*: 'Metaphoric images were often wonderfully composed, and naturally speed and excitement reach their peaks in Olavi's rapid-shootings.'[14] However, in the sound era the lack of dialogue and sound effects was a problem for many viewers, even if Tulio did not think about it as such. 'In many scenes one is harshly distracted by the missing sound recording. One cannot hear the roar of the rapids, the gypsies move as silently as mice and the child cries as in a silent film',[15] one reviewer wrote of *In the Fields of Dreams* (1940). Thus, as fast and dynamic as Tulio's films were, they were also old-fashioned due to their heavy reliance on the conventions of silent cinema. For this discrepancy, Tulio's film style was paradoxically both praised and scorned at the same time. Considering that the lack of sound was already a problem for some reviewers in 1940, we can easily imagine how old-fashioned Tulio's aesthetics must have felt to many spectators in the following decades. This partly explains why Tulio and his melodramas were forgotten in the 1950s.

CINEMATOGRAPHY IN FIGURES AND CHARTS

Statistical analysis that focuses on ASLs and supplements the figure with median shot lengths (MSL) and standard deviations in seconds (StDev) provides tools for analysing the stylistic development and coherence of Tulio's oeuvre.[16] This data, gathered with the Cinemetrics webtool, is presented in Table 6.1.

Clearly, Tulio is a consistent director when it comes to shot lengths – remarkably so considering his career spanned the mid-1930s to the mid-1970s. In these decades, the aesthetics of world cinema changed drastically, a point that is discussed in more detail below. The mean ASL of Tulio's cinema is 7.6 seconds. The data that accounts for twelve of Tulio's films can be illuminatingly divided into quantiles so as to bring into sharper focus an underlying pattern and possible outliers. The ASL of the first quantile (1938–40) is 8.6 seconds, the ASL of the second quantile (1944–6) is 7.3 seconds, the ASL of the third quantile (1946–9) is 7.8 seconds and the ASL of the fourth quantile (1953–1973) is 6.7 seconds. The figures reveal an overall trend: the editing tempo of Tulio's films increased towards the end of his career, but not considerably.

Looking at the ASL of the first quantile, *Jiggs and Maggie* (1939), the ASL of which is 10.3 seconds, is the outlier. This was the only comedy Tulio directed. There are no deviant cases in the second quantile, but the third quantile contains one: the ASL of *A Crooked Woman* (1952), the story of an innocent woman imprisoned, is 8.9 seconds. The final outlier in Tulio's cinema can be found in the fourth quantile: *You've Gone into My Blood*, which tells the story of a woman's descent into alcoholism. These films are the three notable peaks in the ASL data in Table 6.1. Even though *Sensuela* is the fastest film Tulio directed, its ASL is in line with the trend outlined. In terms of shot lengths, the film is not unique in the analysed corpus.

The three identified outliers differ thematically from the rest of Tulio's oeuvre, as they are not melodramas of passion and action. Table 6.2, which is based on the thematic analysis of Tulio's films conducted in chapter 5, indicates that there are fewer archetypal characters in *Jiggs and Maggie*, *A Crooked Woman* and *You've Gone into My Blood* than in Tulio's other films, *In the Grip of Passion* being the notable exception. In his cinema, the archetypes represent universal patterns of human nature. There are no gentle, encouraging fathers in his films (*Jiggs and Maggie* is a farce, and so the father is just plain clownish). As a rule, the fathers are stern. In Tulio's films, female characters often conspicuously lack mothers and many of them are orphans. Discounting *Jiggs and Maggie*, the only real exception to this female motherlessness is *You've*

Table 6.1 Cutting rates in seconds in Teuvo Tulio's films.

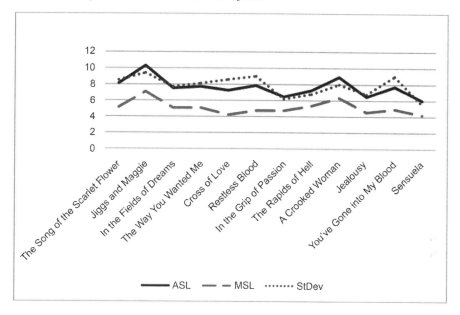

Table 6.2 Archetypal characters in the films of Teuvo Tulio.

	The Song of the Scarlet Flower	Jiggs and Maggie	In the Fields of Dreams	The Way You Wanted Me	Cross of Love	Restless Blood	In the Grip of Passion	Rapids of Hell	A Crooked Woman	Jealousy	You've Gone into My Blood	Sensuela
Stern father	X			X	X							X
Stern mother, granny or aunt	X	X		X		X		X		X		
Female protagonist's mother absent	X		X	X	X	X	X	X	X	X		X
Weak female leading character	X		X	X	X	X		X	X	X	X	X
Strong female leading character	X	X	X			X	X			X		
Reckless young man destroys women's lives	X		X	X	X							X

Gone into My Blood, in which the female character does have a caring, only fairly gently moralising mother – yet she has only a very minor role in the film. Grandmothers and aunts are stern in Tulio's films, much like the fathers. In the latter half of *In the Grip of Passion*, the leading female character has a similar function as these grandmothers and aunts, as she whips her husband as if he were an unruly boy. In Tulio's films after *The Song of the Scarlet Flower*, female characters tend to be protagonists, but there is a strong polarisation between weak and strong leading leading characters. Weak females are as a rule exploited and then dumped by men.

Possibly because of the influence of Regina Linnanheimo as a fellow screenwriter and actress, in the latter half of Tulio's oeuvre, female leading characters tend to be strong enough to fend for themselves. As Table 6.2 indicates, there are two archetypal characters in both *Jiggs and Maggie* and *A Crooked Woman*, but only one in *You've Gone into My Blood*. These are the three films in Tulio's oeuvre in which the ASLs are unusually high. The comparison of the number of archetypal characters in Tulio's films to that of their average shot lengths supports the argument that the filmmaker tended to employ a different editing tempo when he worked on new topics.

When it comes to Tulio's nine melodramas of passion and action, their ASLs sit comfortably between 6 and 8 seconds, if we are willing to overlook the fact that the ASL of *The Song of the Scarlet Flower*, the oldest film in the group, is 8.1 seconds. Discounting the slight back-and-forth movement over the years, the ASLs of Tulio's melodramas decreased from 8 seconds to 6 seconds toward the end of his career, as Table 6.3 illustrates. If one ignores the three outliers, what remains is a steady decrease. Considering that this is a very slight acceleration of editing tempo in terms of ASLs over a thirty-year period, it is fair to say that Tulio is a consistent filmmaker in terms of shot lengths. The ASLs of the lost early films were probably in the range of 8 to 9 seconds, but this is merely an enlightened guess based on the analysis presented. To sum up, the figures in Table 6.1 support impressionistic arguments about the stylistic coherence of Tulio's oeuvre.

As outliers can easily skew the ASL, the figure needs to be compensated with the MSL, which can be defined as the typical shot length. In every film Tulio directed, the MSL is notably lower than the ASL. This indicates that deviant cases significantly distort the latter. At its lowest in Tulio's cinema, the difference between MSL and ASL is 1.7 seconds. The film in question is *In the Grip of Passion*. At its highest, in *The Song of the Scarlet Flower*, the difference is 3.2 seconds. On average, in Tulio's cinema the MSL is 2.5 seconds less than the ASL. There are no notable outliers distorting this figure, as one can see from Table 6.1: the development of the MSL largely parallels that of the ASL, but the quickening pace of the editing rhythm is less noticeable. The mean MSL in Tulio's cinema is 5 seconds. Because of the central discrepancy between silent cinema aesthetics and early sound cinema aesthetics, discussed

Table 6.3 Decreasing average shot lengths in seconds in Teuvo Tulio's films.

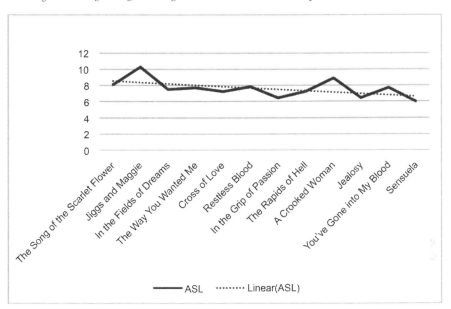

above, the mean ASL is skewed. It is thus best to think about the MSL as the typical shot length in his cinema. Considering that the increasing pace of the MSL is less noticeable than that of the ASL, Tulio can be considered as an even more stylistically consistent director in the light of the latter. It is worth keeping in mind that 5 seconds was the most common shot length in Hollywood in the 1920s, which is a further indication of the strong influence silent cinema had on the cinema of Tulio.

In every film Tulio directed, the StDev is higher than the MSL, on average by 2.7 seconds. This indicates there is stylistic variety in each film he directed. When the StDev is compared to the ASL, results get more complicated. The development of the StDev parallels that of the ASL, but there are times when it is either higher or lower than the latter, as one can see from Table 6.1. On average, the StDev is 0.3 seconds higher than the ASL. Tulio's typical shot length may be 5 seconds, but each film he directed contains a notable amount of significantly longer shots as well as a number of shorter shots. To sum up, Tulio is a stylistically consistent filmmaker in terms of his shot lengths, but there is a lot of variety in each film he directed, as he moves between quicker and slower edited sequences. This supports the argument made above about the stylistic discrepancy between silent and sound sequences in his films. On the whole, fast edited sequences outnumber those in which the pace is slower, as indicated by the MSL, which, as already mentioned, is 5 seconds.

When it comes to the identified outliers, two of them were directed in the 1950s; that is, at a time when Tulio's fortunes had already declined. Table 6.1 clearly shows that Tulio's film style was less consistent in his late career. In terms of shot lengths, *A Crooked Woman* and *You've Gone into My Blood* were Tulio's attempts to reinvent himself by trying out new approaches, whereas *Jealousy* (1953) and *Sensuela* were returns to his standard style of editing. As much as he tried to both reinvent himself and please his old audiences, his late attempts did not bear fruit. In the context of sophisticated studio films of the 1950s and modernist art films such as those directed by Ingmar Bergman, Tulio's silent cinema-inspired film style which had won him praise in the 1930s and 1940s failed to please critics and audiences.

The Cinemetrics database does not contain data that would enable us properly to compare Tulio's films to the mainstream of Finnish cinema. Such a comparison would indicate whether Tulio's films were idiosyncratic in the Finnish context in a metrical sense. The question is important due to the many arguments about the uniqueness of Tulio's passionate film style. To circumvent the issue, Table 6.4 presents data on the ASL in Tulio's films and those of some of his Finnish competitors. In Table 6.4, each surviving film Tulio made is paired with a thematically similar film directed approximately at the same time by some other filmmaker operating in Finland. These comparisons give an approximate idea about the metrical idiosyncrasy of Tulio's cinema in comparison to that of other filmmakers working in Finland on similar topics.

In the light of the figures in Table 6.4, Tulio's films are fast edited in comparison to thematically similar Finnish films of the same era. On the basis of this sample, Tulio's ASLs are on average 4 seconds shorter than those of his Finnish colleagues. This is a notable difference. In some cases, Tulio's editing rhythm is more than twice as fast as that of his colleagues. This further suggests that contemporary film reviewers who recognised Tulio's films as cinematic, appreciated their fast tempo. On the basis of the data in Table 6.4, Vaala was the only Finnish filmmaker whose melodramas were faster than those of Tulio. The reason for this is that of all the filmmakers working in Finland, Vaala best mastered the classical Hollywood style.[17] Editing in his rural melodramas *The Women of Niskavuori* (*Niskavuoren naiset*, 1938) and *God's Storm* (*Jumalan myrsky*, 1940) is on average 0.7 seconds faster than in Tulio's *The Song of the Scarlet Flower* and *In the Fields of Dreams*, to which they may well be compared. Not too much should be made of this difference, however. If we focus on the medians presented in Table 6.4, we see that the editing in *The Song of the Scarlet Flower* is 0.8 seconds faster than that in *The Women of Niskavuori*. The MSL of *In the Fields of Dreams* is 5 seconds, which is the same as that of *God's Storm*. On the basis of these figures, it could be argued that Tulio's films were very slightly faster than those of Vaala. Both ASLs and MSLs considered, it is evident that both Tulio and Vaala made fast-edited films. Tulio's ASLs were

Table 6.4 *A comparison of Tulio's cutting rates in seconds with those of his Finnish colleagues.*

Film	Director	Year	ASL	MSL	StDev
Song of the Scarlet Flower	Tulio	1938	8.1	5.1	8.5
The Women of Niskavuori	Vaala	1938	7.4	5.9	6.0
Jiggs and Maggie	Tulio	1939	10.3	7.1	9.4
Two Henpecked Husbands	Tapiovaara	1939	17.3	9.8	18.5
In the Fields of Dreams	Tulio	1940	7.5	5.0	7.7
God's Storm	Vaala	1940	6.9	5.0	5.8
The Way You Wanted Me	Tulio	1944	7.7	5.0	8.1
Anja, Come Back Home	Särkkä	1944	11.4	8.2	9.6
Cross of Love	Tulio	1946	7.2	4.3	8.6
Decoy	Hällström	1946	9.2	6.7	8.6
Restless Blood	Tulio	1946	7.8	4.7	9.0
The Tracks of Sin	Leminen	1946	10.9	7.6	9.9
In the Grip of Passion	Tulio	1947	6.4	4.7	6.2
Sixth Commandment	Saarikivi	1947	12.8	8.7	11.9
The Rapids of Hell	Tulio	1949	7.2	5.3	6.8
Leeni of Haavisto	Salminen	1948	13.6	6.8	19.2
A Crooked Woman	Tulio	1952	8.9	6.3	8.0
Eyes in the Dark	Itkonen	1952	8.9	6.3	8.1
Jealousy	Tulio	1953	6.4	4.5	6.8
Hilja – the Milk Maid	Särkkä	1953	9.8	7.6	8.1
You've Gone into My Blood	Tulio	1956	7.7	4.9	9.0
Harvest Month	Kassila	1956	19.1	11.1	24.0
Sensuela	Tulio	1973	6.0	4.2	5.0
I Want to Love, Peter	Kassila	1972	12.6	8.6	3.2

cut down by his dialogue scenes, which were often 'shot from one side', to once again quote the filmmaker, but those of Vaala were not. Vaala, being inclined toward the classical Hollywood style, systematically favoured the shot-reverse shot technique in conversation scenes instead of two-shots.[18] Tulio's conversation scenes were often filmed in long and immobile takes. Thus, the StDev is on average 2.2 seconds higher in his cinema than in that of Vaala. This indicates that the editing is more even in Vaala's films, as he was able to shoot all scenes in his chosen style. This is where his situation was different from that of Tulio. Vaala worked for Suomi-Filmi, which granted him bigger budgets and better technology than Tulio could afford in small production companies and as an independent producer of his own films. Clunky sound technology, and small budgets that did not permit Tulio to overcome the obstacles the technology caused, slowed down the tempo of his films.

Researchers have collected much ASL data on English-language films, which enables us to make strong arguments about the evolution of cinema in the countries from which the films originate. In English-language films, the mean ASL has been in decline since the 1930s, as filmmakers have been 'shortening their mean durations by the equivalent of about three frames (about 125 milliseconds) per shot per year.[19] Here it is worth keeping in mind that Tulio's ASLs declined as well. In English-language films, the ASL was about 10 seconds in 1940 and about 6 seconds in 1970. This development parallels that in Tulio's cinema, if one focuses on his highest and lowest ASLs, which are 10.3 seconds and 6 seconds: the difference is 4.3 seconds. But when it comes to Tulio's melodramas of passion, the development was not as fast as in English-language films, as the difference is only 2.1 seconds. In the melodramas of passion, the pace of Tulio's editing dropped from 8.1 seconds to 6 seconds in the period under scrutiny. The point here is that in comparison to English-language films, Tulio's editing was exceptionally fast in the late 1930s, but typical in the early 1970s. By the 1970s, the clunkiness of the early sound technology[20] was a thing of the past, but Tulio could not afford properly to exploit the new technology. He claimed that *Sensuela* had been dubbed into Finnish from an English-language version, but it is obvious that the film was shot silent.

When it comes to world cinema, there is not enough data to make concrete comparisons. Focusing on the years when Tulio released a new film, the mean ASL of world cinema seems to have been about 11 seconds at its highest and 8 seconds at its lowest, based on the data collected from the Cinemetrics database and Barry Salt's average shot length table.[21] The figures need to be taken with a grain of salt. They are approximate, as the yearly samplings are too small to make reliable analyses: the smallest yearly sampling consists of sixty-nine films (1946) and the largest of 139 films (1953), the mean being a hundred films. In comparison to the total number of films produced annually in the world, these figures are tiny. The data also mostly consists of European and American films. The approximate figures nonetheless imply that Tulio's films were fast edited also in comparison to the world cinema with which he had to compete in European film markets. On the basis of this sample, the mean ASL is 3.6 seconds slower in Tulio's cinema than in world cinema. The mean MSL, on the other hand, is 3 seconds slower in Tulio's cinema than in world cinema. These figures further indicate that Tulio directed films in which the pace of editing was fast in comparison to most other films.

THE IMPOSSIBLE CINEMATIC SPACE

Backed by strong empiricism, the above analysis indicates that Tulio relied on fast editing, but sheds little light on how he used 'short flashes', as he termed them. To get a better grasp of the matter, his films must be analysed qualitatively. Here it is again useful to compare Tulio's film style to the classical Hollywood style, which had evolved in the United States in the 1910s, from where it spread to other countries and became the international mainstream style. In the classical style, shot dissections are made following the rules of continuity editing, which 'relies on matching screen direction, position, and temporal relations from shot to shot'.[22] Such editing maintains continuous narrative action that is easy for viewers to follow. In studio-era Finland, the classical style was best mastered by Vaala, who admired the smooth narrative flow in Hollywood films and adapted it to his own filmmaking.

A good example of such continuity editing is found in Vaala's film *God's Storm*. The film contains a scene in which a child is rescued from a fast-flowing stream. The scene begins abruptly, interrupting a conversation a young woman is having with her parents in their yard. The camera shows them talking in a full shot when they hear a cry. The following shot is an extreme long shot. In it a small boy carried by the stream shouts for help. The audience sees two buildings and boats on the other side of the stream. The shot is an establishing shot, as it shows all the significant areas of the space from which the film can cut to closer views of the space. Such analytical editing ensures that the audience knows where everything is located in the scene's space. Now the film cuts to a closer view of the boy in peril, making the sequence more exciting, as his expressions of terror are likely to elicit an empathetic reaction in the audience. In the following extreme long shot, the three characters whose conversation was interrupted appear from behind their home, running toward the camera. From the placement of the shot, the audience knows they are now running to the shore to help the child. The next shot is an extreme long shot showing the stream and one of the buildings on the other side of it. A man runs out and takes one of the boats without hesitation. It should be obvious to the audience he has heard the cries for help as well. With these shots the film establishes a scene in which the boy in jeopardy is being carried by the powerful stream, which is located between the three characters on the shore and the man taking the boat on the other side. The man jumps from his boat into the water, catching the boy. The young woman, on the shore with her parents, throws him a rope, which the man uses to get the boy and himself out of the water. The fast-edited scene is fairly complex, as it consists of forty shots representing five characters and their movements in several locations. But as *God's Storm* follows the rules of continuity editing, it is easy for the audience to follow and grasp.

Continuity editing was the standard practice followed by most mainstream filmmakers, some of whom mastered it better than others. Tulio's editing, however, differs from it in notable ways. This can be demonstrated by contrasting the scene analysed above with a similar scene in *In the Fields of Dreams*. In a full shot, the camera shows the audience a young woman looking after her baby resting in a hammock. The woman lifts her gaze from the child and looks past the camera. Her expression is both surprised and worried (figure 6.1). What follows is a series of high-angle shots of a lamb stranded on a small ledge above a powerful stream (figure 6.2). The two locations are presumably close to each other, but the logic by which the two shots are connected is unclear. Here the scene violates the rules of continuity editing. As there is no diegetic sound, the audience does not hear the lamb crying. One might assume that the woman hears the lamb crying, but this appears implausible as the rapids must be some distance away, the lamb is caught quite low in the gorge and its bleat could surely not be heard over the roar of the stream. The shot of the lamb cannot be a point-of-view shot either, as the woman is in the hammock and the lamb is down the cliff, allowing no direct eyeline. The sequence suggests that the woman reacts to the despair of the lamb, but it does not indicate how this actually happens and how the two spaces are physically located to each other.

This sequence is a fine example of what can be termed the impossible cinematic space; it is a cinematic device Tulio regularly uses. It is clear that the woman notices the lamb, even though it would be impossible for her to do so by any real-world standards. Now, ostensibly following the logic of analytical editing, the film cuts to a closer view of the lamb. This shot is reminiscent of the close view of the boy in peril in *God's Storm*. The two following shots represent other sheep, as they appear to get worried about the missing lamb. Tulio cross-cuts between the lamb and other sheep as they hurry toward the cliff. In a full shot, the young woman runs toward the camera from the hammock. The shot is reminiscent of that in *God's Storm* in which the three characters run toward the camera, indicating that there are notable similarities in the two sequences under analysis. As the woman reaches the edge, she then climbs down, trying to reach the lamb, after which the sheep gather to watch her. In a series of melodramatic shots, she hangs and climbs on the rock. All the time it is unclear

Figures 6.1–2

how the woman, the sheep and the lamb are spatially related, as the film has not provided the audience with an establishing shot or logical shot connections. This is where Tulio's editing style differs from that of Vaala. The woman, the sheep and the lamb are all near one another, that much is understood, but there is no way of saying just how much space there is between the three parties. It does not help that the route taken by the climbing woman is long and dangerous and does not seem to relate to the spot where the lamb is. To complicate matters, all of a sudden there is an extreme long shot of a group of vagabonds on a road. Nothing in the shot indicates how close they are to the events taking place by the rapid. The next shot is a full shot of the hammock as a vagabond walks toward the baby. Presumably they noticed the hammock from the road, after which one of them decided to see what was in it, but Tulio does not use conventions of continuity editing to connect the shots. The vagabond steals the baby in revenge because its father, as a flashback informs the audience, has stopped him from stealing eggs. After rescuing the lamb from danger (at a spot which looks quite different from where it appeared first), the woman sees the empty hammock and presumes that the baby has walked into the stream and vanished. This makes little sense, as the child is not old enough to walk.

The important point here is that Tulio did not fail to follow the rules of continuity editing, which by the turn of the 1940s had been absorbed by mainstream filmmakers. He simply was not as interested in the smooth flow of narrative as the vivid sensation and melodramatic power of shots. To put it differently, Tulio's main aim was to evoke strong emotions in the audience by using powerful images. This is precisely what he does in the sequence analysed above. He provides many shots of the young woman climbing down and hanging from the cliff, even though these violate the spatial logic of the sequence. Here the beauty in peril is the key attraction, in relation to which her spatial relation to the lamb is much less important (figures 6.3–7). This is one indication of how Tulio's melodrama of passion harkens back to the blood-and-thunder sensational

Figures 6.3–7

melodrama of the 1910s, which emphasised 'action, violence, thrills, awesome sights, and spectacles of physical peril'.[23] As Tulio's focus is on separate images and compositions instead of continuity, his cinema has a pictorialist quality.[24] For him, it is enough that a narrative sequence is more or less understandable, as long as it is emotionally evocative. This, too, connects his cinema to the sensational melodramas of the 1910s. In those years 'popular melodrama was not in the business of narrative elegance and continuity, but rather the business of graphic thrills'.[25] More often than not, Tulio achieves a loose continuity that is just about understandable. It is important to keep in mind that Tulio grew up watching silent melodramas, which 'tolerated a high degree of narrative intricacy and discontinuity'.[26] At times his scenes are difficult to follow, however. For example, in the sequence analysed above, as the young woman realises that her baby is gone, she is portrayed in a full shot next to the hammock. From here the film cuts to a medium close-up in which the camera pans and tilts from her shocked face to the empty hammock and from there to the baby's cap, which is on the ground. The item was placed there specifically for this shot, as it was not on the ground in the earlier full shot. The woman picks up the cap and runs to look at the stream, illogically thinking that her baby has fallen in. In an extreme long shot, she leaves the cap on the cliff. This detail goes easily unnoticed, as the film does not offer a close view of the action. After the woman has left, the film cuts to a closer view of the cap, but even in this shot the item can go unnoticed, as it is merely a tiny white spot on the ground next to the stream, the movement of which demands attention. Instead of ensuring that the audience knows how the cap got onto the rock, Tulio relies on his approximate editing style and simply hopes for the best. When another character finds the cap, it becomes a salient plot device, but the audience is likely to wonder how it got there in the first place. Such moments of confusion are rare in the films of Vaala.

One editing convention that Tulio uses repeatedly is the impossible eyeline match. It can be understood as a sub-category of the impossible cinematic space, discussed above. In the classical Hollywood style, the eyeline match is a device by which filmmakers achieve seamless continuity. It is a 'cut obeying the axis of action principle, in which the first shot shows a person looking off in one direction and the second shows a nearby space containing what he or she sees'.[27] The impossible eyeline match violates the logic of this convention. A good example of such editing is found in *The Rapids of Hell* (1949). In one sequence the heroine uses a rope bridge as she crosses the dangerous rapid of the title. As she moves from right to left in a high-angle extreme long shot, she sees something in the off-screen space and happily waves her hand. The shot of her looking is followed by another shot that provides an impossible eyeline match: it is a waist-level extreme long shot in which a man working in a field waves back at her as he moves from right to left (figures 6.8–9). Together, the cut and the performances indicate that the characters see one another, even though the eyelines and screen directions do not match at all. Even common logic has it that a character down on a bridge cannot see a man working high on a flat field. Besides, the audience has been shown trees growing on both sides of the rapid, which leads us to ask where the field is located. In practice, Tulio connects two spaces that cannot be located next to one another with an impossible eyeline match. Such shot connections are common in surrealist avant-garde films but rare in melodramas made in the studio era. The impossible eyeline match is yet another indication of Tulio's approximate editing style. Even lesser mainstream filmmakers were

Figures 6.8–9

able to make eyelines at least roughly match, but Tulio does not even seem to be trying.

Narrative sequences that were more or less understandable were good enough for Tulio, but not everyone in the audience agreed. One reader commenting on a review of *The Rapids of Hell* argued that the film 'is a parody that is meant to amuse the audience with its illogicalities, impossibilities and naivety'.[28] Similarly, *Jealousy* (1953) was accused of containing 'by and large all the same mistakes that were present in the first attempts that were made twenty years ago'.[29] 'Editing leaves a lot to be desired',[30] it was stressed. At the turn of the 1950s, such comments were more common than they had been when Tulio began his directorial career. As the years passed, audiences began to demand greater stylistic sophistication. Not only was Tulio's editing awry, his shots were uneven, as shots were often out of focus, which was unacceptable by the 1950s. Times changed, but he kept relying on means that harkened back to the silent era. Tulio's film style was largely driven by financial matters, but one can also suppose that he made the kinds of melodramas that pleased his aesthetic taste. Indeed, there is something fascinating about Tulio's disregard of the classical rules of constructing cinematic space and the consequent impossible spatial relationships. This gives certain sequences in his films an almost hallucinatory quality, which is in perfect accord with his style of excessively melodramatic, even surreal plot development.

NOTES

1. Toiviainen 1992: 234–5; Varjola 2002: 184.
2. S. S.: 'Sellaisena kuin sinä minut halusit', *Uusi Suomi* 16.10.1944.
3. Varjola 2002: 184.
4. Tulio 2002: 33.
5. A. P.: 'Taistelu Heikkilän talosta', *Suomen Sosialidemokraatti* 3.11.1936.
6. Seppälä 2016: 59, 61, 70.

7. Salt 1992: 174.
8. Ibid.: 214.
9. Seppälä 2012: 354–60.
10. Tulio 2002: 24.
11. Toiviainen 1992: 234.
12. Seppälä 2016: 65.
13. S. S.: 'Sellaisena kuin sinä minut halusit', *Uusi Suomi* 16.10.1944.
14. S.: 'Laulu tulipunaisesta kukasta', *Helsingin Sanomat* 5.12.1938.
15. Anon.: 'Unelma karjamajalla', *Satakunnan Kansa* 24.9.1940.
16. Whereas ASL stands for the mean shot length of the film, MSL is the length for which half the shots in the film have longer lengths and the other half have shorter lengths. The median gives us the likely shot length, as it does not let deviant cases distort the data. StDev measures the extent of the spread of the data about the mean value. It can be used to tell whether the editing is even or not. The higher the number is, the more uneven the editing is and vice versa.
17. Laine 2016: 108–10.
18. Ibid.: 108–9.
19. Cutting and Candan 2015: 45.
20. Thompson and Bordwell 2010, 179–84.
21. Cinemetrics database: http://www.cinemetrics.lv/database.php (accessed on 5 July 2018). Barry Salt's database: camera movement, shot scale, average shot length database on Cinemetrics portal: http://www.cinemetrics.lv/saltdb.php (accessed on 5 July 2018). Only data collected by experienced Cinemetrics users was used. Notable mistakes were removed from Barry Salt's average shot length table.
22. Bordwell, Thompson and Smith 2017: G-1.
23. Singer 2001: 48.
24. Laine 2016: 110.
25. Singer 2001: 210.
26. Ibid.: 209.
27. Bordwell, Thompson and Smith 2017: G-2.
28. Jouko Hytönen: 'Arv. T. A.', *Suomen Sosiaalidemokraatti* 13.3.1949.
29. Camera: 'Elokuvakatsaus', *Satakunnan Kansa* 19.8.1953.
30. Ibid.

NEWSPAPERS AND PERIODICALS

Helsingin Sanomat 1938.
Satakunnan Kansa 1940, 1953.
Suomen Sosialidemokraatti 1936, 1949.
Uusi Suomi 1944.

FILM DATABASES

Cinemetrics database: http://www.cinemetrics.lv/database.php.
Barry Salt's database: camera movement, shot scale, average shot length database on Cinemetrics melodramatic plot development.

BIBLIOGRAPHY

Bordwell, David, Kristin Thompson and Jeff Smith (2017), *Film Art: An Introduction*, New York: McGraw-Hill Education.

Cutting, James and Ayse Candan (2015), 'Shot Durations, Shot Classes, and the Increased Pace of Popular Movies', *Projections: The Journal for Movies and Mind* 9:2, 41–62.

Laine, Kimmo (2016), 'Conceptions of National Film Style During the Studio Era', in Henry Bacon (ed.), *Finnish Cinema. A Transnational Enterprise*, London: Palgrave Macmillan, 87–114.

Salt, Barry (1992), *Film Style & Technology, History & Analysis*, London: Starword.

Seppälä, Jaakko (2012), *Hollywood tulee Suomeen: Yhdysvaltalaisten elokuvien maahantuonti ja vastaanotto kaksikymmentäluvun Suomessa*, Helsinki: Unigrafia.

Seppälä, Jaakko (2016), 'Finnish Film Style in the Silent Era', in Henry Bacon (ed.), *Finnish Cinema: A Transnational Enterprise*, London: Palgrave Macmillan, 51–80.

Singer, Ben (2001), *Melodrama and Modernity: Early Sensational Cinema in Its Context*, New York: Columbia University Press.

Thompson, Kristin and David Bordwell (2010), *Film History: An Introduction*, Boston: McGraw-Hill.

Toiviainen, Sakari (1992), *Suurinta elämässä: Elokuvamelodraaman kulta-aika*, Helsinki: VAPK-kustannus.

Tulio, Teuvo (2002), 'Elämäni ja elokuvani', in Sakari Toiviainen (ed.), *Tulio: Levottoman veren antologia*, Helsinki: Suomalaisen Kirjallisuuden Seura, 23–157.

Varjola, Markku (2002), 'Tulion näkemys ja merkitys', in Sakari Toiviainen (ed.), *Tulio: Levottoman veren antologia*, Helsinki: Suomalaisen Kirjallisuuden Seura, 183–99.

CHAPTER 7

Art of Repetition

'Here I am, just the way you wanted me', the prostitute named Gazelle remarks with a hefty dose of cynicism in her voice to the man who once loved and then abandoned her. The film in question is *The Song of the Scarlet Flower*, which Teuvo Tulio directed in 1938. The film is based on a novel of the same name by Johannes Linnankoski, but the quoted line does not appear in the book. Six years later, a film titled *The Way You Wanted Me* (1944) premiered. It, too, tells the story of an innocent woman who succumbs to prostitution. She is Maija, a young woman grown up in a small island community. Her lover abandons her after she becomes pregnant, which leads her to look for customers in a port tavern. One night in the tavern she meets her former lover and with bitter irony repeats Gazelle's line from the earlier film, which now also serves as the title of this film. Tulio used the phrase once more in his last film, *Sensuela*, which premiered in 1973. Over thirty years had passed, but *Sensuela* tells the same old story: a young and innocent woman, this time from the Sami community, falls in love, is abandoned and has to prostitute herself to make ends meet. Encountering her former lover in the Reeperbahn district in Hamburg, she too says to him contemptuously, 'Here I am, just the way you wanted me.' Throughout his career Tulio depicted men who fall in love with virgins and, without thinking about the consequences of their desire-driven romancing, turn them into prostitutes. The repeated line is a key topos in Tulio's oeuvre; it is a feminist admonition aimed at eliciting self-disgust in the men.

Repetition was a fundamental component of Tulio's authorship. A degree of repetition is 'a common and multiform phenomenon in cinema and in art in general'.[1] In classical cinema, 'the principle of repetition and regulated difference [. . .] is the basis of narrative progression and expansion'.[2] It serves that purpose in Tulio's cinema as well, but as the above example indicates, one rather unique aspect of his art is repetition in an excessive and conspicuous form. Tulio's repetitions are difficult not to notice, and they have received a lot of critical attention. But the extent to which repetition characterises Tulio's oeuvre and the various ways in which he uses it have not been systematically analysed. This chapter explores how repetition in its many modifications contributes to Tulio's film style, making it not only recognisable but also aesthetically rewarding.

In previous studies, Tulio's films have been analysed mostly in terms of genre and auteur theory. In both paradigms, the idea of repetition is essential. 'Most aesthetic theories of genre take as their starting points the issues of repetition and variation, similarity and difference, and the extent to which the elements repeated and varied are simple or complex.'[3] Throughout his career, *Jiggs and Maggie* (1939) being the only exception, Tulio was first and foremost a genre filmmaker directing melodramas that contain sensational elements. He was drawn to topics related to the suffering of women because of their own sexuality and male abuse, which is a long-standing topic in fiction. As Richard Dyer has put it, 'everything in the end is a copy of something else and we know it and we can never get out of it'.[4] This is particularly so when it comes to Tulio's films. Relying on themes and conventions of old forms of melodrama, such as silent films and stage shows of different kinds (discussed in chapter 2), Tulio's films depict the guilt and punishment that result from falling from grace in a world of strict morality laws and social roles.[5] The repeated pattern obviously connects Tulio's films to Christianity, the pathos of which has influenced the development of melodrama in various ways.[6] 'In the centre of Christian misogyny is the idea of the female body as the locus of original sin',[7] and the same can be said of Tulio's films. But Tulio was not a religious filmmaker by any means, even though he is rumoured to have been an ardent Catholic;[8] he merely used devices that can be easily associated with religion, but without aiming for religious awakening. 'One may well ask, whether there are any new kinds of conflicts between people,' Tulio remarks in his autobiography. 'They are all in the Bible.'[9] He seems to have believed that the Bible reflects universal human nature.

As contemporary film reviews indicate, by the turn of the 1950s Finnish audiences often found Tulio's generic influences old-fashioned. The problem was that Tulio had a monolithic understanding of melodrama, even though it is only by adapting to new historical circumstances that a genre can survive.[10] 'Melodrama's continual process of renewal is based in part on its propensity to transmute, adapting to wider cultural changes, technological innovations, and aesthetic ends.'[11] Tulio's melodramas changed remarkably little, even though his film career spanned over thirty years. The filmmaker was so closely attached to archetypical situations of various old forms of melodrama and so disinterested in social changes, that he eventually lost his audience. In the 1950s he explored female imprisonment in *A Crooked Woman* (1952) and alcoholism in *You've Gone into My Blood* (1958), but even these are heavily connected to old melodrama aesthetics. There were new kinds of conflicts between people that Tulio appears to have been unaware of. Art-house films were on the rise, many of them challenging conventional social notions as well as revising old forms of melodrama. By the time Tulio completed his final film, *Sensuela*, in 1973, Rainer Werner Fassbinder had made Douglas Sirk-inspired modernist melodramas such as *The Merchant of Four Seasons* (*Händler der vier Jahreszeiten*, 1971) and *Fear Eats the Soul* (*Angst essen Seele auf*, 1973) that depict troubled human relations in uncaring West Germany. As Anton Kaes argues, these melodramas thematise the failure of these 'uncompromising ideals [of the mid-1960s] and the final shattering of illusions'.[12] In comparison, Tulio was badly out of sync with his time. As Linda Williams has put it, 'in modernity, nothing dates like yesterday's melodrama'.[13]

Tulio's repetitions have also been discussed in terms of auteur studies. To identify an auteur, the critic must identify consistent stylistic traits across his or her films. Tulio's radical repetitions perfectly fit the criteria. 'Auteurism does not just observe or welcome continuity from film to film; it insists on continuity.'[14] Martti-Tapio Kuuskoski argues that Tulio repeats with variations and thus 'repetition is never repetition of the same'.[15] While there is some truth in this claim, on the whole Tulio's repetitions are more eye-catching and obvious than his variations. Kuuskoski's argument brings to mind adaptation studies. 'Adaptation is repetition, but repetition without replication.'[16] It is productive to keep in mind the many attitudes adaptation can take: 'version, variation, interpretation, continuation, transformation, imitation, pastiche, parody, forgery, travesty, transposition, revaluation, revision, rewriting, echo'.[17] Illustrating this, Antti Alanen has insightfully pointed out how many of Johannes Linnankoski's themes, especially the struggle between ethics and eroticism, are present not only in Tulio's actual Linnankoski adaptations, but in his oeuvre as a whole.[18] Tulio even adapted his own films, as *Sensuela* is a remake of *Cross of Love* (1946), which Tulio advertised as being based on Alexander Pushkin's short story *The Stationmaster* (1831), even though it is obvious that it was the German adaptation *The Postmaster* (*Der Postmeister*, 1940) that provided the immediate narrative and stylistic inspiration. Similarly, *In the Grip of Passion* (1947) is a remake of Tulio's now lost film *The Fight over the Heikkilä Mansion* (1936). To get a better understanding of Tulio's repetitions, they are discussed in terms of adaptation in its widest sense, as Tulio recycled elements not only from other artworks but also from his own films.

REPETITION AS A STRUCTURING ELEMENT

Repetition functions as an important structuring device in Tulio's films. By repeating cinematic elements, the filmmaker increases the cohesion of his or her works. This counters some of the effects that result from Tulio's loose editing style and plot holes, as they lessen the narrative flow of the films, making them unnecessarily complicated for viewers to follow. A prime example of pictorial repetition as a structuring device that reduces cognitive dissonance is found in *The Song of the Scarlet Flower*. In one of the key scenes, Olavi Koskela's mother catches him in the act of a sexual encounter with the servant maid Gazelle in a granary. What follows is a sequence in which the mother climbs down from the building with her son behind her, right after she has discovered the affair. The characters move exaggeratedly slowly, taking heavy steps that express shame (figure 7.1). The mother is humiliated, as her son has violated the rules of the landowning family of not having sexual affairs with servants. Olavi, on the other hand, is embarrassed for having been caught in the act and thus hurting his mother's feelings, not for what he has done. Indeed, he later explains to his mother that he loves Gazelle and wants to marry her, suggesting that the rules are outdated. Tulio depicts the characters walking in five long takes, which are intercut with two shots of a dog barking at the characters. Even though the dog is a domesticated animal, it is as if nature itself is on the side of the mother and appalled by Olavi's actions. The sequence echoes the moment in *Sunrise* (1927) in which the husband, who is about to murder his wife for the love of a city woman,

Figure 7.1

takes slow steps as their dog barks, as if sensing that something is wrong. Having reached their house, the mother informs Olavi about a similar encounter, which took place twenty years earlier. The film cuts to a flashback in which the mother wakes up in the middle of the night to breastfeed Olavi. Realising that her husband is not by her side, she goes out to look for him. She finds him in the granary caressing a servant maid. Having discovered the shameful adultery, the mother walks back to the house, taking similar steps as after having discovered Olavi in the self-same granary. 'I'm afraid your father's blood runs in your veins,' the mother informs Olavi as the flashback ends. This suggests that Olavi's night-prowling is not entirely his fault, but it is up to the spectator whether or not to agree with the mother, who believes that Olavi is destined to repeat the sins of his father.

Scenes of such walking are repeated throughout the film. Approximately in the middle of *The Song of the Scarlet Flower*, after having met Gazelle as a prostitute, Olavi walks on a desolate road with his head hung in shame, again taking slow heavy steps (figure 7.2). These steps are a continuation of the ones before and the ones to follow. The act of slowly stepping 'is only meaningful because it is to be repeated again',[19] as Raymond Bellour would put it. Doing his best, Olavi attempts to strive in the world, but again and again his encounters lead to humiliation and shame. In this sequence the setting is different: the granary has been replaced with the brothel in which Gazelle works. In the earlier scene Olavi was ashamed, as his act had hurt his mother's feelings. This time his shame stems from him having realised how severe the consequences of his 'innocent' sexual encounters can be. After five long takes that depict Olavi walking, he enters a house at which he asks for water. A woman Olavi has at their first encounter named Rowan Berry, lives there with her husband and son, who have not been previously introduced to the audience. The moment is under-determined, as the film gives little information about the new characters, but the repetition structure guides the audience to interpret that another man is raising Olavi's son, whom he now sees for the first time. The consequences get more and more severe. As Olavi returns to the road, the film once again shows him walking slowly, but this time with a major difference: the shots of Olavi taking heavy steps are superimposed with shots of the different women he has loved. This cinematic device implies that the protagonist finally understands that each of his sexual encounters has led to a personal tragedy he has known nothing about. Finally Olavi reaches his childhood home, where he meets his mother dying in bed. 'Until now, you've broken things,' his mother tells him. 'Now it's time to start building.' In the opening of the film, when Olavi's mother found him in the granary, he was not willing to follow her advice. Having now repeated the sins of his father and seen the damage they have caused, he is ready to begin a permanent relationship with Kyllikki Moisio.

Figure 7.2

The third time Olavi is seen slowly walking in shame occurs toward the end of the film, soon after he has married Kyllikki. 'You've been another man's wife, out of wedlock,' Olavi shouts in rage at her on their wedding night, choosing to believe a rumour spread by a man jealous of him, and thinking his dreams and desires about a virginal wife are shattered. He even swears to kill her, if only he had his revolver. Olavi is, in a sense, repeating his decadent father's act of trying to kill his wife with an axe after having been caught in the granary with the servant maid. Kyllikki vows that she is innocent. Being disgusted both at himself and at his wife, whose purity he suspects, Olavi leaves their home. Tulio relies on long takes that depict the protagonist taking slow and heavy steps with his head hung ever deeper in shame (figure 7.3). This is something the audience might expect. Soon Olavi reaches a shore where Dark Girl, another one of his many lovers, has drowned herself while he was celebrating his wedding feast. This is by far the severest of the consequences his actions have had. In a state of despair, Olavi walks slowly back to the house. He finally fully regrets his licentious sexual encounters. He is about to shoot himself to redeem his actions, but Kyllikki tells him that it would not atone for his sins. 'I will help you live,' says this woman who is just as strong as Olavi's mother was, appearing like an angel

Figure 7.3

of redemption. Only now when Olavi fully regrets his deeds and is ready to build instead of destroy, is he worthy of Kyllikki. The audience is implicitly guided to think that Olavi need not walk in shame ever again.

Structurally, the three pictorial instances of similar expressionistic walking appear at the beginning, in the middle and at the end, building a pattern of repetition and variation. In each sequence Olavi is in shame, but the narrative connotations are different. In the first instance, Olavi does not understand the consequences his irresponsible sexual encounters can have. He is merely ashamed for having been caught. Then, in the middle of the film, he grasps that he has caused personal tragedies to the women he has loved. Finally, he comes to fully regret his conduct and deep in self-disgust wants to redeem himself, something that he can only do by living honourably and working hard with his wife by his side. In the walking scenes, to use the words of V. F. Perkins, 'the assertion of similarity is put in tension with the sense of transformation'.[20] The sexual dreaming and walking in shame dichotomy embodies 'all the characteristics of the opposition between Eros and Thanatos, the principle of pleasure and the principle of reality'.[21] Over and over again Olavi wishes to overcome the strict morality rules, but there is no escape from the consequences of his sexual encounters.

Another example of structuring repetition in the cinema of Tulio is found in *The Rapids of Hell* (1949), in which the mother of two competing brothers follows their actions from an open window, as if she were their superego. Relying on impossible eyeline matches, she seems to see them almost wherever they are. In *The Rapids of Hell*, the role of the mother is very much like that seen in *The Song of the Scarlet Flower*, as both films centre on men who are unable to keep their sexual desires in check.

In addition to repeating similar shots and sequences as structuring devices in his films, Tulio uses narrative themes in a similar manner. A good example of such use of theme is found in *Cross of Love*, which tells the story of a young woman named Riitta who succumbs to prostitution after her lover has become tired of her. Late one evening at a harbour, a handsome man in a fancy suit spots the melancholic woman gazing at nearby ships while indifferently smoking a cigarette. 'You are the lady I have been looking for,' the stranger informs her. The man is an artist looking for a model who can inspire him. Riitta agrees to pose for him for money. From here the film cuts to an extreme long shot of a studio where the man is painting her as she hangs tied to a gigantic cross. Only Riitta's legs are visible to the audience, as the camera is stationed behind the cross looking at the artist in his work. 'Do you know what the cross of love is?' the artist asks her, and tells her the story behind the painting he is working on:

> Almost two thousand years ago there lived in the great Roman empire a patrician who fell in love with a beautiful slave girl and made her his lover. A few years later the patrician grew tired, drove her away and she became a prostitute. Then one day the patrician's own son met the same woman and they fell in love. When the father heard of his son falling for a prostitute, the girl was captured. And so, the girl was crucified like all the criminals at that time. She was crucified for the only pure love she had. And the son, he forsook his loved one, because . . . well, she was only a woman from the street.

As the artist tells the story, the camera shows close views of him and the canvas on which he is sketching. It is only when his story gets to 'the girl was crucified like all the criminals at that time' that the camera shows Riitta. She is shot from a low angle as she hangs on the cross. While the studio is atmospherically lit, echoing French poetic realism, the cross is lit in full expressionist manner against a pitch-black background: the image is nightmarish. Riitta's life is echoing the life of the slave girl. She, too, has been the lover of a powerful man who has grown tired of her, which has driven her to prostitution. The film cuts to a close-up of her face, which dramatises her tiny act of closing her eyes, as she hears the words 'she was only a woman from the street'. Clearly Riitta is all too aware of the analogy, unlike the artist who knows nothing about her past.

The story is an instance of what in literary theory is known as 'mise-en-abyme'. As the artist continues his work on the painting, he becomes obsessed with Riitta. 'Don't you understand, girl, that I'm in love with you?' The dramatic irony of the situation lies in that the artist is about to repeat the role of the son of the story, who has fallen in love with the prostitute. The difference is that despite the visible signs, which are most evident to the audience, the artist is unable to see that Riitta has succumbed to prostitution. They begin an affair. Toward the end of the film, when he learns the truth about her past, he verbally humiliates her and then abandons her. The film ends with Riitta committing suicide. As she lies dying, her body is shaped like a cross. Expressionist lighting further emphasises the analogy, as it forms a large cross above her. The film suggests that the story of the cross of love expresses a universal truth, as people are destined to repeat the tragic roles of the patrician, his son and the virtuous prostitute whose pure love goes unrecognised. Tulio's cinema is Manichean, as his world is made up of good and evil forces in conflict. Repetition in *The Song of the Scarlet Flower* and *Cross of Love* is aesthetically legitimate repetition, as Kuuskoski understands it.

REPETITION FROM FILM TO FILM

Recognising repetitions and similarities from one film to another is one of the pleasures of watching Tulio's cinema. As Raymond Bellour has put it, the mind takes 'special delight in playing on the joint effects of repetition and variation'.[22] The many repetitions and similarities that run through Tulio's oeuvre can be roughly divided into two categories. The first category consists of comparable cinematic techniques that are repeated in similar sequences in the films. The second category is rarer in the history of world cinema, as it consists of the repetition of shots, songs and suchlike that have already been used. This first section will first delve into comparable elements used in similar sequences, analysing them in comparison with internationally better-known melodramas. The second section examines how Tulio recycles material from his older films, and how the new contexts alter the meanings and functions of these elements.

After the Second World War, Tulio developed a peculiar lighting pattern he used in most of his films. It can be productively compared to that of Josef von Sternberg, the genius of excessive Hollywood melodrama who mastered the use of light and shadow better than probably any other director of his time. 'The proper use of light can embellish and dramatize every object,' von Sternberg writes in his autobiography. 'Each light furnishes its own shadow, and where a shadow is seen there must be light. Shadow is mystery and light is clarity. Shadow conceals, light reveals.'[23] In many of the films von Sternberg made with his muse Marlene Dietrich, he plays with moving light and shade on the star's face. An illuminating example is found in *The Scarlet Empress*, a film about the legend of Catherine the Great and 'the associate myth of her sexual and political omnipotence'.[24] By the second half of the film a formerly innocent and naïve Prussian woman is unhappily married to the Grand Duke Peter. She has lovers among the officers of the Russian army and with their support stages a coup. The film ends with a spectacular scene in which she rides her horse up to the Russian throne and becomes Catherine the Great. As she stands at the throne with her horse, whose white colour perfectly matches her uniform, the film shows her in a medium shot. The glamorous lighting pattern casts shadows on both sides of her face and beautifully highlights her cheekbones. At the same time, the shadow of a flag wildly flapping off-screen casts a dark shadow that keeps concealing and revealing her radiant face. Lighting is of prime significance in the sequence, as it captures the dual theme of sexual (the radiant face) and political (the flapping flag) omnipotence, while also creating a playful tone of mystery and clarity.

The lighting pattern Tulio developed can be termed a poor man's von Sternberg lighting, as it aims to enhance mystery and clarity as well, but has been carried out with the most modest means. This is not to say that the strategy was consciously adapted from Sternberg, as similar lighting effects had been used already in melodramas in the silent era. A good example is the famous sequence in *Flesh and the Devil* (1926) in which Felicitas (Greta Garbo) and Leo von Harden (John Gilbert) are about to smoke a cigarette in a romantic garden under a tree at night. The camera shows them in a dreamy close-up as Gilbert lights a match, which casts a moving shadow on their beautiful faces, which radiate in the light of the flickering fire: soon they kiss passionately.

Reviewers admired Tulio's lighting. It was never on the level of the best Hollywood films, but with his modest budgets he managed to do much. *In the Fields of Dreams* contains a sequence in which Aarne Ylitalo has returned to his childhood home from the United States, where he has spent two years during which his sweetheart Sirkka has been innocently incarcerated in prison. As he learns the tragic news from his brother, Sirkka is shown in a medium shot standing outside a door, listening to them talking inside about her. As she stands still in the evening light, birch leaves cast a flickering shadow on her face. The play of light and shade heightens her wish of being with Aarne again and her fear of being abandoned for good. In *The Way You Wanted Me* Tulio experimented with lighting that looks, probably unintentionally, mechanical and artificial. The new tendency peaked in *Cross of Love*, in which it is a major stylistic tactic. The film opens with a sequence set in lighthouse on a stormy night. Kalle, the master of the lighthouse, climbs to the lantern room at the top of the tower to watch the raging sea. The spectator may find it difficult to ignore that the lantern room is a cheaply made set. Standing in a corner of the room, the camera shows Kalle in the foreground of a medium close-up that guides the audience to pay special attention to his facial features as he laughs insanely. The static lights give the shot a noirish touch, which adds to the horror overtones of the sequence. In addition, a bright light supposedly from the lantern moves mechanically back and forth. Its major function, however clumsily, is to make the set look like a real lighthouse. Here Tulio's lighting tactic is comparable to that of von Sternberg, as it adds mystery and clarity to the expressionist sequence. In formalist terms, the lighting is realistically motivated while it may also be understood in terms of transtextual and artistic motivation.

In a later sequence, Kalle's daughter Riitta is standing at a harbour looking at nearby sailing vessels. In the first shot, her static body is shown in a medium shot. She is bathed in a bright light supposedly coming from the moon. Numerous shadows move mechanically back and forth on her, apparently coming from the masts of the tall sailing ships (figures 7.4–5). The moving shadows make the sequence beautiful and melancholic, reflecting the mood of the innocent island woman who has succumbed to prostitution. The flickering shadows in *Cross of Love* differ from those in *In the Fields of Dreams* in that they look artificial as they move in the most mechanical manner. The last film in which Tulio used this technique was *Restless Blood* (1946). Sylvi has fallen in love with the handsome doctor Valter Sora, who is taking care of her sister. Late one night, Sylvi predicts Valter's future from a deck of playing cards in a small cabin. As they lie on the floor looking at the cards, the camera shows them from a high-angle perspective. Shadows move artificially on the couple, enhancing the mysterious and romantic atmosphere of the sequence. As mechanical as the effect appears, the audience may assume that Sylvi and Valter have lit a fire, which is casting lively shadows on them. Similar lighting effects are also used in *In the Grip of Passion*.

Tulio's use of light and shade is more refined in *The Rapids of Hell*, which premiered three years after *Restless Blood*. In *The Rapids of Hell*, the flickering

Figures 7.4–5

light has been replaced with lamps placed strategically in the off-screen space to create a play of light and shade on the faces of moving characters. At the climax of the film, drunken Artturi realises that his wife Lea has deceived him and made him raise his brother's child. Coming to understand that Lea in truth loves his brother, full of jealousy he approaches her and the baby with three long steps. The first two Artturi takes begin in light and end in darkness, but the third step breaks the pattern and brings him from shade to light. In other words, as the character moves, his face is hidden and revealed by light and shadow. From this nightmarish encounter Tulio cuts to another room where Artturi's mother is lying on the floor. She has been carrying a kerosene lamp, which has fallen on the floor and set the house on fire. The camera shows her from a high angle in a full shot in which she is lying in the background with the fire burning between her and the camera. Here, too, Tulio uses light and shade: the flickering flames and the thick smoke rising up keep hiding and revealing her face as she dies.

In some of his later films, *Jealousy* (1953) and *Sensuela* being good examples, Tulio superimposed flames on the characters' faces in passionate love sequences. In all likelihood he found it easier to use superimpositions than actual fires. A good example of this technique is found in *Jealousy*. Riitta and Jyri are falling in love, as they sit in a small cabin in front of a lit fire. The camera shows them first in a medium shot and then in a medium close-up with flames superimposed on them as they are about to kiss passionately (figure 7.6). The function of the fire, of course, is to serve as a metaphor for the sexual passion that drives Riitta and Jyri. The sequence echoes Tulio's use of mechanically moving lights and shadows, as it creates a flickering lighting effect. The superimposition creates a mechanical and rather obviously fake effect. Tulio repeats the device yet again in his last film. *Sensuela* features a sequence in which Laila and Pekka have just been in a sauna. They sit on the floor of a cabin on a large blue towel, with a red towel wrapped around their

Figures 7.6–7

bodies. The orange flames are superimposed on them once again, signifying burning passions. Here, too, the superimposed shot is mechanical and artificial in nature (figure 7.7).

One key topos in Tulio's oeuvre is a shot of a fast-trotting horse. In his autobiography Tulio describes himself as a horseman,[25] which explains why horses have a prominent position in his cinema. In Tulio's surviving films, the topos first appears in *In the Fields of Dreams*. In the sequence in question, the pure and innocent milkmaid Sirkka is walking on a country road carrying a basket of berries. Using parallel editing, the film cuts between her walking and Aarne Ylitalo wildly driving his horse-drawn cart. The camera shows medium close-ups of the trotting horse's head, which emphasise its strength and speed: the camera is in a low-angle position, shooting the horse against the sky. The footage is actually composed of two horses (figures 7.8–9). The horse that is first seen is in one shot superimposed on a roaring rapid. It echoes the sequence in *The Song of the Scarlet Flower* in which Olavi tames the dangerous rapid by shooting it on a log. Similarly, in the sequence under analysis, Aarne moves as fast as he can and without caring at all about the possible consequences of his reckless driving. He accidentally almost hits Sirkka, who falls over on the muddy road, dropping the berries to the ground. Unlike bashful Sirkka, Aarne is passionate and yearns to live his life to the full. As his horse stands on the road while Aarne speaks with Sirkka, the sharp-eyed spectator will notice that it is the second animal that was trotting at full speed in the close views. The shots of the first horse were presumably repetitions from some earlier work, possibly from Tulio's lost film *The Fight over the Heikkilä Mansion*. However, it has been rumoured that the footage originates from Uuno Eskola's lost silent film *No Tears at the Fair* (*Ei auta itku markkinoilla*, 1927). Wherever the material originated, Tulio found it spectacular, even though the trotting horse was not in sharp focus and the footage was a bit dark. It seems that Tulio tried to recreate the old sequence he admired for *In the Fields of Dreams*. But the

Figures 7.8–9

close-ups of the fast- trotting horse were difficult to pull off with the equipment his crew had to hand. The results were twofold: the quality of the new material was considerably better, but there was too little of it. This interpretation explains why Tulio composed the sequence under analysis combining the old footage with the new footage.

There is a similar trotting sequence in *In the Grip of Passion*, which Tulio directed seven years after *In the Fields of Dreams*. Unlike critics have claimed,[26] the shots the sequence in *In the Grip of Passion* consists of have not been borrowed from an older film, but have been shot specifically for this one: the horse in the close views of the trotting sequence is the same animal as that seen in other sequences in the film; one notices this by paying close attention to its mane and bridle. The quality of the new footage is great and there is a lot of it. In the sequence under analysis, Paavo Iso-Ylitalo wildly wields a whip as he drives a horse-drawn cart. The film offers a montage sequence of medium close-ups of the horse's head against a cloudy summer sky as it trots as fast as it can, and a madly shouting Iso-Ylitalo reining the animal. With this new footage (figure 7.10), Tulio has outdone his earlier efforts. The quality of the shots is better, as the lighting is bright and the horse is in sharp focus. Furthermore, there are more close views of the horse than in *In the Fields of Dreams*. Pictorially, this

Figure 7.10

is repetition with a slight difference. The meaning of the sequence also differs from the earlier film. The close views of the trotting horse do not convey a sense of Iso-Ylitalo's zest for life, but instead his drunken lunacy. To put it differently, here the wildness of the earlier sequence has been taken further, as the driver is drunk and angry.

Clearly, Tulio had worked hard to get similar footage to that audiences had seen and probably admired in his earlier films. He was not unwilling to spend time and money recreating old shots with a qualitative difference. This raises his art of repetition to a whole new level. In the analysed repetitions, Tulio's decisions were not economic, but aesthetic. Tulio repeats these new tour-de-force shots of the fast-trotting horse in *The Rapids of Hell*. At the climax of the film, furious Artturi Yli-Koskela drives his horse-drawn cart as fast as he can. His wife Lea is sitting beside him, asking questions about his brother Antti, and beginning to realise that because of his jealousy Artturi has framed Antti for murder. Lea, who is in love with Antti, accuses Artturi of lying to everyone. Artturi pushes her off the cart. But the cart hits a stump on the road, and he and the cart are thrown into the nearby rapid. Here the madness of the earlier cart rides is taken to a new melodramatic extreme, as it leads to a spectacular death sequence.

This time the trotting horse divided reviewers. 'The horse with the flying mane, close-ups of which I remember seeing before in our films, deserves admiration,'[27] one of them argued. The shots of the horse had been re-contextualised and even given a degree of new meaning, but now at least reviewers noticed the repetition. Another of them stated bluntly that 'the horse ride, which seems to be one of the filmmaker's favourite elements, could very well soon be left out'.[28] Clearly, the trotting horse was recognised as one of Tulio's signature elements. The problem with it was that its repetition broke the cinematic illusion by reminding the audience, in the words of Steven Rawle, of 'the constructed basis of the film'.[29] Seemingly, such criticism did not bother Tulio.

The footage of the fast-trotting horse was repeated for the last time in *Jealousy* in 1953. The film in fact contains a plethora of material from Tulio's previous films. The reasons for this were economic, as the filmmaker had lost his audience and had to work with shoestring budgets. In *Jealousy*, Riitta is happily reining the horse as she sits on a cart with her sister Anja. The medium close-ups of the horse are associated with good moods and happy times. The smiling women are clearly enjoying the thrill of the ride. There is no implication that they are in a hurry or much less that they are in danger. *In the Fields of Dreams* contrasted the virginal Sirkka with the wildly driving passionate man, but here the two women are together living their lives to the full.

Whereas men are reckless drivers of horse-drawn carts, in the cinema of Tulio women are dangerous when driving cars. The trotting horse does not appear in any of what could be termed Tulio's urban films. However, some of these feature similar footage of cars driven by unstable or even hysterical women. At the climax of *Restless Blood*, Sylvi has been driven mad by jealousy, as she realises her husband is in love with her sister. Sylvi takes her car in the middle of the night and drives down from what seems to be a high hilltop. In a montage sequence, Tulio provides static shots in which the car drives past the camera at high speed. He also cuts to extreme close-ups of the car's speedometer and Sylvi's foot pushing the accelerator. These views have the same function as the shots of the trotting horses in that they provide a sense of strength and speed. As Sylvi is driving, the camera portrays her in various medium shots taken from a low angle. The views echo those of the men driving their carts. The montage sequence in *Restless Blood* also contains images of the road as Sylvi perceives it while she is driving much too fast. There is no equivalent for these point-of-view shots in the rural films. As her madness gets the better of her, Sylvi loses control of the car and it goes over a cliff, killing her. Artturi faces a similar fate in *The Rapids of Hell*, as he drives his cart too fast.

There is also a mad driving sequence in *You've Gone into My Blood* that resembles the one just analysed. As Erkki drives to pick up his drunken wife Rea from a party, she becomes hysterical thinking that something terrible has happened to her daughter. Rea rushes to their car and jumps in the driver's seat. Erkki barely manages to get in. The camera provides two shots of Rea driving recklessly and Erkki sitting next to her, doing his best to keep the car on the road. The shots of the car driving past the camera resemble those seen in *Restless Blood*. As the couple fight in the car, Rea pushes Erkki out just like Artturi pushes Lea out of his cart in *The Rapids of Hell*. Clearly, these car sequences are the equivalent of the horse sequences in the rural melodramas.

In addition to recycling shots in his films, Tulio tirelessly used the same pieces of classical and popular music.[30] The popular song he repeated most often is *The Last Raft* (*Viimeinen lautta*). This is a Finnish adaptation of *For me and my Gal*, which had been composed by George W. Meyer in 1917. The version Tulio used in his films was performed by Helsingin Teatteriorkesteri and sung by the male-voice choir of the Finnish Opera.[31] Tulio uses *The Last Raft* to accompany sequences of log drivers shooting rapids. Daring rapid-shooting had already become one of the big topics of Nordic film melodrama by 1919, when Mauritz Stiller directed *The Song of the Scarlet Flower* (*Sången on den eldröda blomman*), which Erkki Karu tried to top in 1923.[32] Tulio first used the song in *The Song of the Scarlet Flower*. In the sequence in question, a group of log drivers have finished their work on the shore beside the village where Olavi's sweetheart Kyllikki lives. As the men prepare to head off, one of them shouts from their raft to the small group of young women standing on the shore: 'Don't be sad, girls, we'll be back next year.' At the same time, Olavi is asking for Kyllikki's hand from her father, but his request is turned down. For a moment he walks with his head hung in disappointment, but soon runs cheerfully toward the bank of the river. Having just missed the last raft, Olavi goes after his colleagues by riding a log. The film provides a montage sequence in which it cross-cuts between tour-de-force footage of the log drivers on the raft, Olavi riding the log and Kyllikki watching him from the shore. *The Last Raft* plays on the soundtrack. In many ways it is the perfect match for the sequence: the lyrics are literally about the last raft of the summer departing and log drivers promising to come back the next year to meet the women whom they now have to leave behind. In *The Song of the Scarlet Flower* the song appears in para-diegetic fashion. There are no instruments to be seen, of course, but the spectator can easily imagine the log drivers singing the song. As Tulio depicts them in extreme long shots, their facial expressions are difficult to see, which hides the fact that the actors obviously were not really singing in the dangerous rapid. The cheerful melody and upbeat tempo of the song correlates seamlessly with Olavi's emotions. He has left his sorrows behind him and is now riding toward new adventures, knowing he will be back next year.

Considering that *The Song of the Scarlet Flower* was widely praised for its rapid-shooting sequences, it is no wonder that Tulio wanted to use this same footage in his later films. *The Last Raft* was heard again nine years later in *In the Grip of Passion*. The film was Tulio's return to the rural topics he had explored in his earlier works. As it begins, villagers are having a celebration on a riverbank where violins play and couples dance. Unexpectedly, the celebrations cease and everyone goes to look at the rapid from a high rock. The diegetic accordion music ends abruptly and *The Last Raft* begins to play on the soundtrack. The film cuts to an extreme high-angle long shot of log drivers arriving on their raft. More shots of rapid-shooting follow, all of which Tulio has borrowed from *The Song of the Scarlet Flower*. Even the shots of Olavi riding the lone log are repeated here, although there is no explicit narrative motivation for their use. The material is cross-cut with shots of people standing on the rock looking down. In a sense the sequence is a mirror image of that in *The Song of the Scarlet Flower*, as the log drivers are now arriving for timber-rafting instead of departing. Pictorially, the sequence is a fitting return to Tulio's old themes, but the use of *The Last Raft* is not as well justified. As the lyrics are about the last raft of the summer departing and log drivers promising to return next year, it is ill-suited to the sequence that depicts the arrival of the first raft. The spectator can overcome the mismatch by interpreting this as the promised return after a long year. Even so, the song is hardly as perfect a match for the sequence as it was for that in *The Song of the Scarlet Flower*. Approximately ten minutes later in *In the Grip of Passion*, the song is repeated again. This time the log drivers depart and one of them, a young man named Olavi, just like the hero in *The Song of the Scarlet Flower*, is willing to stay behind, as he has fallen in love with a local woman. In this sequence as well, old footage of log drivers shooting rapids accompanies the music.

The Last Raft was heard yet again two years later in *The Rapids of Hell*, where it accompanied a sequence of log drivers arriving, composed again of the same old footage from *The Song of the Scarlet Flower*. In *In the Grip of Passion* the song marked Tulio's return to the rural themes of his early works, but this sequence is merely a repetition. As the song and the footage had been used by Tulio only two years earlier, it is no wonder reviewers noticed to their dismay that the material had been borrowed from the filmmaker's earlier works.[33] Just like in *In the Grip of Passion*, the song is played twice in *The Rapids of Hell*. This time the song accompanies footage of the first raft of the summer arriving. At least part of the audience is likely to have recalled Tulio's previous usage of the piece in a similar context.

The Last Raft was heard for the last time in a Tulio film in *Jealousy* in 1953. Here the song accompanies shots of a couple listening to log drivers competing and playing, a sight they want to go and see. Here Tulio is playing with the anticipation of repetition, as audiences familiar with his films had learned to associate the song with the spectacular footage. But this time Tulio does not provide his old footage of log drivers. Instead, the film offers new rapid-shooting footage, which seems to have been shot in a real rapid-shooting competition. Whereas Tulio had outdone his earlier efforts with the new footage of the trotting horse in *In the Grip of Passion*, the rapid-shooting sequence composed of newsreel material in *Jealousy* is a much lesser achievement, as it lacks drama. Furthermore, the lyrics of *The Last Raft* are ill-suited to the footage, as it does not have anything to do with men leaving after a summer's work. Spectators familiar with Tulio's films probably got a sense that he merely wanted to play the song as often as he could when depicting log drivers. The song itself is about repetition, as the phrase 'we'll come again' is heard again and again; the Finnish words 'me tulemme taas' can be understood as meaning present or future. Later in *Jealousy* the log drivers depart and Tulio repeats the song, just like he had played it twice in *In the Grip of Passion* and *The Rapids of Hell*. Now, for the last time in his films, Tulio uses his tour-de-force footage. Here, as in so many of his films, spectacle is rooted in repetition, which easily renders it unspectacular. In *The Song of the Scarlet Flower* the song is the perfect match for the sequence of log drivers departing, but as time goes by, the song becomes a more and more clichéd element accompanying log drivers shooting rapids. In these scenes, repetition really is just repetition, as it ceases to produce anything noteworthy. While Kuuskoski's argument is productive in the analysis of Tulio's individual films, it is less useful in the analysis of his oeuvre as a whole.

THE ART OF EXCESSIVE REPETITION

Tulio's strong faith in the notion that all human relationships worth discussing in films are present in the Bible made him neglect topical issues his audiences were interested in. His characters were, in a sense, trapped in an endless cycle of repetition. Tulio wanted his art to be universal, but because of his relentless repetition of old themes and conventions, his audiences often saw his works as old-fashioned, no matter how cinematic they were at their best.

In individual films, Tulio uses repetition as a structuring device, as he repeats similar shots, sequences and themes. A degree of repetition is an intrinsic part of almost all narration. Tulio, however, repeated certain elements much more than most filmmakers. Stylistic and thematic repetitions added structure to the films that were characterised by features such as negligence of the 180-degree rule and broken eyeline connections, not to mention tour-de-force shots that do little to advance the narrative and often actively distract from it. Tulio's disregard for the principles of classical style often made his films complicated to follow, as the previous chapter demonstrated. Noticeable repetitions, however, made the common threads of his films easier to follow, emphasising them and at times even adding new meanings to old meanings.

In constantly repeating material from his old films, Tulio was both conventional and radical, not to mention economical. Like celebrated filmmakers often do, Tulio used similar stylistic solutions in similar sequences. But much more uniquely in the history of cinema, Tulio used his greatest shots and songs again and again. His attempts to produce new meanings by re-contextualising them provided some results, but with the exception of the trotting horse in *In the Grip of Passion*, they tended to lack bite. Indeed, meanings associated with the shots and songs got weaker, milder and even counterproductive. Considering the amount of repetitions that catch the eye and ear, it is fair to conclude that excessive repetition is a major aesthetic principle that governs Tulio's cinema.

NOTES

1. Shaham 2013: 438.
2. Bellour 2000: 223.
3. Neale 2000: 207.
4. Dyer 2007: 173.
5. Toiviainen 1992: 234.
6. Allen 2018.
7. Koivunen 1995: 141.
8. Alanen 2002: 261.
9. Tulio 2002: 140.
10. Evans and Deleyto 1998: 1.
11. Shingler 2018: 137.
12. Kaes 1996: 618.
13. Williams 2018: 171.
14. Perkins 1990: 57.
15. Kuuskoski 2002: 353.
16. Hutcheon 2013: 7.
17. Sanders 2006: 18.

18. Alanen 2002.
19. Bellour 1979: 71.
20. Perkins 2003.
21. Eco 1979: 153.
22. Bellour 2000: 66.
23. Von Sternberg 1965: 311.
24. Wilson 2005: 60.
25. Tulio 2002: 31.
26. Alanen 2002: 160.
27. T. A.: 'Hornankoski', *Suomen Sosiaalidemokraatti* 9.3.1949.
28. Pena.: 'Tähdellistä', *Riihimäen Sanomat* 26.4.1949.
29. Rawle 2009: 59.
30. Seitajärvi 2002.
31. Ibid.: 292.
32. Seppälä 2017.
33. –N–g.: 'Elokuvat', *Etelä-Suomen Sanomat* 4.5.1949.

NEWSPAPERS AND PERIODICALS

Etelä-Suomen Sanomat 1949.
Riihimäen Sanomat 1949.

BIBLIOGRAPHY

Alanen, Antti (2000), 'Tulio ja Linnankoski', in Sakari Toiviainen (ed.), *Tulio: Levottoman veren antologia*, Helsinki: Suomalaisen Kirjallisuuden Seura, 247–63.

Allen, Richard (2018), 'The Passion of Christ and the Melodramatic Imagination', in Christine Gledhill and Linda Williams (eds), *Melodrama Unbound – Across History, Media, and National Cultures*, New York: Columbia University Press, 31–47.

Bellour, Raymond (1979), 'Cine-Repetitions', *Screen* 20:2, 65–72.

Bellour, Raymond (2000), *The Analysis of Film*, Bloomington and Indianapolis: Indiana University Press.

Dyer, Richard (2007), *Pastiche*, London and New York: Routledge.

Eco, Umberto (1979), *The Role of the Reader: Explorations in the Semiotics of Texts*, Bloomington and Indianapolis: Indiana University Press.

Evans, Peter William and Celestino Deleyto (1998), 'Introduction: Surviving Love', in Peter William Evans and Celestino Deleyto (eds), *Terms of Endearment: Hollywood Romantic Comedy of the 1980s and 1990s*, Edinburgh: Edinburgh University Press, 1–15.

Hutcheon, Linda (2013), *A Theory of Adaptation*, London and New York: Routledge.

Jameson, Fredric (1991), *Postmodernism, or, The Cultural Logic of Late Capitalism*, London and New York: Verso.

Kaes, Anton (1996), 'Rainer Werner Fassbinder', in Geoffrey Nowell-Smith (ed.), *The Oxford History of World Cinema*, Oxford: Oxford University Press, 618–19.

Koivunen, Anu (1995), *Isänmaan moninaiset äidinkasvot*, Turku: Suomen elokuvatutkimuksen seura.

Kuuskoski, Martti-Tapio (2000), 'Melodraman tuolle puolen – Tulion modernismi ja sen johtomotiivit', in Sakari Toiviainen (ed.), *Tulio: Levottoman veren antologia*, Helsinki: Suomalaisen Kirjallisuuden Seura, 307–59.

Neale, Steve (2000), *Genre and Hollywood*, London and New York: Routledge.

Perkins, V. F. (1990), 'Film Authorship: The Premature Burial', *CineAction!* 21/22, 57–64.

Perkins, V. F. (2003), 'Same Tune Again! Repetition and Framing in *Letter from an Unknown Woman*', *16/9 Filmtidsskrift* 1:3. http://www.16-9.dk/2003-09/side11_inenglish.htm (accessed 7 August 2019).

Rawle, Steven (2009), 'Hal Hartley and the Re-Presentation of Repetition', *Film Criticism* 34:1, 58–75.

Sanders, Julie (2006), *Adaptation and Appropriation*, London and New York: Routledge.

Seitajärvi, Juha (2002), 'Tulio ja hänen elokuviensa säveltäjät', in Sakari Toiviainen (ed.), *Tulio: Levottoman veren antologia*, Helsinki: Suomalaisen Kirjallisuuden Seura, 265–305.

Seppälä, Jaakko (2017), 'Stumbling on Technology: Erkki Karu's Notions of Rapid Shooting and the Lack of Telephoto Lenses', in Kimmo Laine, Pasi Nyyssönen, Hannu Salmi and Jaakko Seppälä (eds), *Noin seitsemännen taiteen poika: Kirjoituksia elokuvasta ja muista taiteista*, Turku: Faros-kustannus, 65–73.

Shaham, Inbar (2013), 'The Structure of Repetition in the Cinema: Three Hollywood Genres', *Poetics Today* 34:4, 437–518.

Shingler, Martin (2018), 'Modernizing Melodrama: The Petrified Forest on American Stage and Screen (1935–1936)', in Christine Gledhill and Linda Williams (eds), *Melodrama Unbound – Across History, Media, and National Cultures*, New York: Columbia University Press, 135–50.

Sternberg, Josef von (1965), *Fun in a Chinese Laundry*, London: Columbus Books.

Toiviainen, Sakari (1992), *Suurinta elämässä: Elokuvamelodraaman kulta-aika*, Helsinki: VAPK-kustannus.

Tulio, Teuvo (2002), 'Elämäni ja elokuvani', in Sakari Toiviainen (ed.), *Tulio: Levottoman veren antologia*, Helsinki: Suomalaisen Kirjallisuuden Seura, 23–157.

Williams, Linda (2018), 'World and Time: Serial Television Melodrama in America', in Christine Gledhill and Linda Williams (eds), *Melodrama Unbound – Across History, Media, and National Cultures*, New York: Columbia University Press, 169–83.

Wilson, George M. (2005), 'Narrative and Visual Pleasures in *The Scarlet Empress*', in John Gibbs and Douglas Pye (eds), *Style and Meaning: Studies in the Detailed Analysis of Film*, Manchester: Manchester University Press, 53–67.

CHAPTER 8

Tulio's Legacy

A s we have seen in this book, Teuvo Tulio's reputation as a filmmaker declined steadily through his active career. While his critical status, starting with his early collaboration with Valentin Vaala, was never unequivocal, it can be generalised that until the mid-1940s he was regarded as a welcome innovator within Finnish cinema, a filmic-oriented alternative for the literary- and theatrically-minded majority of studio filmmakers. The sensationalism present in almost all of Tulio's works guaranteed that controversy and disputes often accompanied his premieres, often provoked by the director himself, but early on in his career, he usually managed to turn this to his advantage. From the late 1940s on, critics more and more often regarded Tulio's sensationalism as an objective in its own right, based on a repetitive repertoire of cheap thrills. However, after hitting a low point in the 1960s and 1970s, Tulio's critical reputation started gradually to rise again: his films achieved a kind of a cult status, as critics and enthusiasts raised after the studio era began to see them as intriguing anomalies from, rather than conventionally representative of, the period.

THREE FELLOW FILMMAKERS

In an interesting way, Tulio's critical reputation partly parallels and partly contrasts with that of two of his coeval filmmakers, Valentin Vaala and Nyrki Tapiovaara (Vaala was born in 1909, Tapiovaara in 1911 and Tulio in 1912). All three were, at least at some point in their careers, among the most respected filmmakers of the studio era, and all three now have an established position in Finnish film history. They are, for example, among the rather few filmmakers with a monograph devoted to their careers: a book on Tapiovaara by Sakari

Toiviainen came out in 1986, a collection of essays on Tulio, edited by Toiviainen, in 2002, and a collection of essays on Vaala, edited by Kimmo Laine,
Matti Lukkarila and Juha Seitajärvi, in 2004.[1] However, the respective roads
of these three filmmakers to the canon of Finnish cinema differ considerably.
These differences shed light on the excessive idiosyncrasy of Tulio's style, as
well as on the uneasy cultural position of melodrama as a genre.

To begin with Valentin Vaala, his early collaborations with Tulio/Tugai were
generally received with, sometimes reserved, interest. Since critics and journal-
ists were fully aware that Vaala and Tugai were in their teens when they started,
comments on their first films were often somewhat patronising, but nevertheless,
a certain charming enthusiasm was recognised. Three themes seemed to stand
out in the reviews and journalistic comments. Positive attention was paid to the
fact that both Vaala as a director and Tugai as an actor were children of cinema.
Thus, it was appreciated that they thought of films in genuinely filmic terms,
without being burdened by theatre or literature – criteria that often dominated
the criticism of studio-based films. Against the background of the assumedly
ethno-symbolic 1920s cinema,[2] dominated, albeit not exclusively, by adaptations
of novels and plays, typically with a rural setting that reflected and even constructed national culture, Vaala and Tugai's films were welcomed by many as
bringing a breath of fresh international air. Furthermore, even though their films
rarely featured narrative or visual elements that would count as experimental in
a strong sense, they were readily associated with the European avant-garde of
the 1920s. A nice summary of the early positive views on Vaala is provided by the
critic Roland af Hällström, who later became a film director himself, cooperating
with Tulio in making *The Rapids of Hell* (1949):

> Belonging to a generation that had grown up with cinema . . . Valentin
> Vaala instinctively saw and felt filmically, and he had the courage and
> the guts to try over and over again . . . And the last silent film by these
> young filmmakers, *The Wide Road*, was already partly genuine film art.
> Valentin Vaala was at the time the only one in Finland who represented
> the 'avant-garde' of European cinema; his perseverance and his natural
> filmic eye were a gift from God to a film director.[3]

As a production unit, Vaala and Tugai were usually discussed together, quite
rightly so, since they both contributed, in varying degrees from film to film, to
the scripts, the settings, the costumes, etc. However, as the director, Vaala was
the one who received more positive attention for the filmic expression, whereas
Tugai as the leading actor was the more likely target for prejudice concerning the sexually and ethnically ambiguous features of his star image. As Harri
Kalha has remarked, even for those modernist-minded critics who welcomed
the films as novelties, Tugai's excessiveness proved to be too much.[4]

After accepting the job offer from Suomi-Filmi in 1935, Vaala became one of the most respected studio directors, even if innovation was sometimes seen to have been replaced by professionalism: 'His films nowadays are [exemplars of] exquisite craftsmanship, with traces of his courageous artistically experimental period', wrote af Hällström; 'what is unfortunately lacking now, however, is his aspiration for specific artistic and filmic effects'.[5]

Vaala became known as a fine studio director who, although specialising in sophisticated comedies and subtle melodramas, was able to handle any genre with quite respectable results. Even in the late 1950s and early 1960s, when he was assigned by Suomi-Filmi to work on projects that were not of his own choice, he was given credit for his previous merits. Jörn Donner, generally highly critical of the studio system, wrote in his landmark essay in 1961:

> Valentin Vaala embodies the best qualities of Finnish cinema in a distinguished way. He is part of the literary tradition of rural depiction where Edvin Laine [the director of, for example, *The Unknown Soldier* (*Tuntematon sotilas*, 1955)] has achieved success too. The dominating mode is that of a lyrical sense of the nature. The films become almost sociological documents, as the faiths of the characters affect us on account of their plausibility and, sometimes, their monumentality. However, Vaala should be credited mainly for his technical skill, for directing decently. At this moment, having reached the bottom, we have to admit that we long for the know-how he once stood for.[6]

It is telling that when Suomi-Filmi gave Vaala notice in 1963, he met with a remarkable amount of public support. Firing a well-respected and faithful director earned Suomi-Filmi such bad publicity that they were forced to find him work in their documentary department.

Vaala's critical reputation has remained steady since his feature film career ended. The emphasis has changed, though. Whereas the 1960s and 1970s generation of critics cherished him as the master of the pastoral tradition, since the 1980s both critics and scholars have found new interest in his early experiments with Tugai on the one hand, and in his sophisticated comedies, now reframed as women's films, on the other.[7]

As for Nyrki Tapiovaara, just like Tulio, he gained recognition as a promising young film director during the late 1930s. As opposed to Vaala and Tulio, he had become a renowned cultural figure already before his first film, as a leftist stage director and a radical film journalist. Tapiovaara's career was short: he directed only five films before he died in the Finnish–Soviet Winter War in 1940. Of Tapiovaara's five films, *Juha* (1937) and *One Man's Fate* (*Miehen tie*, 1940, finished by Hugo Hytönen after Tapiovaara's death) were rural (melo) dramas, *Two Henpecked Husbands* (*Kaksi Vihtoria*, 1939) and *Mr Lahtinen Takes*

French Leave (*Herra Lahtinen lähtee lipettiin*, 1939) were musical comedies, and *Stolen Death* (*Varastettu kuolema*, 1938) was a political thriller. In terms of filmic expression, Tapiovaara's works are not as consistent as Tulio's. The common denominator in Tapiovaara's films is possibly the way they synthesise popular film genres with a variety of modernist and avant-garde devices.[8]

As different as Tapiovaara, Tulio and Vaala were in terms of their backgrounds and as filmmakers, they still had a lot in common. All three were associated with the modernist art group Tulenkantajat, Tulio and Vaala more distantly than Tapiovaara, who became an active member in the 1930s, as the previously apolitical group turned left. All three were also members of the film club Projektio, discussed in chapter 4.

Unlike Vaala, both Tulio and Tapiovaara worked outside the major studios. Tapiovaara's first film was produced by Aho & Soldan, a short-film company specialising in often experimental-flavoured documentaries. The second was produced by the young cinematographer Erik Blomberg, who also acted as an executive producer of Tapiovaara's last three films, released though Eloseppo, a small and short-lived company set up for producing alternative narrative films. Before teaming with Tapiovaara, Blomberg had shot Tulio's first three films. And after Tulio's cooperation with Adams-Filmi ended in 1938, Blomberg rented the studio facilities he had constructed with Tulio for Adams-Filmi for the shooting of Tapiovaara's *Stolen Death*.[9]

Even if the variety of Tapiovaara's limited output was greater than Tulio's ever was, both in genre and in style, two of his films resonate closely with Tulio's early work. Like *Silja – Fallen Asleep When Young* – and, indeed, like Vaala's *People in the Summer Night* (*Ihmiset suviyössä*, 1948) – Tapiovaara's *One Man's Fate* is based on a novel by the Nobel Prize-winning author F. E. Sillanpää, and like *Jiggs and Maggie*, Tapiovaara's *Two Henpecked Husbands* is inspired by George McManus' comic strip *Bringing Up Father*, with Eino Jurkka starring in both films. The last film Vaala directed before joining Suomi-Filmi, *When Father Wants to . . .* (1935) is actually an (uncredited) adaptation of McManus' strip too.

Despite such parallels, many of which are obviously much more than coincidences, and the critical appreciation both gained early in their careers, the status Tapiovaara's oeuvre achieved during the following decades differed decisively from that of Tulio's, partly (but far from exclusively) explained by Tapiovaara's untimely death. In the post-war era, with the emergence of a new film culture, which included festivals, film societies, journals and archives (the Finnish Film Archive was founded in 1957), Tapiovaara's reputation began to grow in Finland. The new cinephile generation valued him as an independent filmmaker capable of breaking out of the limitations of studio production. To take just one example, during the first three years (1952–4) of one of the most notable of the new ciné-clubs, Studio, the only Finnish feature films screened were Tapiovaara's *Stolen Death* and *One Man's Fate*.

The reasons for Tapiovaara's renown, however, have varied over the decades. In the early 1950s, when Italian neorealism represented the highest aesthetic ideal, he was seen as an early realist. Jörn Donner, a prominent young critic and later a filmmaker, wrote in 1955 of Tapiovaara in an article that reflected on the future of Finnish cinema:

> We do have a national, realistic film tradition. It is represented by one name, albeit a good one, Nyrki Tapiovaara, who has been considered 'undoubtedly the most talented filmmaker we have had so far'. Tapiovaara wanted to tell about the people of Finland and their struggle. The legacy of Tapiovaara is the only one in Finnish cinema that encourages us and points to the future.[10]

With the emergence of the *politique des auteurs* in the late 1950s and early 1960s, Tapiovaara represented the possibility of individual expression on the fringes of the studio system.[11] And among the new left of the late 1960s and early 1970s, he was seen as a radical filmmaker, who not only survived the cultural and political suppression of the 1930s, but was able to make, at least allegorically, progressive films. In 1975 Toiviainen analysed *Two Henpecked Husbands* as an allegory of class relations:

> Tapiovaara lays bare the dreamed-up sham world behind these circum-stances [Jiggs as a new-rich henpecked husband, Maggie as a domestic tyrant and a social climber] by mercilessly and sharply, and yet hilari-ously, exposing the duality of the characters, the conflict between appearance and reality, the class status of the characters, and the illu-sion of the dreams of success and happiness. . . . Manners of behaviour and attitudes are on display in such an exaggerated and visible way that they are made to speak for or against themselves. We see a conception of a world in which money measures human relations and class and power relations are made overt.[12]

Lately, as some of Tapiovaara's key films have been reconstructed – *Mr Lahtinen Takes French Leave* is partly lost and *Stolen Death* was shortened and re-edited in a more classical narrative form in the early 1950s – a grow-ing interest has focused on Tapiovaara as an avant-gardist.[13] Yet, whether the prevailing emphasis is on realism, auteurism, political activism or the avant-garde, Tapiovaara has sustained his place in the pantheon of Finnish filmmakers.

All in all, despite the fact that their careers intersected in many ways during the 1930s, Tapiovaara's, Vaala's and Tulio's reputations headed in separate direc-tions in the post-war decades. Whereas Tapiovaara was hailed as an exceptional independent filmmaker and Vaala was respected as a skilful professional, even when at the mercy of the ruthless studio system, Tulio was, between the early 1950s and the late 1970s, generally either disdained or forgotten. With respect to Tapiovaara, independent film production was regarded as an aesthetic and political alternative to the restraints of the studio system, but Tulio's independence was seen rather in terms of commercial profit-making. Vaala, for his part, proved that melodrama remained a culturally tolerable cinematic mode when produced with the resources and within the restrictions of major studios, while Tulio, in the eyes of the 1950s and 1960s cineaste generations, became the embodiment of the exploitative and sensational excesses of melodrama.

VAGARIES OF CRITICAL RECEPTION

As we have seen, until the 1950s many critics still acknowledged Tulio's extraordinary style of cinematic expression, while increasingly often complaining about the repetitious, banal, overblown and implausible qualities of his films. Such qualities were typically associated with the alleged popular success of the films, whereas the actual box-office appeal seems to have been in decline too. No box-office figures exist, but judging by all available evidence (the number of copies made of the films, the number, the status and the geographical location of the theatres where the films were first released, etc.), it appears that it was increasingly difficult for Tulio to distribute his films in the 1950s. While a 1950 book on Finnish film industry, aimed at the popular audience, still introduced Tulio as a sole exception to the general rule that films can only be produced with any success within the major studios,[14] a few years later he was no longer in such an exceptional position.

It thus appears that during the 1950s, Tulio's critical status as a film director and independent producer declined simultaneously with the popular appeal of his films. After *You've Gone into My Blood* (1956) he drifted ever further into the margins of the rapidly changing film culture, so that not even his potentially sensational late films, *In the Beginning Was an Apple* (1962, a quasi-biopic of the controversial celebrity Tabe Slioor[15]) nor *Sensuela* (1973, a soft-porn remake of *Cross of Love*, 1946), caused much debate.

General overviews of the history and present state of Finnish cinema followed the same pattern. In 1957 Aito Mäkinen and Bengt Pihlström wrote in the *Studio* yearbook:

In the mid-'30s Teuvo Tulio (1912), influenced by foreign films, turned out some picturesque productions. But he has now chosen the easier commercial way and has in his recent works scripted by him and his star Regina Linnanheimo hit all-time lows.[16]

Typically, Tulio's early films were looked upon somewhat kindlier than his recent output, but it is, in fact, quite unlikely that the younger generation of critics and film intellectuals had seen any of these films, especially after 1959, when all surviving copies of his first three features were (as far as we know) consumed by a massive fire in the storage building of Adams-Filmi. Even some of those who had seen one of the early films were critical. Often quoted is an article on Sillanpää adaptations by the literary critic Aarne Laurila:

> In 1936–37 [Sillanpää's *Silja*] was adapted as an appalling film by Teuvo Tulio. Actually, he did not adapt Sillanpää's brilliant epic, since there is nothing in the film that originates from the author himself, apart from the short preface signed by him. Not only is the story torn apart . . . but what is most repulsive is the constant embroidering and lying . . . Regina Linnanheimo is mostly just silly and sour as the best-known Finnish maid of all time, and the calculating manner she opens and shuts her inexpressive eyes is annoying.[17]

Even more telling than such thoroughly negative assessments is the fact that in some of the key texts of the era, reflecting and promoting the sense of rupture in Finnish film culture, like Pekka Lounela's thirty-page 'Suomalainen todellisuus' ('Finnish Reality', 1957)[18] or Jörn Donner's forty-page manifesto 'Suomalainen elokuva vuonna o' ('Finnish Cinema Year Zero', 1961),[19] there is no mention of Tulio whatsoever.

In 1974, at the low point of his popularity and critical reputation, following the premiere of what proved to be his final film, *Sensuela*, Tulio brought out his memoirs. They were published in serialised form in a women's magazine, which was hardly a prestigious forum. Being very much aware of the difficulties he had run into in his career, Tulio summed up the previous decades from the perspective of an independent filmmaker. The Second World War years were the golden age, since films were just about the only entertainment available, and the number of imported films was limited. However, Tulio himself spent most of the war years at the front, thus not being able to have his share of the gold. During the silver era, the post-war years, due to the better availability of other forms of entertainment and goods, film attendances started to decline. This was followed by the bronze era, as high-quality foreign films started to pour in once again and cars and other attractions competed with cinema, causing evermore problems, especially for domestic production. Finally, after the emergence of television, film business reached its iron age that, according to Tulio's prophecy, witnessed the inevitable, silent death of Finnish cinema.[20]

Whether it was because of bitterness caused by years of bad reviews or general distrust in the contemporary film trade, after the commercial and critical failure of *Sensuela*, Tulio became reluctant to give permission for showing his films. This meant that until his death in 2000, his films were screened only on a few special occasions. The most important of these were probably the television screenings for which Tulio gave permission, receiving a reasonable payment for the one-time television rights, first around the mid-1970s and then again in the early 1980s.

Generally, television had become the main channel for showing old domestic films. In 1963, on the brink of bankruptcy, Suomen Filmiteollisuus, the biggest of the major production companies, sold the permanent rights for nearly all of its films to the Finnish Broadcasting Company, and the other majors followed suit later. Even though film attendances declined through the post-studio decades, old domestic films proved highly successful on television. It is usually thought that the basis of this success was the older generations' willingness to maintain a relationship with their favourite films and stars, now seen almost exclusively on television. However, old domestic films were often seen by younger audiences as well, if only for the reason that Finnish television's 'age of scarcity'[21] lasted until the late 1980s, with only two television channels and a limited volume of programmes and programme hours. Such contemporary filmmakers as Aki Kaurismäki and Markku Pölönen, who have found inspiration in studio-era cinema, grew up watching old domestic films on television, not in cinemas.

Yet, even if old domestic films were aired regularly on Finnish television, Tulio's films seemed to stand out, having been out of circulation for some time. This becomes evident when reading the reviews of the television screenings of the 1980s. Film critics of the new generation were still often ambiguous in their attitude toward Tulio, albeit with a decisively more positive tone than those of the previous generation. 'Tulio is absolute', wrote Harri Moilanen of *The Restless Blood*. 'He exaggerates and he is naive, even harsh. True, but all of this leads to a romantic glow with a total lack of insincerity.'[22] Another critic, Markku Tuuli, considered *The Way You Wanted Me* (1944) a bad film as such, 'since the story with its over-dramatic turns and pathetic events exaggerates so much that one cannot take it seriously. After 40 years, however, the melodrama has gained a new glitter of camp, especially because Tulio's vision is truly impressive . . . Every second of the film is exaggerated, but there is an irresistible glow in this exaggeration.'[23]

An essential element in the critical rehabilitation of Tulio was the spread of VCR technology in the 1980s. Even if his films were only aired once in the 1970s and once in the 1980s, the latter screenings were recorded by many on VHS tapes, after which pirated copies circulated among the growing body of fans. The limited availability and the element of mystery undoubtedly added to the cult status of Tulio's work. Despite their origins in popular cinema, these films were not for all tastes anymore, but rather for cineastes and connoisseurs, with a promise of marginal rather than mainstream pleasures. Further, an atmosphere of mystery surrounded both Tulio and Linnanheimo as public figures. They had not completely shut themselves out, as growing rumours would have it, but both systematically refused to give interviews, even when the new interest in their films became evident.[24]

Another component in the new coming of Tulio, from the point of view of criticism and scholarship, was the growing interest in melodrama in international film archives, festivals and film studies in the 1970s. Retrospective screenings of the works of, for example, Douglas Sirk and Vincente Minnelli, the enthusiasm toward melodrama expressed by art-house auteurs like Rainer Werner Fassbinder, as well as scholarly articles on melodrama by Thomas Elsaesser, Laura Mulvey, Geoffrey Nowell-Smith and others, caught the attention of young Finnish cineastes.[25]

An early sign of this is Tarmo Malmberg's essay 'Traditional Finnish Cinema: An Historical Overview' in the 'little book'[26] anthology *Cinema in Finland* published by the British Film Institute in 1975. Generally, Malmberg's essay, as well as the whole collection, is highly critical toward studio-era cinema, with the exception of, once more, Tapiovaara. Nonetheless, if somewhat reluctantly, Malmberg suggests that Tulio's melodramas might be worthy of reassessment:

> A co-script writer as a young enthusiast at the age of only 16, Teuvo Tulio . . . made his debut as director in 1936 and soon won questionable fame for his banal romantic stories with heavy theatrical acting, sensuality and moral overtones. It might seem strange to mention Tulio in a short introduction of this kind, but seeing some of his films, particularly *Cross of Love* . . . in the perspective of the 1970s and the Douglas Sirk tradition of melodrama it is perhaps possible to see the kind of interest the films have generated.[27]

The first signs of a true Tulio renaissance appeared in the 1980s when the film magazine *Filmihullu* published a series of articles on Tulio by, for example, the critic Markku Varjola. On the one hand, this coincided with a newly rising general intellectual interest in studio-era cinema in Finland, manifest in journalism, scholarly studies, VHS releases, film festivals, television documentaries, etc. On the other hand, as Malmberg had predicted, the growing interest in Tulio related to the international rise of melodrama studies: indeed, one of Varjola's essays[28] was published in 1987 in a special melodrama issue of *Filmihullu*, along with translations of pioneering essays on melodrama by Elsaesser, Mulvey, Nowell-Smith and Jean-Loup Bourget. Further, as fascinated as Varjola was by the idiosyncratic excesses of Tulio, he was clearly inspired by the views of the early 1970s melodrama critics, who celebrated Sirk as a Brechtian modernist, and who used melodrama as a means to expose the contradictions within bourgeois society.[29] 'The bourgeois family idyll in Tulio's films is always extremely fragile', wrote Varjola accordingly. 'Under the surface is a black hole, an abysmal recess of the mind that might drive the characters insane, if ever opened.'[30] In the last resort, Varjola reads Tulio's films as – unconscious, unlike in the case of Sirk – Marxist analyses of the capitalist society destroying itself:

> Tulio's work is a monument of the old Finnish class society, and at the same time a visionary account of its collapse . . . In an extremely unconscious way, Tulio documents the material and spiritual conflicts and the ruptures in work, practices and values, brought by structural changes in society.[31]

In the following years, Tulio's films asserted themselves as legitimate objects of scrutiny in several fields of film, genre and gender studies. For example, Toiviainen devotes an entire chapter to Tulio in his 1992 general history of film melodrama, arguing that Tulio was the most genuinely melodramatic of all Finnish filmmakers, and that the moral universe depicted in his films remained sharply dualistic, even though the focus shifted (male to female protagonist, rural to urban melodrama, etc.).[32] Anu Koivunen and Kimmo Laine discuss *The Song of the Scarlet Flower* (1938) and *The Rapids of Hell* in the context of another more or less indigenous genre, the log driver film, and see them as symptoms of the 'male crisis', of the uneasy encounter between traditional agrarian values and the changing conceptions of masculinity in modernity.[33]

In Anu Koivunen's study on Finnish women's films of the 1940s, Tulio's *The Way You Wanted Me* and *Cross of Love* feature as emblematic parts of the fallen woman cycle, locating a variety of assumedly topical social problems, such as prostitution, crime, venereal disease and alcoholism, in the body of the female protagonist. As a result, Koivunen argues that at the core of the postwar social-problem films is a view of the female body as a potential threat not only to women themselves, but also to the nation.[34] Kalha, for his part, focuses on the male body in a series of queer readings of Tulio's public image as the national, racial and sexual other, concentrating mainly on Tulio as the film star Theodor Tugai in his early films with Vaala:

> Putting the stigmatized body of the *other* on public display, failing to 'repeat loyally', Tugai's screen persona urges us to see the ontologies of Nation and Gender as the factitious structures they are. The film star's dis-articulated, impossible body – his impossibly *moderne* body – thus points to the fractures, instabilities and ambiguities of Modernity – but it also bespeaks a crucial moment of transgression, subversion and, eventually, liberation.[35]

POSTHUMOUS REPUTATION

Tulio's death in 2000 marked a new phase in the Tulio renaissance. Sticking with his decision not to give permission for screening his films almost to the end, he nevertheless allowed the Finnish Film Archive to arrange a retrospective of his work in 1996, and after his death the Archive (from 2013 the National Audiovisual Institute, KAVI) received all rights for his films. Also, the Archive received into its collections all the surviving scripts and other materials relating to the production of his films. This gave KAVI the opportunity not only to exhibit the films in its own theatre but also to make them available for festivals and special screenings, as well as to grant permission for television broadcasts. Furthermore, starting in 2006, KAVI has released all of Tulio's surviving films on DVD, excluding *In the Beginning Was an Apple*, for which it does not hold the rights, but including Tulio's surviving collaborations with Vaala, *The Gypsy Charmer* (1929) and *The Wide Road*, as well as the film Tulio produced for Matti Kassila, *The Radio Goes Mad*. These high-quality releases with English and Swedish subtitles, featuring as extras the alternative Swedish versions of the films and surviving scenes from the lost films, have considerably paved the way for Tulio's new status as one of the most highly valued Finnish filmmakers of the studio era. This is further consolidated by the fact that the two screening venues run by KAVI have been named Kino Tulio and Kino Regina, the latter opening as part of the new Helsinki Central Library in 2019.

A few years before his death, Tulio had already donated hundreds of original negatives of production stills to KAVI. This enabled KAVI to organise photographic exhibitions, including a large exhibition at the Helsinki Art Museum in 2003, as well as to invest in book publishing. Of the two books published by KAVI and the Finnish Literature Society in the early 2000s, *Intohimon vallassa* ('In the Grip of Passion') is a coffee-table book, built around production stills, but also containing essays by Toiviainen and Kalha.[36] *Tulio – Levottoman veren antologia* ('Tulio – An anthology of the Restless Blood', edited by Sakari Toiviainen) is a lavishly illustrated collection of essays including thematic readings – for example, a thorough exploration of Tulio's film music by Juha Seitajärvi – as well as personal reminiscences from Tulio's acquaintances and an edited version of his 1974 memoirs.[37]

Tulio's co-workers have never failed to give him credit. Practically all of the cinematographers he worked with, including Erik Blomberg, Osmo Harkimo, Pentti Lintonen and Esko Töyri, seemed to be unanimous in praising him for two reasons when interviewed after their active careers: first, for his visual sophistication and his ability to 'think in pictures'; and second, for his readiness to share his knowledge of filmmaking. Often he would grab the camera himself, wanting to be in control of every visual detail.[38]

In 1983 Tulio received a life achievement Jussi Award, which is the Finnish equivalent of the Academy Award, presented since 1944. During his active years he never received an award, as opposed to Vaala's four Jussis. Linnanheimo, however, did win the best actress category in 1946 for her roles in *The Restless Blood* and *Cross of Love*. In 1988 Tulio was chosen as the first honorary member of the Association of Finnish Film Directors. According to the archives of the Association, he did not show up for the event, but afterwards he presented the Association with a bottle of brandy.[39]

Among present-day filmmakers, the most enthusiastic cherisher of Tulio's legacy has been Aki Kaurismäki. As early as 1983, when starting his career as a film director, Kaurismäki stated in an interview: 'To my mind, Teuvo Tulio is, perhaps, the greatest Finnish film director ever, the most modern and the most European of them all.'[40] Critics have been aware of Tulio's influence on Kaurismäki. '*The Match Factory Girl* [*Tulitikkutehtaan tyttö*, 1990] and *Juha* [1999] can both be seen as homages to Tulio', writes Varjola: 'The set-up in both is *Tulionesque*, and although the taciturnity in the former is not typical of Tulio, the latter with its melodramatic language is very Tulio-like. Aki Kaurismäki just made an international breakthrough, never experienced by Tulio.'[41]

True, Tulio did not have a remarkable international career, despite industrious efforts and some relatively modest success with the Swedish-language versions he made for the Scandinavian markets. However, in the 2000s a number of retrospectives have been organised at international film festivals and film archives. Indeed, this book would never have come into being had the editors of the *ReFocus*-series not encountered a Tulio retrospective at the Brooklyn Academy of Music in 2008.

NOTES

1. Toiviainen 1986, Toiviainen 2002 and Laine, Lukkarila and Seitajärvi 2004.
2. See Kääpä 2010: 15–18.
3. Hällström 1936: 241.
4. See Kalha 2009.
5. Hällström 1936: 251.
6. Donner 1961: 21–2.
7. This change of emphasis is exemplified in Anu Koivunen's work on Finnish women's film: Koivunen 1995. See also Laine, Lukkarila and Seitajärvi 2004.
8. See Laine 2019.
9. Toiviainen et al. 1980: 14.
10. Donner 1955: 69.
11. See, for example, Lounela 1957, 31–3.
12. Toiviainen 1975: 45–6. Toiviainen's later monograph (Toiviainen 1986) is an excellent synthesis of the realist, auteurist and political views on Tapiovaara.

13. See Laine 2019.
14. Toni 1950: 35. Granted, one of the two authors of the book, Nisse Hirn, might have been partial, being the scriptwriter for several of Tulio's films. The other one, Topo Leistelä, however, made a long career working for both Suomi-Filmi and Suomen Filmiteollisuus.
15. For an analysis of Slioor's celebrity image, see Saarenmaa 2010: 45–139.
16. Mäkinen and Pihlström 1957: 13.
17. Aarne Laurila: 'Nuorena nukkunut', *Projektio* 1/1961.
18. Lounela 1957.
19. Donner 1961.
20. Tulio 1974: 87.
21. See Ellis 2000.
22. Harri Moilanen: 'Levoton veri', *Kansan Uutiset* 14.4.1984.
23. Markku Tuuli: 'Sellaisena kuin sinä minut halusit', *Katso* 3/1982.
24. Nikula 2000: 222–8.
25. On the Sirk renaissance, see Rentschler 2005.
26. See Mark Betz's analysis of the 'little book' phenomenon, typical for the pioneering era of academic film studies in the 1960s and 1970s. Betz 2008: 319–49.
27. Malmberg 1975: 5.
28. Varjola 1987: 39–41.
29. See Gledhill 1987: 7.
30. Varjola 1985: 35.
31. Varjola 1987: 40.
32. Toiviainen 1992: 231–55; see also Alitalo and Alitalo 1990: 38–42.
33. Koivunen and Laine 1993: 136–54.
34. Koivunen 1995: 107–45.
35. Kalha 2009: 141.
36. Marttila et al. 2003.
37. Toiviainen 2002. Another notable publication from the early 2000s is the biography of Regina Linnanheimo by Jaana Nikula: Nikula 2000.
38. See the interviews in Töyri 1983: 45, 103, 164, 253; and Kirjavainen, Pensala and von Zansen 2013: 149.
39. Pulkkinen 2016: 7.
40. Mikko Piela, '"En ole löytänyt vielä omaa tyyliäni"', *KU-Viikkolehti* 24.12.1983.
41. Varjola 2002: 185.

NEWSPAPERS AND PERIODICALS

Kansan Uutiset 1984.
Katso 1982.
KU-Viikkolehti 1983.
Projektio 1961.

BIBLIOGRAPHY

Alitalo, Simo and Tuike Alitalo (1990), 'Regina Linnanheimon silmät. Näkökulmia suomalaiseen melodraamaan', *Lähikuva* 3/1990, 38–42.
Donner, Jörn (1955), 'Tie elokuvamme tulevaisuuteen', in Jörn Donner and Aito Mäkinen (eds), *Studio 1*, Helsinki: Studio, 68–77.

Donner, Jörn (1961), 'Suomalainen elokuva vuonna 0', in Aito Mäkinen (ed.), *Studio 6*, Helsinki: Suomen elokuva-arkisto, 17–58.

Ellis, John (2000), *Seeing Things: Television in the Age of Uncertainty*, London and New York: I. B. Tauris.

Gledhill, Christine (1987), 'The Melodramatic Field: An Investigation', in Christine Gledhill (ed.), *Home Is Where the Heart Is – Studies in Melodrama and the Woman's Film*, London: BFI Publishing, 5–39.

Hällström, Roland af (1936), *Filmi – Aikamme kuva. Filmin historiaa, olemusta ja tehtäviä*, Jyväskylä & Helsinki: K. J. Gummerus osakeyhtiö.

Kääpä, Pietari (2010), *The National and Beyond. The Globalisation of Finnish Cinema in the Films of Aki and Mika Kaurismäki*, Oxford: Peter Lang.

Kalha, Harri (2009), 'The Case of Theodor Tugai: The Filmstar and the Factitious Body', in Tytti Soila (ed.), *Stellar Encounters. Stardom in Popular European Cinema*, New Barnet: John Libbey, 132–42.

Kinisjärvi, Raimo et al. (1979), 'Varastettu kuolema – Itsetietoisen ohjaajan vapautunutta ilmaisua', in Jukka Rossi (ed.), *Vuosikirja 2*, Kajaani: Oulun elokuvakeskus, 30–45.

Kirjavainen, Sakari, Marja Pensala and Kati von Zanse (eds) (2013), *Konnia ja huligaaneja. Elokuvasukupolvien kohtaamisia*, Helsinki: Gaudeamus.

Koivunen, Anu (1995), *Isänmaan moninaiset äidinkasvot. Sotavuosien suomalainen naisten elokuva sukupuoliteknologiana*, Turku: Suomen elokuvatutkimuksen seura.

Koivunen, Anu and Kimmo Laine (1993), 'Metsästä pellon kautta kaupunkiin (ja takaisin). Jätkyys suomalaisessa elokuvassa', in Pirjo Ahokas, Martti Lahti and Jukka Sihvonen (eds), *Mieheyden tiellä. Maskuliinisuus ja kulttuuri*, Jyväskylä: Nykykulttuurin tutkimusyksikkö.

Laine, Kimmo (2019), 'Nyrki Tapiovaara – Between Avant-Garde and Mainstream Cinema', in Benedikt Hjartarson et al. (eds), *A Cultural History of the Avant-Garde in the Nordic Countries 1925–1950*, Leiden and Boston: Brill and Rodopi.

Laine, Kimmo, Matti Lukkarila and Juha Seitajärvi (eds) (2004), *Valentin Vaala*, Helsinki: Suomalaisen Kirjallisuuden Seura.

Lounela, Pekka (1957), 'Suomalainen todellisuus', in Jouko Tyyri (ed.), *Elokuvan maailmat*, Helsinki: Gummerus, 11–35.

Malmberg, Tarmo (1975), 'Traditional Finnish Cinema: An Historical Overview', in Jim Hillier (ed.), *Cinema in Finland*, London: British Film Institute.

Mäkinen, Aito and Bengt Pihlström (1957), 'The Finnish Cinema Today', in Aito Mäkinen and Bengt Pihlström (eds), *Studio 3*, Helsinki: Studio, 11–23.

Marttila, Markku et al. (eds) (2003), *Intohimon vallassa. Teuvo Tulion kuvamaailma*, Helsinki: Suomalaisen Kirjallisuuden Seura.

Nikula, Jaana (2000), *Polttava katse. Regina Linnanheimon elämä ja elokuvat*, Helsinki: Like.

Pukkinen, Antti (2016), *Suomen elokuvaohjaajaliitto Selo ry. Historiikki*, Helsinki: SELO.

Rentschler, Eric (2005), 'Douglas Sirk Revisited: The Limits and Possibilities of Artistic Agency', *New German Critique* No. 95, 149–61.

Saarenmaa, Laura (2010), *Intiimin äänet. Julkisuuskulttuurin muutos suomalaisissa ajanvietelehdissä 1961–1975*, Tampere: Tampere University Press.

Toiviainen, Sakari (1975), *Uusi suomalainen elokuva*, Helsinki: Otava.

Toiviainen, Sakari (1986), *Nyrki Tapiovaaran tie*, Helsinki: Valtion painatuskeskus and Suomen elokuva-arkisto.

Toiviainen, Sakari (1992), *Surinta elämässä. Elokuvamelodraaman kulta-aika*, Helsinki: VAPK-kustannus and Suomen elokuva-arkisto.

Toiviainen, Sakari (ed.) (2002), *Tulio – Levottoman veren antologia*, Helsinki: Suomalaisen Kirjallisuuden Seura.

Toiviainen, Sakari et al. (1980), 'Kuvaajan matka menneeseen' (an interview with Erik Blomberg), *Filmihullu* 8/1980, 8–21.

Toni [Topo Leistelä and Nisse Hirn] (1950), *Haluatko elokuvanäyttelijäksi. Filmitietoa elokuvasta kiinostuneille*, Hämeenlinna: Nide.

Töyri, Esko (1983), *Vanhat kameramiehet. Suomalaisen elokuvan kameramiehiä 1930–1950*, Helsinki: Suomen elokuvasäätiö.

Tulio, Teuvo (1974), 'Suomalaisen elokuvan yksinäinen susi', *Jaana* 3–18/1974.

Varjola, Markku (1985), 'Paratiisista kadotukseen', *Filmihullu* 3–4/1985, 35–7.

Varjola, Markku (1987), 'Tuli on', *Filmihullu* 5–6/1987, 39–41.

Varjola, Markku (2002), 'Tulion näkemys ja merkitys', in Sakari Toiviainen (ed.), *Tulio – Levottoman veren antologia*, Helsinki: Suomalaisen Kirjallisuuden Seura, 183–99.

Filmography

THE FIGHT OVER THE HEIKKILÄ MANSION (TAISTELU HEIKKILÄN TALOSTA, 1936)

Actors: Regina Linnanheimo (Anni), Heikki Tuominen (Anni's father), Siiri Angerkoski (Anni's mother), Matti Lehtelä (Toivo Erkkilä, the young master of Heikkilä), Pentti Viljanen (Matti Väliportti), Elli Ylimaa (Manta), Waldermar Wohlström (secretary), Lars Åberg (farmhand), Valter Tuomi (provost), Ekku Ylimaa (Little-Jaakko), Unto Saliminen (Jaakko Heikkilä), Henny Valjus (Katri).

Director: Teuvo Tulio; Producer: Abel Adams; Script: Yrjö Kivimies (and Teuvo Tulio, uncredited); Cinematography: Erik Blomberg; Editor: Teuvo Tulio; Set Design: Jan Tschifschis; Sound Recording: Lauri Pulkkila; Music: Leevi Madetoja; Conductor: Martti Similä.

Production company: Adams-Filmi Oy

Length: 95 min

Opening night: 1.11.1936

SILJA – FALLEN ASLEEP WHEN YOUNG (NUORENA NUKKUNUT, 1937)

Actors: Regina Linnanheimo (Silja), Otso Pera (Armas), Kille Oksanen (Oskari), Kaarlo Angerkoski (Väinö), Kaarlo Vares (professor), Rakel Leino (Laura, professor's daughter), Aku Peltonen (Nukari's master), Elsa Rantalainen (Nukari's matron), Valter Tuomi (Ville of America), Elli Ylimaa (Aunt Sofia).

Director: Teuvo Tulio; Producer: Abel Adams; Script: Yrjö Kivimies (and
    Teuvo Tulio, uncredited); Cinematography: Erki Blomberg; Editor: Teuvo
    Tulio; Sound Recording: Leo Salminen; Music: Kauko Ero; Set design:
    Kille Oksanen.
Production company: Adams-Filmi Oy
Length: 97 min
Opening night: 25.12.1937

TEMPTATION (KIUSAUS, 1938)

Actors: Regina Linnanheimo (Raili), Unto Salminen (Provost), Yrjö
    Hämäläinen (Martti), Aku Peltonen (sailor – Nikko), Ida Kallio (Leena),
    Seija Rauni (Paula).
Director: Teuvo Tulio; Producer: Abel Adams; Script: Yrjö Kivimies;
    Cinematography: Erik Blomberg; Editing: Teuvo Tulio; Set design: Kille
    Oksanen; Sound Recording: Leo Salminen; Music: Toivo Lampén.
Production company: Adams-Filmi Oy
Length: 95 min
Opening night: 25.3.1938

THE SONG OF THE SCARLET FLOWER (LAULU TULIPUNAISESTA KUKASTA, 1938)

Actors: Kaarlo Oksanen (Olavi Koskela), Rakel Linnanheimo (Kyllikki
    Moisio), Mirjami Kuosmanen (Annikki), Nora Mäkinen (Gazelle), Birgit
    Nuotio (Dark girl), Maire Ranius (Rowan Berry), Sylvi Palo (prostitute),
    Aku Peltonen (head of log drivers), Veikko Linna (master Moisio), Lauri
    Korpela (master Koskela), Ida Hallikainen (matron Koskela), Onni
    Veijonen (Toivo), Elli Ylimaa (midwife).
Director: Teuvo Tulio; Producer: Teuvo Tulio; Script: Yrjö Kivimies,
    Regina Linnanheimo and Teuvo Tulio; Cinematography: Fred Runeberg;
    Editing: Teuvo Tulio; Set Design: Kosti Aaltonen; Music: Toivo Lampén;
    Sound Recording: Leo Salminen.
Production company: Teuvo Tulio
Length: 110 min
Opening night: 4.12.1938

JIGGS AND MAGGIE (VIHTORI JA KLAARA, 1939)

Actors: Eino Jurkka (Vihtori Vuorenkaiku), Verna Piponius (Klaara Ritva
    Vuorenkaiku), Turo Kartto (Nisse Vuorenkaiku), Nora Mäkinen (Vappu
    Vuorenkaiku), Leo Lähteenmäki (engineer Peter von Schaslick), Kirsti

Hurme (Ritva Vuorenkaiku, alias Ritva Vuorenrinne), Tauno Majuri
(Klasu Tullari).
Director: Teuvo Tulio; Producer: Teuvo Tulio; Script: Teuvo Tulio and
Turo Kartto; Cinematography: Felix Forsman and Charlie Bauer; Editing:
Teuvo Tulio; Set Design: Viljo Rummukainen; Sound Recording: Harald
Koivikko; Music: Toivo Lampén.
Production company: Tarmo-Filmi Oy
Length: 99 min
Opening night: 19.8.1939

IN THE FIELDS OF DREAMS (UNELMA KARJAMAJALLA, 1940)

Actors: Sirkka Salonen (Sirkka Valkama, Ylitalo's young maid), Olga Tainio
(Ylitalo's old matron), Kille Oksanen (Aarne Ylitalo), Kyösti Erämaa (Urho
Ylitalo), Kirsti Hurme (Kirsti Turja, Ylitalo's maid), Aku Peltonen (Matti,
Ylitalo's farmhand), Varma Lahtinen (Aino, Ylitalo's maid), Eino Jurkka
(shopkeeper), Ida Kallio (old Kerttu), Väinö Kangas (judge), Evald Terho
(old gypsy), Taito Mäkelä (prosecutor), Timo Jokinen (Sirkka's son).
Director: Teuvo Tulio; Producer: Teuvo Tulio; Script: Ivar Johansson
and Teuvo Tulio; Outdoors Cinematography: Eino Heino; Indoors
Cinematography: Felix Forsman; Editor: Teuvo Tulio; Set Design: Felix
Forsman and Viljo Rummukainen; Sound Recording: Harald Koivikko;
Music and Musical Adaptations: Tapio Ilomäki under the pseudonym T.
Tumma.
Production company: Tarmo-Filmi Oy
Length: 108 min
Opening night: 22.9.1940

THE WAY YOU WANTED ME (SELLAISENA KUIN SINÄ MINUT HALUSIT, 1944)

Actors: Marie-Louise Fock (Maija Kantola), Ture Ara (Aarne), Kunto
Karapää (Erkki Holmberg), Lauri Korpela (Aukusti, Aarne's father),
Annie Sundman (Mrs Holmberg, Erkki's mother), Ida Salmi (Maija's
foster mother), Sven Relander (director Auronen), Paavo Jännes (director
Henrik Karo), Frans Kampman (Kalle).
Director: Teuvo Tulio; Producer: Teuvo Tulio; Original topic: Ahti H. Einola;
Script: Niilo Hirn under the pseudonym Filmimies; Cinematography:
Gunnar Juselius, Olavi Gunnari, Eino Heino, Auvo Mustonen and Esko
Töyri; Editing: Teuvo Tulio; Sound Recording: Yrjö Saari; Set Design:

Kosti Aaltonen; Music: Tapio Ilomäki; Director's Assistant: Roland af Hällström.
Production company: Oy Filmo Ab
Length: 102 min
Opening night: 15.10.1944

CROSS OF LOVE (RAKKAUDEN RISTI, 1946)

Actors: Regina Linnanheimo (Riitta), Oscar Tengström (lighthouse keeper Kalle), Ville Salminen (Consul Mauri Holmberg), Rauli Tuomi (artist Henrik Hormi), Pentti Viljanen (Pekka), Hilly Lindqvist (Saara), Elli Ylimaa (owner of dressmaker's shop), Lauri Korpela (pilot), Senja Soitso (Maija).
Director: Teuvo Tulio; Producer: Teuvo Tulio; Script: Niilo Hirn under the pseudonym Filmimies; Cinematography: Uno Pihlström and Pentti Lintonen; Set Design: Kosti Ahonen; Editor: Teuvo Tulio; Sound Recording: Yrjö Saari; Music: Tauno Tuomisto.
Production company: Teuvo Tulio
Length: 99 min
Opening night: 22.2.1946

RESTLESS BLOOD (LEVOTON VERI, 1946)

Actors: Regina Linnanheimo (Sylvi Sora, née Kahra), Eino Katajavuori (doctor Valter Sora), Toini Vartiainen (Outi Kahra), Elli Ylimaa (Sylvi's and Outi's aunt), Nora Mäkinen (prostitute), Lauri Korpela (ophthalmologist Brauner).
Director: Teuvo Tulio; Producer: Teuvo Tulio; Script: Niilo Hirn under the pseudonym Filmimies, Teuvo Tulio and Regina Linnanheimo; Cinematography: Pentti Lintonen; Set Design: Kosti Ahonen; Editing: Teuvo Tulio; Sound Recording: Yrjö Saari; Music and Musical Adaptations: Tauno Tuomisto.
Production company: Teuvo Tulio
Length: 91 min
Opening night: 22.3.1946

IN THE GRIP OF PASSION (INTOHIMON VALLASSA, 1947)

Actors: Regina Linnanheimo (Aino Iso-Ylitalo, née Ylitalo), Kullervo Kalske (Olavi), Eric Gustafsson (Paavo Iso-Ylitalo), Aku Peltonen (hunchback), Elli Ylimaa (Mrs Andersson), Oscar Tengström (Ylitalo's old master),

Kaija Suonio (Ylitalo's old matron), Ruth Luoma-aho (Laila), Matti
Oravisto (Niilo Iso-Ylitalo), Matti Aulos (vicar), Veikko Linna (Paavo's
father).
Director: Teuvo Tulio; Producer: Teuvo Tulio; Script: Niilo Hirn under the
pseudonym Filmimies; Cinematography: Osmo Harkimo; Set Design:
Pentti Hämäläinen; Editing: Teuvo Tulio; Sound Recording: Ensio
Lumes; Music: Tauno Marttinen under the pseudonym Musicus.
Production company: Teuvo Tulio
Length: 90 min
Opening night: 16.2.1947

THE RAPIDS OF HELL (HORNANKOSKI, 1949)

Actors: Regina Linnanheimo (Lea), William Markus (Aarne Yli-Koskela),
Åke Lindman (Artturi Yli-Koskela), Annie Mörk (Yli-Koskela's old
matron), Rauha Rentola (Irma, Yli-Koskela's maid), Heikki Savolainen
(Kalle, Yli-Koskela farmhand), Eero Leväluoma (Ali-Koskela's master),
Helge Ranin (provost).
Director (actual): Teuvo Tulio; Director (as credited) Roland af Hällström;
Producers: Yrjö Rannikko and Yrjö Norta; Script: Jussi Talvi;
Cinematography: Esko Töyri; Editor: Teuvo Tulio; Set Design: Kosti
Aaltonen; Sound Recording: Ensio Lumes; Music (also conductor):
Tauno Marttinen.
Production company: Fenno-Filmi Oy
Length: 105 min
Opening night: 25.2.1949

A CROOKED WOMAN (RIKOLLINEN NAINEN, 1952)

Actors: Regina Linnanheimo (Eeva Isokari, alias 'Veera Puranen'), Eija
Karipää (Riitta), Tauno Majuri (judge Lauri Isokari), Kurt Ingvall
(Kristian, doctor), Elli Ylimaa (Kristian's mother), Paavo Jännes (vicar),
Anton Soini (prison guard), Martti Petsola (Kari Isokari).
Director: Teuvo Tulio; Producer: Teuvo Tulio; Script: Regina Linnanheimo;
Cinematography: Osmo Harkimo and Veikko Laakso; Set Design: Kosti
Aaltonen and August Lindström; Sound Recording: Ensio Lumes; Music:
Tauno Marttinen.
Production company: Teuvo Tulio
Length: 110 min
Opening night: 1.2.1952

JEALOUSY (MUSTASUKKAISUUS, 1953)

Actors: Regina Linnanheimo (Riitta Maras), Eero Paganus (forester Jyri
    Maras), Assi Raine (Anja), Annie Mörk (grandmother, director of the
    sawmill), Paavo Jännes (doctor), Lauri Korpela (sawmill administrator).
Director: Teuvo Tulio; Producer: Teuvo Tulio; Script: Niilo Hirn under the
    pseudonym Filmimies; Cinematography: Erkki Imberg; Set Design: Lauri
    Ahokas; Editor: Teuvo Tulio; Sound Recording: Ensio Lumes; Music:
    Tauno Marttinen.
Production company: Teuvo Tulio
Length: 93 min
Opening night: 13.3.1953

YOU'VE GONE INTO MY BLOOD (OLET MENNYT MINUN VEREENI, 1956)

Actors: Regina Linnanheimo (Rea), Ami Runnas (composer Tauno Tarras),
    Rauha Rentola (Eeva), Åke Lindman (Erkki, master mariner), Elli
    Ylimaa (Rea's mother), Kirsti Hurme (Tauno's wife), Kauko Vuorensola
    (policeman), Laila Rihte (Mari, Tauno's maid).
Director: Teuvo Tulio; Producer: Teuvo Tulio; Script: Regina Linnanheimo
    under the pseudonym Arel; Cinematography: Veikko Laakso; Editing:
    Teuvo Tulio; Set Design: Lauri Ahokas; Sound Recording: Hugo Ranta;
    Music: Tauno Marttinen.
Production company: Teuvo Tulio
Length: 102 min
Opening night: 21.9.1956

IN THE BEGINNING WAS AN APPLE (SE ALKOI OMENASTA, 1962)

Actors: Tabe Slioor (Tabe), Tauno Majuri (general director), Kunto Karapää
    (artist), Kalle Rouni (major), Eija Hiltunen (wife of the general director),
    Esko Saha (other man), Anne Maria Hindell (Tabe as a child), Tuija
    Halonen (narrator).
Director: Teuvo Tulio; Producer: Anelma Vuorio; Script: Reino Arras;
    Cinematography: Esko Töyri, Olavi Aaltonen and Teuvo Tulio; Editor:
    Armas Vallasvuo; Set Design: Ensio Suominen; Sound Recording: Gösta
    Salminen; Music (also conductor): George de Godzinsky.

Production company: Mainoselokuva Oy
Length: 37 min
Opening night: 20.4.1962

SENSUELA (SENSUELA, 1973)

Actors: Marianne Mardi (Laila Walk), Ossi Elstelä (Aslak Walk, Laila's
father), Mauritz Åkerman (Hans Müller), Ismo Saario (Pekka), Marja
Pertamo (Greta Kujala), Armas Ek (Sami), Yrjö Tähtelä (narrator).
Director: Teuvo Tulio; Producer: Teuvo Tulio; Script: Teuvo Tulio and Yrjö
Norta; Cinematography: Teuvo Tulio and Yrjö Norta; Editing: Teuvo
Tulio; Set Design: Teuvo Tulio; Sound Recording: Lasse Hjort; Sound
Mixing: Yrjö Norta.
Production company: Teuvo Tulio
Length: 104 min
Opening night: 29.5.1973

Index